CAPPUCCINO AND CHICK-CHAT

Debbie Viggiano

For my family, because we're in this together!
xx

Welcome to my world, lovely reader. If you like daft jokes and ditzy *blonde* situations (I am one, after all) then you might enjoy reading random excerpts from the last ten years of my life.

There is no given timeline so you might find, for example, that my daughter is a fourteen-year-old in an early chapter but, a few pages on, she's twelve months older!

The years go quickly, as have these events in my life. The ups, the downs, and wrestling to try and maintain balance somewhere in between. Let's have a chat. Chick-chat. Make yourself a cuppa and join me...

Time for a BBQ?
There's too much at steak...

'What lovely weather,' said my husband, peering at a sunny sky full of spring sunshine. 'We'll soon be having barbecues again. I can't wait!'

For us, barbecues are a huge event. I say *huge* because, since my husband first uttered those words, it is actually my father who now takes charge of any al fresco cooking. This is because he kindly bought us a grill for our wedding anniversary. It was the size of a small car. Unfortunately, my husband couldn't get to grips with it, and I have no desire to mess about with gas tanks and hot tongs.

This enormous contraption mostly resides under a tarpaulin in the garage and pretty much takes up all the floor space. Depending on the mood of the Great British Summer, the grill is wheeled out, at best, six times a year. But at least my neighbours can sigh with relief seeing my father at the cooking helm, and not Mr V. You see, a few summers prior to this, and not long after moving into our current home, my husband made a similar comment to above.

'What lovely weather,' he said, all those years ago. 'Let's have a barbecue!' And, back then, I joyfully embraced his enthusiasm. Except we didn't have a BBQ. That was soon resolved. Whilst on the supermarket run, I picked up a couple of disposable barbies – foil containers full of coals. Once home, I presented them to my husband.

'Here you go! And look... here are the sausages. So get barbecuing!'

It's only in hindsight that I realised the stupidity of this action. After all, much as I love my hubby, regrettably this is a man who can wreck the house with a single screwdriver from the Pound Shop. In no time at all, Mr V had surpassed himself. He had transformed into someone who might just wreck several houses... this time by barbecue.

I stared in horror as the two lightweight containers, now lit and merrily blazing away on the garden table, floated upwards on a gust of wind before frisbeeing off towards our open patio doors and – uh-oh – the curtains flapping away in the breeze. I gulped and dashed off to the kitchen to grab a jug of water to do some hasty extinguishing. The wind picked up, and the blazing barbecues headed closer. Terrified, I charged back outside with the jug of water, and almost crashed into Mr V coming in the opposite direction.

'Quick,' I screeched, 'fling this on them.'

'I'll do no such thing,' said my indignant husband, as the spinning barbecues crash-landed at our feet. He grabbed the curtains and folded them out of the way. 'Look at that,' he said in delight as he gazed at the flaming containers, 'aren't they burning well?'

Which was an understatement.

'Fantastic,' I said, smiling sweetly. 'So what are we having for dinner? Barbecued patio?'

But before my husband could answer, the wind once again lifted the burning barbies up again, but this time took them off to the sun-dried trees, parched shrubs, wooden fence and decking area. To the left I could see my neighbour's curtains violently twitching and caught a glimpse of a pinched, horrified face. Forget the jug of water. This was a hosepipe job. Shoving my husband to one side, I smartly extinguished the barbecues.

'What did you do that for?' he asked, retrieving the sodden foil trays. 'How am I meant to get them lit again?'

I didn't bother answering. To hell with barbecuing dinner. Retrieving the raw sausages, I chucked them in the oven instead. Except, by a strange twist of fate, I realised we might well need to revert to barbecuing, because when I went to open the oven, the door fell off. Yes, really. Things like that seem to happen to me.

Which reminds me. Why did the skeleton go to the BBQ? For the spare ribs...

What kind of dog chases anything red?
A bulldog...

This year is a special wedding anniversary. Special enough that, at the time of tying the knot, Mr V promised that when we reached this milestone, he would buy me an eternity ring. Now, like all my sisters of the fairer sex, I'm not averse to the odd sparkler. Especially a sparkler that has all sorts of official papers declaring quality, clarity, weight, and then – upon the sun shining at a certain angle – frazzles your eyeballs with lots of sparkly diamond light.

However, a recession has been going on. Things are tight. Money is required not so much for diamond rings, but astronomical – and very necessary – payment of bills. So I suggested foregoing the eternity ring and instead asked my husband if he'd agree to me having a second pooch instead.

'Another beagle?' asked Mr V, looking aghast. 'Won't our Trudy Beagle be upset?'

'I don't think so. I think she'd love the company.'

'I'm not sure,' said my husband, shaking his head. 'It's taken years to train Trudy Beagle, and I think two beagles would be a nightmare.'

I could identify somewhat with my husband's fears. After all, it has been challenging to drum any sort of obedience into our ancient girl's head. It's a bit like having kids. Just when you've toilet trained them, taught them not to scratch their armpits, snarl at you, loll around on beds that don't belong to them, and to stop eating you out of house and home... they go and leave you.

Such is how it has been with our kids. We are down to one teenager left in the nest. Every now and again we think about downsizing. Mr V is keen for us to move into a smart apartment and for me to swap country dog walks for running on a treadmill in a posh gym. Having tried the gym-bunny thing, I can honestly say I was bored silly running on a treadmill after just ten minutes. So an apartment is definitely out. I love surfing Rightmove's website and have spent many a happy hour idly looking at properties by the sea with romantic visions of walking a dog along a picturesque coastline... waves pounding against a rugged shoreline... then later holing-up to write in a gorgeous attic room overlooking the untamed ocean.

Of course, this is a little pipe-dream. A flight of fancy. A wish that will likely never come true. Probably just like that diamond ring. So, back to reality. I shall instead take myself off to the supermarket to do the weekly shop and, whilst trolleying around, will work out a strategy on how to hound (no pun intended) Mr V into letting me have that second pooch.

Which reminds me. What do you get if you cross a dog and a calculator? A friend you can count upon...

What kind of tree fits into your hand?
A palm tree...

Spring has most definitely sprung. Suddenly I want to spend all my time in the garden. However, following a recent op I'm not yet able to lift our weighty steamroller of a mower. So I asked Mr V to take care of the lawn. I was a bit twitchy about this request. After all, the garden is my domain and it's fair to say that, where the grass is concerned, I do suffer a touch of OCD. I like the lawn to have blades of grass that stand to attention, with the finished cut looking something like a chessboard with that criss-cross look. Mr V was keen to help, however, and I gratefully accepted his offer to mow the lawn. Leaving him to it, I hunkered down by a flowerbed and set about planting hundreds of mixed bulbs.

So immersed was I in turning over the fresh earth and pleasantly daydreaming about the riot of colour that would eventually poke through the soil, it took me a while to realise that my husband had disappeared. Rocking back on my heels, I looked around. The lawnmower had been put away, but the extension lead remained out. I gaped at it. The lengthy orange flex looked like a giant tangled ball of wool. My husband appeared from around the side of the house.

'All done,' he beamed.

'Er, great. Um, what happened to the extension lead?' I asked, wondering how long it would take to unravel.

'I haven't the faintest idea,' said my husband, scratching his head in puzzlement. 'It somehow got itself all knotted up.'

'I see.'

I didn't really. But as is often the way with my hubby, he does one job and makes another. Fifteen minutes later, I'd unknotted the extension lead, re-wound it on its reel, and put it away in the garage. Walking round to the front of the house, I was brought up short by the sight of bagged-up grass cuttings. But instead of placing them in the compost bin, Mr V had dumped them in my ornamental wheelbarrow. I lifted the bags off to find the wheelbarrow – awaiting a tray of seedlings to bloom – quite broken.

I tried not to be irritated. And failed. My husband is a man who runs a company, is logical about money, wise about teenage tantrums, and rarely loses his temper. It never ceases to amaze me how Mr V can have such amazing qualities in some areas, and yet... well... be so flipping rubbish when it comes to being hands-on! I'm not the cleverest of people, but like to think I'm fairly practical. That what I lack in brain power can at least be made up in common sense. Pushing away feelings of annoyance, I took some deep breaths, told myself the extension lead was at least useable again and the broken wheelbarrow could be repaired. At least it wasn't like the time when Mr V had taken a video tape from my bedside drawer and used it to record a football match... erasing, in the process, every single filmed memory of the children growing up. If ever there had been a time to have a meltdown, then that had been such a moment. By comparison, breaking the ornamental wheelbarrow wasn't an issue.

Feeling a little more soothed, I retraced my steps to the garden... and stared at the lawn in amazement. Instead of resembling an area of manicured green, the grass looked like it had been cut by a chomping herd of goats.

Pushing down feelings of exasperation, I told myself that at least the grass was now short and to go and have a cup of tea and raid my secret stash of chocolate – guaranteed to lift the mood.

As it was such a beautiful day, my husband had left the kitchen door open. I stepped inside, but as my eyes adjusted to the sudden gloom, was horrified to encounter a very muddy Trudy Beagle, enormous lumps of earth scattered across the kitchen floor, and hundreds of muddy flower bulbs. Spinning on my heel, I rushed back to the flowerbed I'd not long since finished planting. Yes, completely dug over. By the dog.

Sighing, I went back inside to clear up, making a mental note to exchange the outstanding cup of tea for something stronger. Which reminds me.

What gets bigger, the more you take away?
A hole...

Mothering Sunday
Remember, advice your child rejected will one day be given to your grandchild...

When we are young, many of us automatically assume we will follow in the paths of our parents, find a partner, and go on to have children. And for most of us this does indeed happen. I can remember excitedly reaching the point in my (first) marriage where a baby was on the agenda. And then waiting in vain as, month after month, nothing happened. The first year of anticipation turned into a second, which then rolled into a third, and still there was no patter of tiny feet.

It is very difficult watching those around you start families without so much as a blip.

'Oh,' – one girlfriend happily told me – 'my hubby only has to *look* at me and I'm big with child.'

Jolly good. Jolly, jolly good. Except it wasn't jolly at all. Although I was always delighted for my friends and wished them and their growing bumps all the love and luck in the world, I would be a liar if I didn't admit that a part of me was beyond envious. I made sure that I never turned into one of those women who couldn't look at a pram without bursting into tears although, again, I couldn't help but feel sad if I ever caught a glimpse of a tiny bundle swaddled in pink or blue.

A visit to a doctor didn't give much of an explanation. These were the days when test-tube babies were only for the very rich, and certainly help wasn't available on the NHS. My GP told me I was probably stressed. Which was a fair comment, because by the third year I was feeling incredibly stressed by the whole thing. *Why* wasn't I pregnant?

In my darkest moments of despair, I'd curled up in a ball and plead with God.

'Please, if you really are the Creator of *All That Is*, then let me create too. Let my body create another human being. I won't ever ask for anything else. I'm begging you. Can you hear me? Just one baby, eh?'

By this point I'd saved enough money to privately see

a gynaecologist to find out what might be wrong. And then, just as I was about to have investigative surgery, I became pregnant.

'Thank you, God,' I whispered. 'Thank-you-thank-you-thank-you-thank-you. I will never ask you for another thing.'

Overjoyed, nine months later I gave birth to a little boy. Hurrah, a mother at last! I suddenly felt as though I belonged... that I was no longer standing on the outside looking in at the other members of the Parent Club. I took great delight in wheeling my own pram around, showing off my own tiny bundle dressed head-to-toe in blue.

But hormones are a funny thing. After promising God that if I had just one baby then I would never ask for another, instead I found myself with a powerful all-consuming yearning for a second child. I told myself to be grateful for the beautiful son I had – and I was. Truly. But it was as if my body wasn't listening. Mother Nature had programmed my body to pro-create. And despite my best efforts to disconnect and zone out from that feeling, the switch to turn off those powerful feelings remained elusive.

I wasn't surprised when, once again, the months turned into years. However, this time around I *did* finally go ahead with investigative surgery – and discovered that, thanks to a burst appendix and peritonitis at the age of nineteen, I had blocked fallopian tubes and adhesions. The gynaecologist was amazed I'd ever achieved a pregnancy and said an operation was necessary in order to become a mother again. Thankfully, my daughter arrived soon after.

Some of us become parents so easily. For others it is a real difficulty. And for some it isn't even an option. And then there are others who simply don't want children. Whatever your choice, whether you are a mum to one... or ten... or are 'mum' to fur babies instead, I wish you a very Happy Mother's Day. Which reminds me.

What's the definition of *minimum*?

A small mother...

You can't have a decent conversation if there is a goat in the vicinity.
They're always butting in...

It's that time of year when the sun wakes up and beams a few warm rays our way. Everybody is deliriously happy about *the good weather*. Suddenly joggers abound, their chalk-white limbs poking optimistically out of sporty shorts.

I love the warmer weather. It means Trudy Beagle and I don't get rained on when going for a walk. It also signals the start of various charities determined to cash in on the sunnier days.

Yesterday, as I was picking up my emails, my daughter stuck her head round the study door.

'It's Sport Relief on Sunday,' she said, 'and I'm doing a sponsored run in London with the rest of my class.'

'Okay,' I said, thoroughly distracted. My eyes skimmed over an email from Neighbourhood Watch. The subject line had me raising my eyebrows.

HAVE YOU SEEN THIS GOAT?

'Will you sponsor me?' asked Eleanor.

'Of course,' I said clicking on the email. There was a mugshot of a goat which had apparently broken out of some neighbouring allotments and buggered off.

'I'm running three miles with the school at Hyde Park,' Eleanor continued, 'so will you give me a pound a mile?'

I read the email's blurb. The heartbroken owner of the goat was begging for anybody with information to get in touch and had him their mobile number.

'Anything you want,' I replied, absent-mindedly.

I failed to spot my daughter's eyes lighting up like a Las Vegas fruit machine, or take on board her gleeful response.

'Fantastic! Thanks, Mum,' she said, before skipping off.

Clicking off the email, I decided to take Trudy Beagle for a walk and keep my eyes peeled for the runaway goat.

That evening, my husband took me out to dinner. I

look forward to Saturday nights as we tend to be like passing ships during the week and it gives us both a chance to actually see something of each other. As the warmer weather also heralds the time of year for me being a golf widow, Mr V likes to update me with a blow-by-blow account of how he fared around the green. As there are eighteen holes on a golf course, and it takes about four hours to go from start to finish, you appreciate that my husband's recital isn't a five-minute tale. I did lots of oohing and aahing, and promptly zoned out. My thoughts wandered to Eleanor saying something about doing a run for Sport Relief on Sunday morning. Was that *this* Sunday or *next* Sunday? And I really must remember to go to the cash dispenser and get some money out so I could pay her maths tutor and then give Eleanor her three quid sponsor money, and perhaps a little extra for effort. I zoned back into my husband's animated chatter.

'... And the ball was stuck in the bunker! But I chipped it out,' – he waggled his wrists by way of demonstration – 'and I said to myself, "Ha! Eat your heart out, Tiger!"'

'Amazing,' I said, nodding my head whilst privately thinking that Tiger Woods might possibly have not been in the bunker in the first place.

'And then,' my husband continued, causing me to immediately zone out again.

I decided to bring up the subject of booking our summer holiday when he'd finished his next golfing instalment, which seemed to be on par (no pun intended) with the Rider Cup. I took a sip of Bacardi and, for a moment, pondered where we could afford to go that might offer turquoise waves and white-sand beaches.

'So what do you make of that?' asked Mr V.

'Amazing,' I repeated.

'That's what I thought,' said Mr V, smugly. 'I mean, it's not every day you see a goat trundling along the Top Dartford Road.'

Like a rubber band, my concentration sprang back to my husband's last words.

'What goat?' I asked, straightening up.

'I just told you,' said Mr V. 'There was this goat trotting

merrily along the main road.'

'Did you stop the car,' I asked, sharply.

'What, to give it a lift?' my husband guffawed.

'No, to catch it!' I cried.

'Well... no. I presumed it belonged to somebody,' said Mr V, looking confused.

'But didn't it strike you as odd to see a goat heading towards Dartford?' I said, incredulously.

'Erm... yes... and no,' said my husband. 'I thought that perhaps it was being taken for a walk. You know,' he shrugged, 'like a dog. But off the lead.'

I stared at my husband. 'What, as in the owner wasn't far away and any second now would put his fingers to his lips, let out a piercing whistle and shout, "Oi, Billy! Heel!"'

'Er, yes, something like that,' my husband nodded.

I've since told Neighbourhood Watch that the goat was last seen heading towards Dartford, possibly toward the A2 where it might thumb a lift to London. Meanwhile, I've been presented with Eleanor's sponsored run invoice:

One train ticket to London £5
One Sport Relief t-shirt £8
Restaurant bill after charity run £15
Sponsorship £20 per mile £60
Total £88

Where's that goat? Because I'm joining it. Which reminds me.

What do you call a goat that runs away to sea?

Billy Ocean...

Why don't men do laundry?
Because the washer and dryer don't have remote controls...

Yesterday my son returned home from uni trailing a suitcase stuffed with laundry. Robbie came through the door, keen to tell me about his latest laboratory dissection. I always do my best to be an enthusiastic listener, but it's hard. I like human bodies to be alive, kicking and in one piece. Not smelling of formaldehyde with bits missing from the previous lot of medical students who had to remove a brain, or something.

As Rob chatted away, I unzipped the suitcase. His scrubs were perched on top of the pile.

'Give that a good wash, Mum,' he said, with a mischievous wink, 'because it reeks of death.'

Donning a pair of rubber gloves, I gingerly set about doing my own dissection – in this case, my son's laundry. The scrubs were handled in the same way one might touch a stick of lit dynamite.

I'm thrilled my son wants to be a dentist and has embraced his medical studies with such passion. My mother is too. As a retired nurse, she was always privately disappointed her two daughters hadn't gone into the profession, especially in the days of us husband-hunting. My mum is from the *Carry On, Doctor* era, where Matron was always a feared Hattie Jacques-type character, and all the nurses aspired to walk down the aisle with either a Consultant or an anaesthetist waiting at the altar.

Being raised by a nurse rubbed off on my sister and self in other ways. For example, we're both OCD about germs. We wash our hands. A lot. We were taught that microbes – and possible death – lurked in every public toilet.

To a certain degree, my son has morphed into my mother. Little did I know as I later stood at the kitchen sink running my fingers under the tap, that my actions were being scrutinised.

'You call that hand-washing?' Robbie spluttered. 'Let me show you how us medical students have been taught.'

And with that my son set about thoroughly soaping between each finger, right down to the webby bits, making circular motions over both palms, washing each fingertip and both thumbs in alternating clockwise and anti-clock directions, then proceeded to work his way up to the elbow.

'I'm not scrubbing up for surgery,' I protested, 'I just want to peel the vegetables.'

Sigh. I must apologise. It wasn't my intention to chat about corpses and scrupulous food preparation. Which reminds me.

What did the skeleton say before eating his dinner?

Bone appétit...

What do you get if you cross a telephone with a pair of scissors?
Snippy answers…

I find accents extremely challenging. Especially when on the telephone. It doesn't matter whether the caller is from Ireland or India, Scotland or Singapore, anybody listening will hear me frequently repeating, "Sorry, could you say that again, please?" Sometimes it's quite embarrassing.

'Are you taking the mickey?' snarled one exasperated person at the other end of my telephone earlier this week.

As a Londoner, I pronounce J as *jay*. However, a Scott will say *ji*. Or, depending on the region, *jee*. Earlier this week one Scotsman was telling me his email address. I wrote down *beale @ blah blah dot co dot uk* and read it back for confirmation.

'Och, no,' said the disembodied voice. 'It's Beale.'

'Beale?' I repeated.

'No, Beale!' came the reply.

'That's what I said… Beale.'

'Lassie, ah seed BEALE! B – I – L – L.'

Gotcha.

Mind you, even if things are spelt out to me, it doesn't necessarily mean I'm out of trouble. I emailed another Scotsman via *air dot haig @ blah blah dot co dot uk* but it bounced back as an incorrect address. So, I rang the person up to clarify.

'Och, how strrrrange,' said the voice at the end of the telephone, 'because it's definitely *air*. *Air* for *Rrrrrobert*. Ah! Or should I say *arrr*?!

Another accent that challenges me is that of my husband's family. When I first met my mother-in-law, I assumed she was still talking in Italian. I smiled politely and did lots of miming with my hands, while my husband guffawed into his cappuccino. Nowadays I have my mother-in-law sussed. She leaves the last syllable off everything. So, if she starts telling me about somebody's *dort*, I know that she's telling me about a person's *daught*-er. And if she's chatting about a recipe involving *macar-own, tom-art, oyn, re-cot* and *parmez* then it is generally understood we're talking about macaroni, tomatoes, onions, ricotta and parmesan. Confused? Not half as much as I first was.

When my own parents met my in-laws, they were even more confused than I had been. Mr V and I took both sets of parents out to a restaurant. Yes, Italian. Once inside, the two mothers – unbeknownst to the rest of us – kicked off their respective shoes to do some serious unimpeded toe-wiggling under the table. All four parents began chatting away to each other and I was quietly impressed at each of them working out what the other was saying... until I realised everyone was at cross-purposes. My mother-in-law said Italy was very beautiful, to which my mother nodded but expressed sadness at never having visited *Israel*, but were the beaches any good?

'Yes, lovely sand. But not much parking,' said my father-in-law, in his heavy accent.

My father, who is quite deaf, caught the last word and thought he was being asked about his new car's parking camera, and proceeded to tell everyone about how the vehicle drove, whereas my father-in-law – who was trying to work out what cars had to do with holidays – decided that perhaps my father was talking about driving to the continent?

'I prefer to travel by plane,' he said.

'Really?' My father looked confused. 'What, even to the supermarket?'

Now it was my father-in-law's turn to look bewildered.

'Si, in *Italia* we have lots of *supermercati*,' he replied.

It was all a bit of a muddle. Even more so when our respective mothers left the restaurant. Because they both had each other's shoes on. Which reminds me.

What sort of shoes do secret agents wear?

Sneakers...

Patient to Psychiatrist:
Ever since I signed up for Twitter, I get this feeling I'm being followed...

This week I joined Twitter. Very reluctantly, I might add. On many, many occasions, I've been reminded that – as an author – I should be more *Out There*. Up until now, this advice has been steadfastly ignored. After all, I've only just settled into Facebook. And that's taken three years. Could I cope with Twitter? Should I even try? And anyway, what did Twitter actually *mean*? A few years ago, the answer would maybe have been something like the noise an owl makes. Anyway, I digress.

I signed up. And I did my first tweet. A mini essay. Up came a prompt box.

You'll have to be cleverer than that! You only have one hundred and forty characters.

One hundred and forty characters? Twitter is expecting a writer whose fingers spew thousands of words to sum something up in one hundred and forty characters? Flash fiction has never been my forte, which meant that Twitter and I were already not off to a good start.

As my genre is contemporary romance (okay, chick-lit) I decided to kick off with putting two words in the search box. Up came Twitter's suggestions on who to follow... fellow lovers of the written word... romantics... writers... and naturally chick-lit fans. I began clicking the button to follow them. After a while, my eyes glazed. But I let the mouse keep on clicking.

First lesson on Twitter: pay attention to who you are following!

I was astounded to receive messages from 'chicks' eager to tell me their tips on... *ahem*... spit or swallow. And we're not talking cuckoos or feathered friends. Some hasty "unfollowing" took place.

Forty-eight hours later, I quietly congratulated myself. Yay, I was getting the hang of it! Why, I'd even discovered a link and managed to open it – how exciting! But it turned out to be the thrill was for the sender only.

Second lesson on Twitter: don't open a link unless you know who sent it!

Suddenly I was receiving hundreds of nasty messages. Even worse, so were my followers. And apparently all those nasty messages were from me. H – E – L – P!

By this point I'd dropped the smug self-congratulations, and instead wanted to metaphorically flush Twitter down the toilet.

A spot of password changing then took place. After that I wondered why I couldn't sign back in. Transpired I'd mis-typed *Twitter* with *Titter*, except I wasn't laughing. Hopefully, one of these fine days, I'll be tweeting like a pro, and maybe even posting pictures of what I had to eat. Which reminds me.

Why were the breakfast potatoes chasing each other? Hash tag...

Controversy over breast implants.
Are we making mountains out of molehills?

I spent all my teenage life with a chest as flat as a pancake. It didn't bother me too much until, hitting my teens, and gaining an overnight interest in boys. I quickly discovered that the lads from the boys' school were more interested in the girls at my school who had... *ahem*... boobs.

Every Saturday night, you absolutely HAD to be seen at the local disco – along with every other fifteen-year-old in the vicinity, all clutching their older siblings' driving licences and making out they were over eighteen. The weekly disco was a cause of great excitement. And stress. How could that flat chest be coaxed into rising for the occasion? Often, my girlfriends would raid their dads' sock drawer and swagger into the disco sporting an instant pair of Dolly Partons. But I didn't have the bravado to do that. Spot the teenager who nobody asked to dance standing on the outside looking in.

These days, that is no longer the case. By that, I don't mean I lurk on the edge of dance floors. I mean that I no longer have a flat chest. And very recently I have been reminded how bits of our body can either make us see the funny side of things, or actually be quite upset. For example, the exterior of our house is currently being painted. I am faintly amused by the decorator ringing the doorbell in the morning but always addressing my chest. I doubt he knows what my face looks like. But I bet if you ask him what top I'm wearing, he'll tell you whether it's cotton, wool, scoop-lined or V-necked. However, for some ladies the attention is hard to cope with, especially if they also have the "fuller figure" and are extra top-heavy as a result.

The misconceptions people have about their bodies is quite staggering. I don't watch television and haven't for years. I'm not au-fait with *Boot Camps for Big Girls*, or *Britain's Next Anorexic Model* or *I'm An Attention Seeker Do Not Evict Me*, but such programmes are watched by millions. And a high percentage of the viewing audience are very impressionable. Like my teenaged daughter.

We recently attended The National TV Awards. I was oohing and aahing about various celebrities, but who did my daughter rush off to talk to? Some thirty-year-old reality star with the body of a child, fake breasts, fake hair, fake nails, fake eyelashes, fake tan, an obvious nose job, and such over-filled lips that – in profile – she resembled Donald Duck.

'Oh my God,' sighed my daughter, enviously, 'she is *so* beautiful.'

Was she kidding? Apparently not.

If I told my daughter that my idea of beauty was a young and voluptuous Sophia Loren, she'd probably squeal with horror and say that a young Sophia today would be begging to audition for the next *Lipo Or Live With It* programme. And THAT is what hacks me off. That reality television programmes, magazines, social media sights like Instagram etc, are full of ridiculous ideals and influences that are bang out of order.

The bottom line is: BRING BACK THE BOTTOM!*

Which reminds me.

Cosmetic surgery used to be such a taboo subject. Now, when you talk about Botox, nobody raises an eyebrow...

*Re-reading this several years later, the big bottom is back. Yes... bum implants. ARGH!

When does it rain money?
When there is 'change' in the air...

Holidays are being discussed. We have been fortunate enough to come up with enough dosh to go away this year, and I can't wait to exchange a temperamental British summer for two golden weeks of sunshine somewhere else in the world. I love going away, and it's round about this time of year that I find myself literally *yearning* for the anticipated break. A fortnight of stress-free bliss. Bring it on! Except... so far, no holiday has been booked. I can see a *last minute dot com* being the result.

Mr V is privately hoping we will be having a family holiday. With three children aged nineteen, seventeen, and almost fifteen, that is unlikely. I knew last summer was, realistically, the last time we'd all go away together. Indeed, my son has already booked a jaunt to Turkey without us. My step-daughter doesn't want to go away at all, and my daughter doesn't want to go on holiday without her step-sister or brother. So, at this rate it could be just me and Mr V – which, quite frankly, I'm more than happy to entertain (where's that brochure for the Maldives?)!

Currently, as I type this, the British weather is dismal. However, the Government is still emphatically advising everyone that we are experiencing drought, to shower instead of bath, and if we use our hosepipes, we will be heavily fined. Although I can't see anybody in my area wanting to use their hosepipe to water the lawn. Right now, many lawns are under water and a good many of our local roads are flooded. Walking Trudy Beagle requires Wellingtons and a storm mac – for her, as well as me. Sleeping at night is difficult because the torrential endless rainfall sounds like a firing squad pelting against our bedroom's skylights. But when all is said and done, I don't really care where we go on holiday, just so long as the sun shines all day long for fourteen days solid, and there is a lounger to loll around on whilst reading my Kindle and sipping a cool drink. Meanwhile, I think I'll order a new umbrella off Amazon. Which reminds me.

What happens when it rains cats and dogs? You must be careful not to step in a poodle...

How do crazy joggers run through the woods?
They take the psycho path...

Recently I started jogging again. Not because I like it. Rather to tone up, lose weight and get fitter. To date I look no different. Nor has any weight been lost. However, fitness might be up a notch. This was put to the test last Thursday when Mr V and I caught a plane to Prague.

Following EasyJet's advice, we arrived at Stansted Airport two hours prior to take-off. We checked in, got rid of the luggage, and congratulated ourselves on having plenty of time to relax. Strolling into one of the many coffee shops, we sat in a corner with our cappuccinos and immediately put the world to rights. And also lost track of time. Stupidly, we hadn't gone through the X-Ray bit and, as luck would have it, there was a horrendously long queue. A lady swathed from head to toe in long flowing garb was repeatedly setting the alarms off and flatly refusing to co-operate. The queue ground to a standstill. The crowd of waiting people began chuntering. Staff started to look harassed. Twenty minutes later it was finally our turn. I didn't get cleared. Boots, belt and wristwatch had been removed. A stern woman with a huge metal detector scanned me. More demented bleeping. Next, I was being thoroughly frisked by hand. Behind me, the queue were muttering. Loudly. Red-faced with embarrassment, I was finally waved through when airport staff decided the bleeping was down to the numerous decorative studs on the backside of my jeans.

We now had just ten minutes to catch our flight. Even worse, the monorail wasn't working. At various points around this part of the airport, large black-and-white notices proclaimed: *IF YOU ARE LATE, WE WON'T WAIT!*

Gulp.

And so began our manic run through Stansted Airport as we searched for Boarding Gate 2. We belted along corridors, skirted trolleys, bypassed dawdlers, leapt two stairs at a time up the escalator, flew round corners and finally found Gate 2. The area was devoid of people and

23

the gate was shut. At that moment there was an announcement.

Bing bong.

'Last call for Prague! Please go to Gate 13.'

Not Gate 2?

'I thought you said Gate 2,' I gasped to Mr V, panting hard.

'Well, I *thought* it was Gate 2,' he wheezed, bending forward and trying to catch his breath.

Now wasn't the moment to remind him, for the hundredth time, that he should have an eye-test. I'd nag him in Prague. Or murder him. One of the two – if we ever got there.

We turned and thundered off in the opposite direction. Don't ask me how we made it. I lost sight of my husband and assumed he was ahead of me. I burst into the aircraft and flapped my arms at the waiting flight stewards.

'Here... sorry... my husband waiting...' I waved a hand expansively at the unsmiling passengers.

'Your husband?' asked one of the stewards, checking my boarding pass. 'We are still one short.'

'He's not here?' I croaked in horror. Oh my God. Had I got on to the wrong plane? Or... *hell*... was my husband on the wrong plane instead? 'Does this go to Prague?' I wheezed, trying to resist the desire to drop to the floor and quietly expire.

'Yes – if we don't miss our slot!' said the other steward, sounding peeved.

'Cabin crew to doors,' crackled an overhead announcement.

'No!' I said, stretching my arms across the aircraft door and blocking both stewards. 'We can't go without my husband.'

The man in question chose that precise moment to stagger into view. We heard him before seeing him. The noise was a bit like someone having an asthma attack... but through a tannoy. Mr V's heart was hammering so hard I swear his shirt was visibly palpitating, whereas I was puffing but not in imminent danger of having a coronary. So, the good news is: regular jogging is good for your health. Oh, and we got to Prague.

The following morning we set off to explore. Like all good tourists I'd downloaded a map of Prague the day before using all my printer cartridges in the process, along with an entire roll of cellotape to stick numerous A4 sheets together. Whereupon the receptionist gave us a dinky map all neatly folded up, immediately rendering mine useless.

We wandered outside and stood on the pavement where Mr V studied the map.

'Catch the Number 22 tram,' I read from my tourist guide, 'to the river.'

As if on cue, a Number 22 tram rattled to a standstill in front of us. We hopped on, and off we went. In the wrong direction. An hour later we still hadn't found the river, but we'd checked out some diverse market stalls where you could buy fresh flowers. And cannabis.

Totally lost, we came across a church.

'Let's go in,' said Mr V.

Inside, a few people sat in pews, heads bowed in prayer. The silence was so profound it was literally deafening. As I'm a firm believer that God is everywhere and not just in a church, I didn't imitate Mr V who was frantically crossing himself and clearly muttering apologies for not having been inside a holy place since his nephews were baptised. Fifteen years ago. The interior of the church reminded me of Madame Tussauds – but a Godly version. Eerie giant-sized statues of saints jostled for space with a dying Jesus. A padre glided silently out of a confessional box and greeted us. Mr V did lots of bowing and scraping and reversed towards an exit. The padre put up a hand to halt us. Terrified that he was going to be hauled into a confessional box, Mr V made a break for it. Whereupon the real reason for the padre's attempt to stop us became apparent. Only God would know when that particular door had last been opened. It groaned back on its hinges, with thunderous creaks and cracks splintering the air, well and truly shattering the silence and shocking the occupants within.

Finding the metro, we disappeared into the bowels of

the earth. More by luck than design, we ended up in a place that was totally unpronounceable but began with S and was –hurrah! – near the river. And so exploring the Old Town properly began.

Prague is a beautiful city with a plethora of cobbled streets and quaint buildings steeped in history. However, so many have been marred by prolific graffiti, indeed I have never seen so much of the stuff in my life. And any ideas to do a bit of frivolous shopping and buy yet another handbag went right out the window when I saw the number of tramps, beggars and lost souls on the streets. These were people who needed a meal. And although we gave a few some money, I doubt they fed themselves. To say it made you sad is an understatement. Likewise, when I saw a beautiful young girl offering her services to a bunch of drunk stags. All I kept thinking was, 'That's somebody's precious daughter,' and I wanted to shove the leering louts away. But all cities have their dark side. Prague is probably no different to any other city in the world.

Putting the seedier part to one side, it was nice to visit another bit of the world and explore that country's culture and history. Would I go back? Possibly. But next time I'll be paying closer attention to departure gate numbers – and have on my trainers. Which reminds me.

What do running shoes do when they forget something?

They jog their memory...

What do you get if your dog eats beans and onions?
Tear gas...

The downside of owning a dog is that sometimes – well okay much of the time – they parp. And toot. And even occasionally trumpet (especially if they've swiped your beans on toast when you weren't looking). But in the case of my pooch forget the parp, toot and trumpet. There is a whole orchestra of wind instruments going on under Trudy Beagle's tail.

A beagle is a bit of a wotsit when it comes to grub. As far as this breed is concerned, all food is theirs. Even yours. They will eat anything and everything and have no comprehension of their stomach ever being full.

I have a feeling that my pooch went foraging on our last walk and ate something she shouldn't. I also have a feeling that a vet bill might be imminent! Meantime, I've put her on soft boiled rice to calm the gut down. That and throwing all the windows in the house wide open. Which reminds me.

Actually... no, let's not go there!

What did the sign in the vet's waiting room say?
Back in five minutes so... Sit! Stay!

How ironic that my last blog smiling about Trudy Beagle
and her all-too-common *toots* should change – within
twenty-four hours – into something so serious. I felt
horrendously guilty for not taking her to the emergency
vet on Sunday night but, then again, what would I have
said?

'Help! My dog won't stop tooting!'

Realistically, dogs are prone to tooting. Especially
beagles who suck cuddly toys, chomp on socks, lick floors,
chew on plants and, given half a chance, bust into the
dustbin to consume goodness only knows what manner
of manky leftovers. The fact that they survive and
(mostly) escape unscathed, can fool you into believing
they have constitutions of iron. However, by Monday
morning it was evident things Trudy Beagle's tum was
taking a turn for the worse, and we hastened to the local
surgery.

As always, there was a queue. An elderly lady was
nervously perched on a waiting room chair. On her lap
was a carrier containing her pet bunny. She was first in
the queue. Trudy Beagle was second. All was calm. Until
a third arrival came into the waiting room. This patient
was a Staffordshire Bull Terrier, muzzled and sporting a
plaster cast on one leg, which thumped noisily on the
floor as it moved around. Within seconds later, the fourth
patient of the day arrived. This one was a massive
German Shepherd with a flustered owner.

'Stand back, everybody!' he yelled. 'Move out the way!'

Exactly *where* everybody was meant to move to was
unclear. Here we all were in a waiting room which was
rapidly reducing to the size of a postage-stamp. The
elderly lady with the bunny was shrinking back in her
chair, clutching bunny's carrier and looking absolutely
terrified. The Staff turned around to check out the
German Shepherd, and was immediately greeted with a
row of pearly-white teeth and ominous growling,
whereupon it decided to launch itself at the German

Shepherd. There was the sound of its plaster cast clunking against the Shepherd's skull, followed by all hell breaking loose. The dogs tumbled over and over. Leads entangled. Owners shouted. The elderly lady with the bunny tried to blend into wall. At this point, if you are eating or have a frail tummy, stop reading. Or skip the following paragraph.

As canine war broke out, Trudy Beagle did what all terrified dogs do... had a bowel evacuation. But because she wasn't well, what came out was comparable to aerosol mist. My pooch fought against her lead to escape the mayhem, her quarters swinging around the waiting room. And it would be fair to say nobody escaped being sprayed by my dog's backside. The lady with the bunny nearly fainted. The Staff's plaster cast went from grubby white to chocolate brown. The German Shepherd stopped fighting and looked gobsmacked. Or should I say *blob*smacked? And the air turned not just brown but also blue as major swearing broke out. Ever watched *Love Story*? Ali MacGraw famously tells Ryan O'Neal, 'Love is never having to say you're sorry.' Well no matter how much you love dogs, sometimes saying sorry just isn't enough.

'Sorry,' I bleated. 'Sorry-sorry-sorry-sorry-sorry.'

I do not lie when I say that everybody – even that bunny – gave me a shitty look.

The vet appeared in the doorway and insisted my pooch was seen first. We walked off down the corridor with my dog's backside still aerosol-misting, spraying leaflets on worming and a glass wall-mounted unit showcasing a local resident's Designer doggy leads. *Total* nightmare.

Trudy Beagle was diagnosed with Haemorrhagic Gastroenteritis which – I was horrified to find out – can be fatal if not dealt with promptly. She was immediately hooked up to a drip and pumped full of antibiotics. I'm relieved (no, wrong word, Debbie)... I'm delighted to say that one week later, Trudy Beagle is once again fighting fit, and hopefully we won't have to return to the vet's waiting room for a very long time. They hope so too!

Which reminds me.

A man took his beagle to the vet and said, 'My beagle is cross-eyed. Can you do anything for him?'

'Possibly,' said the vet. 'Let's take a good look.'

So he picks up the beagle and peers at its eyes, before looking pained.

'Well?' said the anxious owner.

'Not good,' said the vet. 'I must put him down.'

The owner was distraught. 'Put him down? What, just because he's cross-eyed?'

'No,' said the vet, 'because he's heavy...'

Teacher: Where is your coursework?
Student: I lost it fighting a pupil who said you weren't the best teacher...

Mr V and I recently attended Parents Evening. With three children between fourteen and nineteen, it's fair to say we've ratcheted up quite a collection of evenings huddled around a classroom desk opposite a teacher. We've met a lot of teachers. The truly great and the ruddy awful. This week was no exception.

My husband, daughter and I made our way over to the Physics tutor. A man. And a very uninterested man at that.

'Pleased to meet you,' he said, sounding beyond bored. He shifted one buttock from his plastic chair, and scratched absent-mindedly before looking at Eleanor. 'Your name?' he asked.

My husband's eyebrows nearly shot off his forehead, and I had to stifle an exclamation of surprise. This man had been teaching our daughter for the past year!

'Eleanor,' said Eleanor.

'Okay,' said the tutor, looking none the wiser as he consulted a typed list in front of him. 'Ah. Yes. Here you are. Looks like you're a C student. Obviously, that means you need to work a lot harder.'

The tutor stood up, one hand extended, indicating the meeting was over. We didn't shake his hand. Nor did we stand up. I cleared my throat.

'Actually, this is a subject Eleanor finds quite tough, so much so that we've recently engaged a private tutor.' The teacher shrugged. I ploughed on. 'Do you have any helpful pointers on how Eleanor can increase her understanding?'

'Yeah. Stick with the private tutor.'

We then stood up, wondering what on earth he was doing in the teaching profession. With such utter disinterest, was it any wonder his students lacked higher grades? We moved on to the next appointment.

'Good evening, Mr and Mrs Viggiano,' beamed the Spanish teacher. I beamed back. How refreshing to have a teacher who not only addressed you, but also got your name right. I don't mean in terms of pronunciation; I mean in being *correct*. My children are from my first marriage (their father is deceased) so they have a different surname to me. And whilst my second husband had nothing against my first husband, he'd rather not be addressed as Mr Coveney.

We sat down. The teacher gave us an earnest look before enthusiastically launching into her chat. 'Now I know Spanish isn't Eleanor's favourite subject, but with a little bit of effort she could do *so* well. Her written exam achieved a Grade A, and she was just two marks off an A*. The oral exam was weaker – a Grade C – but, once again, only a couple of marks away from a Grade B. Eleanor has a beautiful accent and *so* much potential.'

The teacher then waxed lyrical about school trips to Spain, recommended some Spanish films to watch and suggested the attendance of lunch-time workshops that she personally held twice a week.

'I'm more than happy to give up a lunch hour for my pupils,' she assured, 'or, if Eleanor prefers, she can seek me out after school with anything she's stuck on.' She smiled at Eleanor as she continued. 'Can I also suggest that you read Spanish gossip magazines to whet your interest in the language and increase vocabulary?'

We thanked the teacher for her time, shook hands and stood up.

Now *that* was a teacher who didn't just know *our* names, but more importantly knew her *pupil's* name including that pupil's strengths, weaknesses and potential. AND was passionate about her job and the subject she was teaching.

Meanwhile Eleanor has noted her Spanish teacher's helpful suggestions and bought a book of Spanish jokes. I don't understand any of them. So I'll stick to English. Which reminds me.

How many Spaniards does it take to change a lightbulb?

Just Juan...

The Queen's Diamond Jubilee
A Bit of a (Royal) Do...

I'm a bit of a royalist. I mean, the Queen has been around for as long as I've lived *and* some more. She's part of all that is British. She's like fish and chips, a cup of tea, or a rainy day in a British summer. In other words, the monarch is part of the fabric of life. Whatever you think about the Queen or, indeed, the Royal family, I do believe she's one amazing woman and that her reign of sixty years is something to celebrate. So, later on today, I will be dishing up the Sunday roast upon a dining table covered with a paper version of the Union Jack flag. There will be red-white-and-blue serviettes with a centrepiece of red-white-and-blue flowers. We shall raise a glass to Her Majesty and then finish off with coffee and red-white-and-blue cupcakes. Happy Diamond Jubilee Your Majesty!

Which reminds me. Did you know that royal chairs are rarely throne out...?

A book fell on my head.
I can only blame my shelf...

After months of procrastinating, I've finally bought a Kindle. As I walked out of PC World clutching my newly boxed prize, I did fleetingly wonder if I'd done the right thing. You see, I love books. As in *proper* books. You know, made of paper with a spine that creases if you bend it back, and pages that come unglued when you drop it in the bath. Not that I've dropped a book in the bath for years. Chance would be a fine thing. But you know what I mean. Anyway, I digress.

As I'm an author of novels that predominantly sell as e-books, it seemed faintly ridiculous not owning such a device. But having now rectified that and taken the leap into Kindle Land, I have been happily taking advantage of all those amazing free downloads that Amazon notifies me about. Indeed, I've had a pleasurable time trawling through freebies, looking inside, having a bit of a read and *umming* and *ahhing* whether to download or not. In all truth, it's been a bit like browsing in a bookstore, except in the comfort of my own home. So far, I've downloaded twenty books. I can't stop marvelling at how hefty this number of books would be – say, in a holiday suitcase – or how much space they would take up on a shelf, before eventually gathering dust. It's fair to say that I'm a total convert to this pencil-thin gadget that slips so conveniently inside my handbag. Which reminds me.

Did you hear about the dog who loved chewing things he shouldn't? One day, he found a Kindle and crunched on it until it fell to pieces. When the dog's owners returned home, the husband said to his wife, 'Oh no, isn't that your Kindle in Fred's mouth?' The wife replied, 'Yes, but never mind, it's only to be expected. After all, he's a Golden E-Reader...

What do you call the father you walk all over? Stepdad...

Being a parent is a tough task. Even more so being a step-parent. My husband should know. He has effectively raised my two children (their father is deceased) and consequently taken a road he most certainly never dreamt he would one day travel.

They say the path of true love never runs smoothly. That is never more bang on the mark when step-children are in the equation. Young children are affectionately called *little monsters*. But what about when they grow older? Yes, they become *big monsters*! But a step-parent never dare utter those words. A step-parent must let a lot of stuff go right over their head.

'You're not my real father!' has been a favourite come-back when one of my teenagers has thrown a massive tantrum. But equally the same chippy teenager has quickly sought refuge with their step-father if I've been on the warpath, verbal guns blazing.

My children have rejected their step-father, loved their step-father, shouted at him, cried on his shoulder, pushed him away, and hugged him. Today they are spoiling him, and rightly so, with cards and presents. It's their way of saying, 'Thank you for being there when my own Dad isn't.'

As Johann Schiller said, it is not flesh and blood but the heart which makes us fathers and sons. So to all the step-fathers out there with a blended family – here's to you! Happy Father's Day. Which reminds me.

Harry: What does your dad do for a living?
Dan: He's a magician. He likes sawing people in half!
Harry: You got any brothers or sisters?
Dan: Yeah. Two half-brothers and a half-sister...

What is the difference between teenagers and parents?
The teenagers still have the faults that the parents outgrew...

Yesterday evening my teenage daughter begged for her boyfriend to come over.

'Um... but it's Saturday night,' I said. My daughter knows full well that my husband and I nearly always go out on a Saturday night. 'It's our date night,' I continued, 'which means nobody will be at home.'

Eleanor glared at me. The words *the two of you will be left alone together* hung, unspoken, in the air. 'Don't you trust me?' she snapped.

'Yes, of course,' I blustered, whilst privately thinking, "I have absolutely no idea. I would hope so. But I can't be certain. Because I remember my own teenage years like yesterday. And I once said the same thing to my own mother. And reneged on my promise."

'You don't *sound* like you trust me,' said Eleanor, eyes narrowing.

'I trust you,' I said, keeping my fingers crossed behind my back.

So Mr V and I went out. Needless to say, my husband wasn't happy about it.

'Are you trusting them?' he asked, as we sat down in the cinema and waited for the film to start.

'Yes, of course,' I said, staunchly. 'Anyway, you were once a teenager. I can remember you telling me stories about your parents leaving you alone on a Saturday night and your girlfriend used to pop over. Your parents trusted *you*, didn't they?' I reasoned.

'Debbie, they didn't *know* my girlfriend used to come over.'

'What? You lied to them?'

'No, I just failed to mention it, that's all.'

'Right,' I said, nervously chewing on my popcorn. 'Well, I'm sure you both behaved, eh? Watched telly. Had a cup of tea.'

Mr V rolled his eyes. 'Don't be ridiculous. I was a

36

sixteen-year-old boy.'

'Shall we change the subject?' I asked, whilst discreetly grabbing my phone and doing some frantic texting.

Me: *Everything okay?*
Me: *Hello?*
Me: *Answer please.*
Me: *Reply in the next ten seconds or I'm coming home.*
Eleanor: *YES I AM OKAY! WAS IN TOILET!*

It's a funny old world. You can torment yourself with a whole list of things that will happen while you're out... like worrying about your child having underage sex. Taking drugs. Raiding the drinks cupboard. Posting a party on social media. Coming home to find the house trashed. Discovering your car with a mysterious prang, even though your teenager swears they didn't illegally take it out the moment your back was turned.

But never in a million years could I have guessed what was actually going on as I tried and failed to concentrate on a film called *The Five Year Engagement*. And no, I haven't the faintest idea what it was about. I was too busy wondering if neighbours had called the police to evict revellers from our house. But I do remember a giant pink bunny making various appearances – in the film, not in my private worries – and a very unappetising love interest. Anyway. Back to *What Was Really Going On At Home*.

Okay. As soon as the key went in the front door, I was aware of deathly silence. And darkness. And a funny smell. Wacky backy? No. Gas. And I'm not talking about Trudy Beagle's rear end. This was *British Gas*. And lots of it. I ran into the kitchen, turned off an unlit burner and then threw open the windows and doors.

'Don't turn on any lights,' I screamed to Mr V, who naturally did just that.

Fortunately the house didn't blow up.

My teenager and the boyfriend were upstairs. In her bedroom. Blissfully unaware we were home. Or that the downstairs stank of gas. In fact, they weren't aware of anything other than the no-good they were up to. Which was... my daughter piercing her boyfriend's ear.

Is that all? I hear you sigh.

Well, I wasn't entirely sure how well my daughter's inflicted piercing would go down with the boyfriend's mum. I had a feeling she might be a teeny bit cross.

And the reason for the gas? Because Eleanor had 'sterilised' a needle from my sewing box over the hob. Except she'd had it in her head that you gassed a needle rather than held it in a flame (so much for all the extra private science lessons we're paying for!). And such was the eagerness at getting on with the job, neither of them had thought to turn the gas off afterwards.

Still, I must look on the bright side. The house is still standing. And nobody is hurt. Other than the boyfriend's ear. Which reminds me.

How much do pirates pay to get their ears pierced?

A buccaneer...

Conjunctivitis.com
Isn't that a site for sore eyes?

They say that eyes are the windows to the soul. That when you look into a person's eyes you can tell in a nanosecond if that person is clean-living, kind, and generous of spirit. Well anybody looking at my peepers right now would probably think I was a shifty sort with a penchant for jam doughnuts. Because that's what they resemble right now. Two puffy slits with red centres.

It all started off with a dose of hay fever and itchy eyes. Within twenty-four hours, my eyes felt as though somebody had poured gravel into them. The optician prescribed some drops. But yesterday, when my eyes were so painful it was like blinking against sandpaper, a nice pharmacist suggested some lubricating stuff for dry eyes.

So last night I went to bed with my eyelashes coated in oily gunk. The eyeballs finally felt a bit more comfortable. But this morning the lids were welded together and, upon waking, there followed a few seconds of blind panic (literally) because I couldn't see anything. Somewhere along the way, conjunctivitis had set in.

At the time of writing this, my in-laws are visiting. I had hopes about properly entertaining my in-laws... you know, being the magnanimous host, not wearing wraparound sunglasses and a grimace. The sunnies are all well and good during daylight, but it's not such a great look at night. Yesterday evening, whilst out, I attempted passing myself off as mysterious. My daughter gave a mirthless laugh and suggested *dodgy* instead. And Mr V has started calling me Roy. As in Orbison.

Ah well. It could be worse. At least eye infections do eventually heal. Which reminds me.

I later had to ring in sick at work.

'What's wrong?' asked my boss.

'I have a problem with my eyes.'

'Conjunctivitis?' he asked.

'No, I just can't see myself working,' I replied.

Why are birthdays good for you?
Statistics show that those who have the most live the longest...

Her Majesty the Queen was born on 21st April 1926, but it has long been customary to celebrate the sovereign's birthday publicly on a day during the summer, when better weather is more likely. Her Majesty's official birthday is marked by *Trooping the Colour*.

As this summer has been pretty much a total wash-out, it would seem my daughter has taken a leaf from the Queen's birthday book. When Eleanor turned fifteen on 6th July, the weather was incredibly wet. Nonetheless we celebrated, taking our brollies with us as we headed out to a local restaurant.

Eleanor continued the celebrations with her school friends the following day. Unfortunately, the weather was still atrocious. Birthday celebrations are now on their third day with (as I write this) a scheduled girlie shopping trip taking place at Bluewater Shopping Centre. And as Eleanor's *bestie* is not available to celebrate until next week, a fourth and final birthday celebration remains outstanding.

This extended run of celebrating has cost me dear. Regrettably, as my bank manager will testify, I do not have the Queen's purse. And transporting ten girls from their restaurant outing last night back to our house was tricky to say the least.

'The trouble is,' I said to Eleanor, 'I don't have the Queen's carriage. I have a Nissan Note. How are ten girls going to fit in my car?'

Eleanor looked thoughtful. 'Can't we at least try?' she finally asked.

Yes, she was being serious.

We resolved the transport problem by dragging Mr V away from his television viewing of the sports channel where he was flicking constantly between tennis, football, golf and motor racing. This is a man who, had he remained a bachelor, would probably now have a bank of television screens on his lounge wall.

Mr V was given orders to transport five girls in his car. That said, it was still a squash. Despite him having the bigger car, it was the girls with the smallest bottoms who made a beeline for his motor. I found myself transporting girls with legs longer than lampposts in my small run-around. One girl, 6'4" in her heels and sporting a towering afro, had to fold herself up like a deckchair to even get into the car. She ended up curling herself into the foetal position across everyone's laps in the back. There was a moment of anxiety when her hair got shut in the door. The door re-opened, the hair was scooped inside, and we set off.

Driving along, I checked my rear-view mirror and was alarmed to see one of the passengers had grown a beard. Closer inspection revealed the girl's jawline had, in fact, been framed by her friend's upwardly flowing afro.

Meanwhile, my daughter is now joyfully ticking off the days to her sixteenth. When you get to my age, you prefer to forget about your birthday because it is no longer a big deal. Which reminds me.

Forget about the past, you can't change it.

Forget about the future, you can't predict it.

And forget about the present, because I didn't get you one...

What are the hottest days during summer? Sun-days…

As any Brit will tell you, our summer has been a total wash-out. Oh we've had a few nice days here and there, don't get me wrong, but they've never fallen within a hoped-for time frame.

For example, earlier this year, when my son was swotting like mad for his finals, it irked him to be cooped up indoors with his computer and masses of notes, whilst outside the sun blazed away, its heat pressing up against the grime-encrusted windows of his London digs.

Likewise, my daughter was unimpressed to be shut up in a boiling-hot classroom trying to get her head around some early GCSE exams, when all she and her mates wanted to do was roll down their socks, hitch up their hemlines and sit in the sunshine turning pale limbs the colour of honey.

Now that exams are out the way and the long summer vacation stretches ahead, it is simply the "Law of Sod" that the sun has packed its bags and naffed off. Trying to do anything – mow the lawn, wash the car, trolley shopping out of the supermarket, walk Trudy Beagle, go for a run – is fraught with dodging cloud bursts and thundery rumbles, not to mention roads that turn into mini lakes within a matter of moments.

But this family has had enough! The suitcases are out, and the flights are booked! We're off to Cyprus. I've heard that temperatures are currently nudging forty degrees. Good. Because earlier this week I actually put the central-heating on for a few hours. I'm looking forward to going abroad and doing nothing other than reading, swimming, sunbathing and walking along a beautiful beach. It will also be a pleasure to wear pretty summer dresses that have, in the main, remained unworn and hanging in the wardrobe. Sunshine here we come! Which reminds me.

What did the pig say whilst sitting on a boiling hot beach?

I'm bacon…

Why did the scientist buy some sunscreen?
Because he was a pale-ontologist...

This time last week I was in Cyprus. Summer holidays, whether home or abroad, are all about taking a step back from busy lives and re-charging the batteries.

It was with a sigh of pleasure that I hopped on a plane and briefly escaped Britain's dismally wet summer and grey skies. Of course, the moment I jetted off, England sniggered behind her Union Jack flag, and temperatures soared to twenty-seven degrees for three whole days! But I didn't care too much. I was about to embrace *forty* degrees.

There was a moment of uncertainty upon touch-down. Having collected our luggage, we couldn't find the rep.

'Follow me,' I said, spotting a lady waving a Thomas Cook placard.

The rep checked her clipboard to see which coach we should get on. The tip of her biro traced the passenger names as she moved through her list.

'Oh dear,' she said, chewing her lip. 'You're not on the list.'

At this point I would just like to say that in the last twelve months I've been dealing with an unwelcome affliction. It's called *Menopausal Memory*. Every now and again the mists of menopausal memory clear giving a moment of clarity. My brain cells did a bit of sifting and – ding! –suddenly I was remembering that I'd booked the holiday with a completely different tour operator. Thomson. And sure enough, there was another rep – a man this time, and not standing a million miles away – waving a placard at the passing crowd.

'Viggiano?' he called in a forlorn voice. 'Anybody seen the Viggiano family?'

Relieved, the three of us gathered our suitcases and trundled over to him.

'Sooooo sorry,' I said, feeling flustered by the stupid mistake. My hair was sticking uncomfortably to my back, not helped by the airport having no air-conditioning. Electric fans were dotted about, but even they seemed to be wilting.

'No problem, you're here now,' the rep smiled. He paused to mop his shiny face with a cotton hanky. 'All I need from you is the name of your hotel.'

Ah yes. The name of the hotel.

'The name of the hotel,' I said, rummaging through my handbag for the paperwork, 'is... er... the name of the hotel is... it's right here... somewhere... it's... um–'

No paperwork. Where was the paperwork? Menopausal memory had returned. I looked at Mr V for inspiration. He looked back at me and shrugged. As well he might. I'd insisted on taking charge of booking this holiday and overseeing everything. The paperwork, therefore, was also my responsibility.

'What hotel are we staying in, Debbie?' asked Mr V. The question sounded innocent enough, but it was delivered through gritted teeth. My husband looked hot – as in puce-faced and in dire need of air-conditioning – and my daughter looked like every other teenager at the airport with their parents... beyond bored.

'Right,' I said, emerging from the depths of my handbag, 'I seem to have mislaid the paperwork. But it's not a problem. I can tell you *exactly* which hotel we're staying in.' Everyone, including the rep, looked relieved. 'Yes, it's the one with the really massive swimming pool.'

Out of my peripheral vision I could see my husband rolling his eyes. My daughter started being dramatic and whimpered about heat exhaustion. We'd only been on Cypriot soil for ten minutes. How was she going to cope with the next fortnight? The grey fog once again shifted.

'Oh, oh, wait... I remember now!' I squeaked, excitedly. 'We're staying at the Hotel Anus.'

There was a stunned silence. Even my teenager momentarily shut up.

'Ah,' said the rep, carefully, 'I think you mean the Atlantica *Aeneas* Hotel?'

Yes. That's what I said. Well, almost.

And so began our holiday. Every day I would stretch out on a sun-lounger. Rivulets of water would run down my sides. I wasn't sure if my body was crying from the heat or some part had sprung a leak. The only exertion was to press the page-turning button on my Kindle, take a tug on the straw of my iced lemonade, or put both aside and take a dip in the pool or sea.

Were there any holiday mishaps? Yes, of course. Like getting on a bus one evening to explore and getting lost. We ended up in Protaras. Not because we wanted to check out Protaras, more because – after forty minutes – we'd had enough of being in a sweat box with hundreds of wannabe clubbers necking booze and rolling spliffs.

Walking through the town, we stuck out like sore thumbs. Clubbers abounded. My daughter, dressed in cheeky shorts, actually looked overdressed compared to the many bare-chested young men everywhere. And whilst the women weren't bare-chested, let's just say that nothing was left to the imagination! Across the road was a nightclub that I myopically mis-read as *Boobies*. Which was quite appropriate in the circumstances.

'Drink,' Eleanor gasped. 'I need a drink.'

We headed towards a familiar neon sign. All the way to Cyprus and here we were in McDonalds.

The following day, back by the pool, I noticed a lady staring at my husband. He'd noticed too and looked mighty pleased with himself.

'I've still got it,' he smirked, before falling asleep on his sun-lounger. I lay back on my own sunbed and settled down with my Kindle, aware that the lady on the other side of the pool was still staring. Now she was nudging her friend. They giggled. What was funny? I lowered my Kindle and looked sideways at my slumbering husband. Or, rather, his old-fashioned swimming trunks. So far Mr V has refused to embrace long swim-shorts covered in neon palm trees. I don't know why. Eleanor even told him it would make him look younger, but his refusal has been steadfast. He is a man who doesn't like change, which includes hanging on to his ancient Speedos which are... well... saggy to say the least. And my husband hadn't realised just how lacking in the elastic department they were until lying sideways on his sun-lounger. And inadvertently exposing himself. Which gave a whole new meaning to that charming English colloquialism *dropping a bollock*.

There was another sticky moment – literally – when my daughter charmingly discarded several pieces of used chewing gum by spitting in the direction of our bathroom's toilet. But her aim was off and several balls of chewed gum landed on the toilet seat. Being a teenager firmly in her own zone, she left them there. In due course Mr V came along, shutting himself away in the bathroom with – yesss! – an English newspaper bought for an extortionate price at the local souvenir shop. I would like to point out that my husband is quite hairy. We're talking... rug-like. So when he eased himself down on the toilet seat, he wasn't expecting to have one thigh adhere to a load of chewing gum. Or to be shrieking in pain half an hour later as his wife cut him free with a pair of nail scissors.

Meanwhile my daughter had packed a suitcase full of shorts that, in all truth, were little more than denim underpants. Boys flocked around, and Mr V did an awful lot of huffing and puffing.

'Debbie, have you seen what Eleanor is wearing?' he asked, as we went to the terrace for a pre-dinner drink. 'Can't you do something about it?'

Ha! As if I have any influence on a fifteen-year-old. But Eleanor had overheard her step-father's criticism and, annoyed, stomped off to the bar.

'And make sure you're only drinking Coke!' Mr V shouted after her.

'Yessss,' Eleanor hissed, face flushed with embarrassment. Somewhere along the pot-holed path of bringing up a teenager, she must have taken on board the word "compromise" that I have so often trotted out in soothing tones when trying to avoid doing battle. Because at the bar she compromised. She had the Coke but also asked for Malibu in it. Mr V, who'd been watching like a hawk, looked ready to blow a gasket. Rather than get caught up in a row between the two of them, I hastened off to the bar and ordered my own Coke. With Bacardi.

Foreign drinks are nothing like British ones and,

within minutes, Eleanor and I were absolutely plastered. Mr V pursed his lips and took himself and his one bald thigh off to the bar too. He ordered a gin and tonic. Five minutes later he was also smashed.

By the time we'd finished our drinks and were ready to stagger in to dinner, it became apparent Eleanor was in difficulties. She was perched on a tall stool, but couldn't move.

'C'mon,' I slurred, 'geddoff.'

'Can't,' said Eleanor, shaking her head.

'Why not?' asked Mr V.

'I've got a wedgie.'

So Mr V and I had to form a screen around Eleanor while she stood up and made the necessary adjustments to her extremely short shorts.

Much later, on the way back to our hotel room, I came across a stray cat. It eyed me suspiciously. It's been years and years since I've had a moggy in my life, but this pitiful creature captured my heart, especially when I spotted five tiny kittens tucked into a nearby geranium plant. Mummy Cat allowed me to peer into the flowery depths. The kittens were adorable, but it was obvious they had an eye infection. A couple of them even had their eyes glued shut by thick green gunge.

I then realised that two small children had materialised by my side and were studying the kittens with joy, until also noticing their eyes.

'What's wrong with them?' asked the tallest.

'They have something called conjunctivitis,' I said.

'That sounds horrible,' said the youngest. 'Can you fix it?'

'I'll try,' I smiled.

I went to the local pharmacy and bought antibiotic eye drops. For the remainder of the holiday me and my two "nurses" – Isabelle and Trinity – would swaddle the kittens with an old t-shirt and drip the drops into their crusty eyes while Mummy Cat looked on, somehow knowing we were trying to help her babies.

Isabelle named all the kittens. There was a dear little tortoiseshell called Tikka. Two tabbies became Tiger and

Mischief, and two tabby-and-whites were suddenly finding themselves addressed as Alvin and Chipmunk.

'I think you need to re-name Alvin,' I said, one day.

'Why?' asked Trinity.

'Because Alvin is female,' I smiled.

We watched as the kittens – now clear of conjunctivitis – pounced on each other and played with their tails in the shade of the flowerbed. Mummy Cat looked on contentedly. Which reminds me.

Did you hear about the cat that swallowed a ball of wool?

She went on to have mittens...

How did the landlord die?
He cashed out...

My son is revving up for his second year of dentistry at uni. A London apartment has been found. Now to me, the words *London apartment* conjure up a host of possibilities like... a lofty penthouse... or a converted warehouse with fabulous high ceilings and state-of-the-art kitchen... or even a snazzy waterside residence where you can see the boats chugging up and down the Thames. So when Rob came home and enthusiastically cried, 'I've found a rental, and it's great,' I was really chuffed for him. Rob's smile was so wide his lips were almost meeting round the back of his head.

'What's it like?' I asked eagerly.

'Well,' he hesitated, picking his words carefully, 'my room is the smallest, but it's really light and airy. And I can see the sky!'

Seeing the sky is very important to Rob. He has spent the last year living in Queen Mary's Halls of Residence overlooking a building site which, in no time at all, turned into a towering new hospital wing completely blocking out all light. The view from his window was bricks, bricks and more bricks punctuated by blacked-out glass which – argh! – reflected back the bricks of the building he was inhabiting. After a while Rob found this view so depressing, he ended up buying huge posters of sun-drenched skies, emerald-free parks and gushing waterfalls, and blu-tacked them all over his walls.

A few days later, I found myself loading up the car and transporting all Rob's gear to this new *London apartment*. An hour later we were parked up in a mean side street adjacent to a squalid looking block of flats that smacked of social housing.

'Are you sure your flat is privately owned?' I asked Rob.

I've heard many a tale about Council tenants illegally sub-letting.

'Oh, Mum,' Rob implored, as we got out of the car, 'don't start stressing, and please don't embarrass me in front of my three flatmates.'

'Of course not,' I said, following my son up a concrete staircase that stank of urine.

And I tried not to. Really, I did.

'You're all paying HOW MUCH?' I shrieked to Rob and his flatmates as we stood in a kitchen sporting lopsided cabinets that were full of mouse droppings. When my son had mentioned the rent was five hundred pounds per month, I'd naively thought the four of them were splitting this sum between them. How any landlord had the cheek to charge two thousand quid every single month for this grime-encrusted s**t-hole (which the lettings agent had assured had been "professionally cleaned") was surely a joke. Except I wasn't laughing.

'Hey, it's not too bad,' quavered Rob.

'You're right,' I fumed, 'it's not too bad, because it's actually ABSOLUTELY DIRE.'

And then I did what any other embarrassing parent would do... despatched all four of them to the local shop for bleach, scouring pads, cleaning fluid, rubber gloves and anti-bac wipes.

Seven hours later, the place had been scrubbed from ceiling to floor, and wall to wall. However, I can't say it looked any better for it. I also think Rob might be re-cycling his posters. You can indeed see the sky from his bedroom window, but only if you crane your neck.

Oh, to have written a novel like *Fifty Shades* and made a comfortable million or three. Then I'd have bought my son one of those gorgeous new *London apartments* half a mile down the road with all mod-cons. Meanwhile, I shall source eBay for a couple of mousetraps. Which reminds me.

What is a mouse's favourite game?

Hide and squeak...

Definition of a flatmate:
Someone who checks the mail but only collects his own...

My son has not yet fully moved into his *London apartment* (also known as *the black hole*) and already squabbling has broken out amongst the flatmates. This doesn't bode well for harmony in the months ahead.

Let me backtrack. There are four students in total, of which my son is one. Three lads and a young lady. Prior to this merry band of four renting the black hole, Rob assured me they all got on like the proverbial house on fire. Which in some respects is true, because in the last few days there have been lots of smoke signals escalating into fireworks.

It all started when Rob and – I'll call them Wayne, Dwain and, um, Jane – went to view the black hole. Well, actually it was just Rob, Wayne and Jane, because Dwain had failed his exams and was swotting for a re-sit.

'Can I leave you guys to view potential rentals on my behalf?' Dwain had asked.

'Sure,' the others had replied.

As their budget was tight, there were only a limited number of properties available – which ranged from the heave-making and disgusting, to the dismally dire. They elected for the dismally dire. A series of photographs were taken, including a video. These were immediately sent off to Dwain, who viewed them before giving the thumbs up.

'That'll do,' Dwain texted, 'and if you guys don't mind, I'd appreciate the bedroom with the desk in it.'

The others agreed and sorted out the remaining choice of rooms between themselves. As mentioned previously, when I helped my son move his stuff into these digs, I was appalled at the state of the place. Filthy wasn't a word which came even came close to describing it. Rob, Wayne, Jane and I spent hours scrubbing the place from top to bottom. Dwain didn't join in with the cleaning because, exhausted from revision and exams, he'd taken himself off for a holiday in the sun. This had annoyed Jane because Dwain had told her he was broke AND he still owed her three hundred pounds for his share of the deposit money.

Over the last couple of weeks Rob has been in and out of the black hole to either oversee men from the gas suppliers or to check dodgy appliances, and Jane has forked out for paint and spent three days tarting-up skirting boards and doors in an attempt to make the place look less of a black hole and more of.. well... a grey hole. At no point has Dwain bothered to put in an appearance. *And* he still owes three hundred quid deposit money to Jane.

And then yesterday, while Rob was at work (his summer job), Dwain phoned to have a moan.

'I'm just moving my stuff in, Rob, and I'm not happy. In fact, I'm livid.'

'What's up?' said Rob.

'This *London apartment* you've chosen is a naffing black hole. So I'm angry. Fuming, in fact. And I've changed my mind about having the room with the desk. It's too dark. I'll have the lounge as my bedroom instead.'

Unfortunately Wayne, Jane and Rob are not in agreement to Dwain having the lounge as his bedroom. The lounge was a deciding factor in them taking the lease because of its size. It can accommodate a dining table for them all, a couple of sofas and is big enough to entertain friends. They've already clubbed together and bought a projector for movies in there – which Dwain also owes money towards. Dwain threatened not to pay Jane the outstanding three hundred pounds deposit money if he didn't get his own way over having the lounge as his bedroom, and Jane promptly burst into tears. So Rob and Wayne joined forces and told Dwain – politely but firmly – that he was bang out of order. It was pointed out that Dwain had been given first pick of the bedrooms, hadn't availed himself to viewing any properties, had failed to do his share of cleaning, and still hadn't stumped up monies owed. Result? Dwain promptly had the mother of all tantrums and called Rob, Wayne and Jane some rather choice names.

So, not a good start. And if it's like this now, I wonder

how tensions will be a few weeks down the line. Which reminds me.

Did you hear about the guy who pushed his friend under a steamroller?

He wanted a flat mate...

How do you avoid getting wrinkles?
Take off your glasses...

Earlier this week I took my daughter to the local photographer to update her portfolio for her drama agent. Whilst there, I asked the photographer if she would be kind enough to take a few *mother and daughter* photographs.

'Of course,' said the photographer.

So, together, Eleanor and I beamed away whilst the camera flashed. At the end of the shoot, the photographer showed us the results on a big screen. Eleanor looked absolutely stunning. But who the hell was the old bag standing next to her?

I don't spend a lot of time in front of the mirror. Well, only to slap some make-up on. It's always been such a rushed procedure, snatching five minutes in a hectic schedule, that I suppose I've been oblivious to the increasingly puffy eyebags and crinkly crow's feet. Putting on lippy is a two-second job. One second for the upper lip, and another second for the lower lip. Whereas Eleanor outlines, fills, glosses, and then sprays on something to make her lippy stay on the mouth and not transfer to a coffee cup. Naturally, being a teenager, she – along with all her classmates – finish off by taking a selfie doing a peculiar pout, before posting it to each other. I know. Weird. But clearly spending time on highlighting, shading, defining and having twenty-plus cosmetic brushes in one's make-up box (yes, a box is required to fit everything in) helps produce immaculate results. It also helps being fifteen and flawless, and not fifty and falling apart. I stared at the giant overhead screen in horror.

'Do you do air-brushing?' I asked.

Since reaching the half-century landmark earlier this year, never have I been more aware of body parts doing things they've never done before. Forget about wrinkles, middle-age spread or sprouting a fluffy chin overnight. That's superficial. It's primarily the brain I'm talking about. Since my last birthday, it has completely re-

54

located. Possibly to my derrière. I laughingly tell my family that my backside is keeping my brain warm. My husband jokingly says, 'That figures, because you talk a load of s**t.' Well, I think he's joking anyway.

Certainly there's a major problem connecting the brain to other parts of the body. Like my mouth for instance. There are moments where I open my chops to speak and wonder exactly what's going to come out. Take last Friday for example. The car needed petrol. So I filled up, and then ambled over to the cashier to pay.

'Hi,' I beamed. 'While I'm here, I'll take the car through the dishwasher.'

The cashier gave me a sympathetic smile before wordlessly passing me a ticket... to the car wash.

Where do these unwanted words come from? Why does the brain misconnect to the mouth causing rubbish to spout forth?

I was caught out again while doing the day job. Whilst it's good to be friendly with folk, when writing to "Paul" it's probably best not to start his letter with "Dear Pal". It could be misconstrued as taking friendliness too far.

The brain is also failing to remember day-to-day things. How many times do I go upstairs to do something, only to find I have no recollection of why I ventured up there? But no matter because, also being a busy housewife and mum, there's always something to do when I get there. If only I could remember what.

One day, Mr V watched me go up and down the stairs, backwards and forwards, without actually *achieving* anything.

'Are you exercising?' he asked.

'No,' I replied, 'I'm trying to remember... something.'

'Well why don't you sit down and think about it?'

'Don't be ridiculous,' I said, rolling my eyes.

Sit down? I was far too busy going up and down the staircase. Mr V shook his head and went back to his telly viewing.

In the last week alone I've tried to get into three cars that belonged to other people, and lost my car in various car parks four times. I just couldn't remember where I'd parked. Should I be worried, or does this happen to other menopausal women?

I'm currently reading a book about taking charge of your life and making your dreams come true. According to this book, you can literally *manifest* things into your life. Currently I'm working on manifesting a really brilliant fully working brain. However, this cosmic calling thing turned a whole new corner last Wednesday.

I was ransacking the larder for a jar of baby porridge for the hamster (yes, sounds odd, but Misty is old in hamster years, lacks a few teeth, and I swear the baby porridge is all that's now keeping her going). Anyway, could I find the jar of baby porridge? No. Frustrated, I grabbed a chair, hoisted myself upwards, and systematically searched the larder's high shelves from top to bottom. No baby porridge. It was late, the shop was shut, and I didn't want the hamster going hungry. So, in desperation, I'm embarrassed to confess that I resorted to my cosmic ordering book and began chanting:

'I am *manifesting* a jar of baby porridge... I am *manifesting* a jar of baby porridge.'

Mr V wandered into the kitchen in search of a late-night snack, found his wife with her head inside a cupboard commanding a tin of soup change into a jar of porridge, and asked just what the hell I was up to. I nearly fell off my chair. It's one thing to attempt manifestations in private, quite another to do it in front of an audience. I clambered down from the chair, put it back under the table... and then froze. For there... *right there,* on the *table top*, was – wait for it – a jar of *baby porridge.*

'OH. MY. GOD.' I said, paling dramatically.

'Now what's the matter?' said Mr V.

I picked up the jar of porridge and waggled it in front of my husband's face.

'I've only gone and done it,' I crowed. 'I've *manifested* a jar of baby porridge!'

Or... *gulp*... had I, in fact, been to the cupboard... removed the porridge... forgotten I'd done so... then spent a futile ten minutes searching the cupboard and behaving like a lunatic?

Meanwhile, I've taken solace in a bit of retail therapy. Autumn is upon us. The shops are full of warm knits, long-sleeved tops and trousers in various shades of wine. I've bought a couple of sweaters and some jeans in this shade. After all, they match my face when an all-too-frequent menopausal hot-flush comes along. Which reminds me.

If scientists ever find a cure for the menopause, what will our biggest problem be?

Global cooling...

**Why was the teacher wearing sunglasses?
Because her students were so bright...**

They say *all good things must come to an end*. And so it was with the school summer holidays.

I always have mixed feelings about the half-term and end-of-term breaks. On the plus side, it's fantastic not having to do the school run and have an extra hour in bed every morning. It's also brilliant enjoying some quality time with my children. On the minus side, my working day is severely disrupted because – oops – they're children only in name. The reality is that I'm living with teenagers. Young adults. And actually, they don't particularly want quality time with their mother. What they absolutely do want, however, is knowing whether I've washed/ironed/sewed a button on their jeans/skirt/shirt/blouse because those garments are required for wearing. Now. This very minute. What's that, you say? Tell them to do it themselves? Oh, but I have. Many a time. But it's always the same. My words fall on deaf ears. Plus, I can't deal with stroppy teenagers. It's draining. So, for a quiet life, I give in. Yep, I'm a wimp. Too often the hope for moments of happy togetherness disintegrate into mutually soaring stress levels.

Over the summer holidays, a typical disruption to my working day was dropping everything to provide an impromptu taxi service. The nineteen-year-old had a habit of suddenly saying, 'Any chance of you quickly chucking me over to so-and-so's house?' By using the words *quickly* and *chucking* I was instantly misled to believe that so-and-so lived just around the corner. Not ten miles away. Or even twenty miles away. Which made for rather prolonged round trips. Especially in rush hour. I only wised-up to this ruse at the end of August.

'I borrowed some stuff that belongs to my mate Harry,' said my son, 'and now he wants it back. I don't really want to see him though. Would you mind *quickly chucking* his stuff back for me?'

As Harry lived thirty minutes away and I was desperate to go to the supermarket, I was swift with my response.

'No problem, just so long as I can *quickly chuck* you at Tesco's en route.'

Touché!

My son looked suitably gobsmacked. But he dutifully did my shopping whilst I returned a stack of CDs to his mate.

My daughter, now fifteen, but not yet ready to totally sever the invisible umbilical cord, had far sweeter tactics.

'I love you, Mum,' she recently cooed, sidling up to me for a hug. 'What about we have some girlie time together, and go shopping?'

For this, re-read it as Eleanor doing the shopping, and me paying. But I fall for it every time. Inevitably we would set off to Bluewater Shopping Centre, me humming joyfully at the prospect of looking in *Next* or *Marks and Spencer*. That idle daydream was immediately scuppered when Eleanor dragged me into stores that were only a paradise for teenagers, with not one middle-aged woman in sight. Well, not on the shop floor anyway. Instead they were spotted standing with hunched shoulders outside changing room cubicles, credit cards clutched possessively to matronly bosoms, while their own teenage daughters slithered into fabulous figure-hugging frocks. Take *Lipsy* for example. Gorgeous dresses in sizes small, medium and large. But, in *Lipsy*-speak, these sizes actually translated as 6, 8 and 10. I do not know any truly "large" woman who would fit into a *Lipsy* dress. Not unless she wanted to look like a particularly porky sausage in the grip of a very tight bandage.

'Let's go to M&S,' I eventually suggested, gravitating towards the store with a reluctant Eleanor at my heels. But as soon as those words had popped out of my mouth, I'd cringed. You see, they were the same words my mother had dared to utter decades earlier when *I* was teenager. Back then, my feelings about M&S had been the same as my daughter's. A shop for old people.

'You sound just like Grandma,' said Eleanor. 'You'll be admiring that polyester dress next,' she said, pointing.

'Don't be ridiculous!' I spluttered, moving smartly

away from a dress that was... no, it couldn't be... hell, it was. Polyester.

Needless to say, the only shopping achieved in M&S was at their cafe, *Revive*. If my credit card had been human, I'd have offered it a cappuccino, because it certainly needed a bit of reviving if my daughter's copious shopping bags were anything to go by.

But suddenly the long summer holidays were well and truly over. Peace reigned. My son went back to university and I had to wipe my tears away with a less-than-fresh tea towel, causing me to instantly break out in conjunctivitis. My daughter went back to school and, within seconds, informed me there was a forgotten academic review we both needed to attend – just typical. So I binned the manky tea towel and took my very sore bloodshot eyes off to meet the new form teacher. Miss G looked about the same age as my daughter. I do hope the form don't gang up on her. Which reminds me.

Did you hear about the cross-eyed teacher?

She had trouble with her pupils...

Why did Mrs Spider buy a computer?
Because she wanted a website...

Remember that nursery rhyme, *Incy Wincy Spider*? When my kids were little, they used to love listening to it. Right now, the words "down came the rain and washed the spider out" have never been truer because, in our house, spiders seem to be everywhere.

Yesterday, I flicked back the kitchen curtains only to have a sizeable spider fall into the palm of my hand. I recoiled in horror and, like a javelin thrower, flung it across the room before smartly stepping backwards. Straight into the dog's water bowl.

The rest of the family haven't fared much better. My daughter leapt into the shower only to discover she was sharing the cubicle with an eight-legged visitor. Walls instantly closed in and hyperventilation took place. And Mr V, comfortably enthroned in our bathroom, was horrified to discover a spider sharing his newspaper (he's not very good with spiders... or sharing his newspaper).

However, pity my poor sister. A friend of hers wanted to get rid of their greenhouse. My sister, a keen grower of fruit and veg, whizzed round to her friend's place and, before you could say *Alan Titchmarsh*, she'd disassembled the whole thing and stowed it in her four-by-four. The friend had cautioned my sister to check it over for spiders first, and one can only assume this warning fell on deaf ears.

The following morning, greenhouse now unloaded from her car, my sister set off to work. As she roared along the M25, in her peripheral vision she saw something black stroll across the ceiling. At this point she was in the outside lane doing ninety (but that's between you and me, and not to be shared with the cops). She most certainly wasn't in any position to take her eyes off the motorway to see exactly what the *something black* was. However, sensing it might be something to scream about, she attempted to move her vehicle across lanes and get on to the hard shoulder in order to investigate. But before she could even find a gap in the traffic, the *something black* released a silvery thread... and dangled in front of her face. Her worst fears were confirmed. A huge spider. The sort that is thick-bodied with legs that could benefit from hair removal cream. As it rotated before her nose, my sister began to scream. She screamed as her vehicle hurtled past a Tesco's lorry, screamed as she carved up a pensioner hogging the middle lane, screamed as she finally edged into the inside lane, and screamed even more upon discovering the hard shoulder had run out and didn't begin again for another two miles. The spider, possibly unnerved by all her noise, stopped rotating and dropped into her lap. My sister nearly fainted. Aware that causing a motorway pile-up simply wasn't on, she managed to keep going until the next hard shoulder mercifully appeared. She later told me that, finally parked on the hard shoulder, she wondered what passing motorists had made of the woman hopping around in one shoe as she thrashed the living daylights out of her car.

Even worse, on her drive home, exactly the same thing happened. And the saying that *All things come in threes* was never truer. Yes, the following morning, yet another horrendous vision was dangling in her rear-view mirror whilst she once again zoomed up the M25.

My sister was convinced that a hoard of spiders had transferred from the disassembled greenhouse and found a home in the lining of her vehicle's roof. Needless to say, the roof lining has been squashed and squashed and squashed in an attempt to squish anything that might have remained lurking. Personally, I'd have traded in the car, and to hell with the expense.

I can always remember my son, when a toddler, having his first encounter with a spider. Without me realising, he'd been repeatedly touching the spider's leg causing it to wave its leg about. This resulted in my son giving a string of delicious baby chuckles. Eventually I went to see what he was finding so funny – and smartly stifled a scream. I didn't want to transfer my fear to my little tot. It was then I had a light bulb moment... train my toddler to adore spiders... and then get him to despatch them!

'Aww, look at the furry spider,' I said (from a safe

distance). 'Give him a gentle stroke, and then pop him outside for Mummy, eh?'

''Pider,'pider,' said my son, lovingly.

It didn't last. Six months later, he'd joined the rest of us folk with arachnophobia. What *is* it about spiders that reduce so many of us to gibbering wrecks? Which reminds me.

Why are spiders happy when it's Halloween?

Because everyone thinks they're fake...

Why do some people nap on the toilet?
Because they think they're in the rest-room...

My son, Rob, recently moved into his *London Apartment*. He's sharing with three other dentistry students. I've written previously about their digs. In a nutshell, it's an expensive rental that looks slightly better than a squat. Indeed, when I first stood in my son's room, the urge to burst into tears was overwhelming. The only thing I seemed capable of uttering was, 'This place is a s**t-hole.' However, the current condition of the toilet has reinforced that statement.

Rob and his flatmates Duane, Wayne and Jane (not their real names) are all getting down to the nuts and bolts of living with one another. Things didn't get off to a great start with Duane and, unfortunately, matters haven't improved.

Jane is an organiser. Rob thrives on pleasing. Wayne is a Yes person. Whereas Duane is just... a prat. Within seconds of moving in, Jane purchased a white board. She wrote up everybody's lecture schedules and worked out a rota for household chores. So far Duane has managed to avoid his share with a succession of excuses. These are now running thin on the ground. The last excuse was, 'I don't know how to mop.'

Jane assigned Robbie to train Duane in vacuuming and mopping, while Wayne cleaned the bathroom and Jane scrubbed the kitchen. Halfway through vacuuming, Rob realised his trainee had lost interest and locked himself in his room – and bolted the door for good measure. Jane, in manager mode, told Rob to carry on mopping and she'd speak to Duane later.

However, Duane later quietly sneaked out of his room to grab a snack from the fridge. He left boot prints over Rob's clean floor, and mess in Jane's spotless kitchen. Before either of them could murder Duane, he'd scarpered back to his room and locked the door. And there he remained until Wayne, Jane and Rob went to bed. At some point in the night, Duane crept out of both his room and the apartment for a night on the town. He returned at around four in the morning with an unknown guest. Music was played at full blast.

Three hours later, Jane blearily opened her eyes, got up and went to use the loo. A charming sight greeted her. (Not really!) The loo was completely blocked. She scribbled warning notes to Rob and Wayne, pushing the bits of paper under their doors. Her message read *Loo Out of Order*. She then took herself off to university. Cross-legged.

When Rob surfaced an hour later, he failed to see Jane's note and groggily staggered off to the loo. Unimpressed with the sight that greeted his eyes, he automatically pressed the flush button. And watched in horror as the water rose and rose, and then rose a bit more. Just when it seemed as if the River Thames was about to surge out of the toilet, the water subsided. But the contents within didn't.

Livid, Rob banged on Duane's door. No answer. He then walked into the kitchen to find a raided fridge, leftovers chucked at the bin – but not in it – and a sink full of vomit. Rob returned to Duane's door and this time threatened to kick it in. But as Duane still refused to answer the door and Rob didn't want a damages bill from the landlord, instead he stomped off to uni.

Who needs to watch telly when there is drama unfolding in an East End dump of a flat? Will Wayne, Jane and Rob share damages between them to break down the door to Duane's bedroom? Will they find Duane hiding in the wardrobe or pressed flat under the bed? Will they disembowel him to stop shock encounters with Duane's bowels? And, more importantly, who is going to unblock that loo? Which reminds me.

What do you get if you cross a Goth with a toilet?

The Cisterns of Mercy...

Did you hear the gossip about germs?
Never mind. I don't want to spread it...

Today I'm talking dirty. Yes. That's right. Pure filth. My working week has been full of workmen. With the filthiest hands.

Now I've got nothing against workmen. Indeed, I'm exceedingly grateful to them for the services they provide. Car mechanics? I love them. Especially when the car won't start. Repairer of roads? I love them too. Particularly when fixing the pothole that gave me a puncture a few weeks ago. I tried to nurture the same feelings of love for the workmen who visited my house this week. Let me start at the beginning.

We needed a new driveway, so I booked a reputable Kent County Council contractor to do the job. The company said they'd do it *soon*. That was months ago.

'We're a very busy company, Mrs Viggiano. Please be patient,' was the standard reply whenever I chased up.

Patience is a virtue. But not mine. And then a leaflet plopped through my letterbox. *WE DO DRIVEWAYS* was the heading.

'We're not using people we know nothing about,' said Mr V.

'Of course not,' I replied.

So naturally I waved Mr V off to work before ringing the number.

Enter Tom. Nice enough chap. Had a squint which made him look a bit dodgy. His sidekick had a thick tinker accent and no teeth. I told myself that one cross eye and a lack of dentures was unimportant. We got down to the business of numbers. They wanted half the money that the KCC's contractor had quoted. I resisted the urge to rub my hands together and cackle with glee.

'The job's yours. When can you start?' I asked.

Tom's right eye met mine while his left eye studied the floor. I wasn't sure whether he was looking at me or the ground. Possibly both.

'Hmm. I'm not sure when I can get hold of the tar,' he said.

Which possibly translated as *we need to wait for the material to accidentally fall off the back of a lorry*.

'I'm a very patient woman,' I smiled. Which I am – where money is concerned.

The tar made an appearance four days later. Suddenly my driveway had pneumatic drills noisily chugging all over the place. A lorry arrived and dumped a steaming mound of tarmac. The lorry driver jumped out of his cab. He looked like an extra from *Lock Stock and Two Smoking Barrels*. He marched up to the front door. Uh-oh. Was he about to ask what I thought he was going to ask?

Ding dong.

'Good morning, Mrs Viggiano,' he smiled. Only two teeth missing. 'Could I be using your toilet now?'

Terrific.

'Right. Well, you'll have to take off those shoes,' I said, pointing to his tarmac-encrusted trainers. My eyes automatically strayed to his hands. They were blacker than the tar being spread across the drive. I sent up a silent prayer of thanks for God creating anti-bacterial wipes for germ-phobic women like me.

The lorry driver disappeared into the downstairs toilet. Seconds later there was the sound of the tap running. Hurrah. A man who washed his hands after using the loo. He thanked me and went out. I immediately went into the loo with my anti-bacs. The hand-towel, clean that morning, was streaked in black. I picked it up and chucked it in the washing machine, before replacing it with a clean one from the airing cupboard.

Ding dong.

I mentally braced myself. Would this be the rest of the tarmac crew wanting a wee-wee? Instead it was a completely different workman.

Enter Joe, from British Gas, summoned after our boiler kept playing up. One minute we had no heating. Then no hot water. Then we had heating but still no hot water. Then hot water, but no heating again. Then, finally, we had both heating *and* hot water but regrettably the thermostat packed up. And then the control box

67

jammed. When the house had reached forty degrees, I took to the fuse box in desperation. Joe has actually been popping in and out these last few days trying to sort out the wretched boiler.

'I've come to fix your boiler,' said Joe, for the umpteenth time this week. He's had a difficult time with our ancient model. It was probably made before he was born, because he only looks fourteen. All this week he's had a habit of looking at the boiler, tapping his teeth with a pencil and then ringing up his brother – also an engineer with British Gas – invariably to hiss, 'I haven't a bleeping clue what's wrong with this customer's boiler.'

But today – hurrah – Joe managed to fix everything… the heating, the hot water… and the dodgy thermostat. And then came the magic words.

'Can I use your loo?'

I couldn't help it. My eyes instantly looked at his hands. They looked as if they'd been coated in black gunk. I made a mental note to chuck yet another replenished hand-towel in the washing machine. As soon as Joe had departed, out came the anti-bacs again, because I'm never entirely sure if the drips all over the floor are from water or… well… quite.

Anyway, it is now Sunday. And peaceful! Not a workman in sight. I have a brand new very black driveway. And there is heating and hot water. And clean handtowels. All is well with the world. Which reminds me.

Why did the germs cross the microscope?

To get to the other slide…

What does a vet's dog do with bones?
Barium...

As far as I'm concerned, my senior pooch is Super Dog. Why? Well, because she's wonderful of course!

Trudy Beagle sleeps at the foot of my bed, beeps her nose against mine when it's time to wake up, and waits patiently to be given the last piece of breakfast toast. When the family go out without her, she transfers herself to the half landing on the stairs in order to gaze through the hall window and wait for everyone's return. And when I'm writing way into the early hours, she lays on my feet snoring. At bedtime, she bounds up the stairs ahead of me. Except this week, she stopped bounding.

It seems only five minutes ago that we gave a home to an unwanted beagle. We have no idea why her previous owner no longer wanted her. Could it have been that it was because a beagle can leap fences, dig faster than a JCB, swipe twenty picnics in as many seconds whilst walking through a park, and bust open every single supermarket shopping bag if you dare to look away for one second? Quite possibly.

Time marches on. None of us are getting any younger. Which includes the pooch. So I took Trudy Beagle to the vet.

Taking a breed like this one on a car journey is always noisy. For our pooch, the car means one of three things:

Either a wonderful destination where there are loads of squirrels to chase...

Possibly a spell at the local kennel while Mum and Dad are on holiday...

Or – every pet's nightmare – suffering a thermometer where the sun doesn't shine.

The moment Trudy Beagle is settled on the back seat, the barking begins. The initial noise is a sort of hopeful yipping sound as she cranes her neck to see the longed-for green space. Upon sailing straight past this, the hopeful yips turn into a noisy protest with her nose pressed up against the glass to see which lesser of two evils the destination will be. When the car bypasses the dirt track to the local kennel, our girl knows we're down to the last option. And then the baying begins. Ever heard a beagle bay? You don't want to.

The veterinary's receptionist looked slightly anxious as my beagle burst into the waiting room. After all, the last time we were here, the walls changed from white to brown in the space of seconds. I won't go into detail. Fortunately, there were no other pet patients about and we went straight into the vet's consulting room. Trudy Beagle was diagnosed with a touch of arthritis, and a prescription was written up.

'One more thing before you go,' said the vet in a very matter-of-fact voice. 'I'd like to check your dog for diabetes. It's easy enough. Simply collect some urine in this.'

'Oh, right, okay,' I said, taking a small pot from him and wondering how I was going to get my beagle to wee in it.

The following morning I instead found an unwanted plastic container which looked more practical for the job. I showed it to Trudy Beagle. She wagged her tail. Food? I shook my head and grabbed her lead. Ah, walkies! Again, I shook my head.

'Wee wees,' I instructed.

Trudy Beagle looked at me with her head on one side as if to say, 'What? In that? Don't be ridiculous.'

Outside in the garden, she wouldn't oblige, so we ventured out after all to try elsewhere. Trudy Beagle had her nose to the pavement sniffing out that all-important precise spot to piddle. The minute her rear bobbed down I shoved the container under her... oh! Which bit, exactly did, the wee...? Damn, she'd stopped.

'Mummy?' said a child's voice behind me. 'What's that lady doing?'

Wasn't it perfectly obvious what I was doing? Bent down, doubled over, hair falling in my face, brow furrowed in concentration. From which blasted keyhole did the wee come out?

Mummy took her child's hand and swiftly crossed the road to get away from the strange lady.

'Can we have a dog?' asked the child.

'Absolutely not,' was the firm answer.

Eventually, Trudy Beagle and I entered the local park which is hallowed ground for weeing. But not in great abundance. Rather, the ritual for Trudy Beagle is leaking a maximum of three drops on a daisy or nettle before sniffing out the next particularly interesting thistle or weed. And so, plastic container poised, I spent the next hour painfully collecting a urine sample. Drip by drip. By the time we'd completed our circuit, the container had collected not just wee, but several flies, a dead leaf and a half a fluffy dandelion.

Anyway, the good news is the pooch doesn't have diabetes, and her experience of having a container shoved under her backside hasn't traumatised her. She's totally chilled. Which reminds me.

What do you call a dog that meditates?

Aware wolf...

My husband said he wanted me to treat him more as an equal.
So I showed him how the washing machine and vacuum cleaner work...

Next month Mr V and I will be celebrating an anniversary ending with a zero. I can't believe where the years have gone.

I've been married before (my first husband is deceased). I met my children's father at the age of eighteen. It was a bit of a whirlwind thing and, back then, we didn't have any spare cash. My engagement ring came from Argos and cost ninety-nine pounds.

I didn't think I'd re-marry, but Fate had other ideas. The great thing about getting hitched later in life is that finances are usually more solid. So when I accepted Mr V's proposal of marriage, instead of pouring over a catalogue for a cheap engagement ring, I was thrilled to peer into the brightly lit jewellery shops of Hatton Garden. At the time I was working for solicitors in London and Hatton Garden was just around the corner. My husband suggested, initially, that I pop along there in my lunch hour for a first recce before...

He didn't finish his sentence. I was off like a dog after a rabbit. Nose down, tail up. Let's face it, no woman is ever going to turn her nose up at a diamond or three.

Hatton Garden is mesmerising. The pavements are lined with jewellers showcasing display after rainbow display of diamonds, rubies, sapphires, emeralds, you name it. The designs are endless. Intricate... complicated... simple... fashionable... retro... traditional... contemporary. I'd barely gone a dozen paces when I spotted 'the one'. I ground to a halt and stood, quivering, as I gazed at *my* ring nestling on a black velvet cushion pad. The shop's strategically placed spotlights bounced off a diamond that made me salivate. I pushed the door open and went inside.

'Hello!' dimpled the jeweller. 'Do sit down. Can I make you a tea? Coffee? Have a sweetie!'

A bowl full of colourfully wrapped chocolates was

pushed towards me, and a sumptuously upholstered chair pulled out. I sank down, feeling like a VIP. Which, in hindsight, I was. Very Important *Purchaser*.

The ring was brought out. The jeweller slipped it on my third finger. And incredibly it was a perfect fit. It had my name all over it. I glanced at the price tag. That bit had Mr V's name all over it.

I floated back to the office with my mobile clamped to one ear.

'I've found it!' I trilled happily.

But Mr V's response wasn't as enthusiastic as mine.

'I'm not buying the first ring you've clapped eyes on. You need to look in more shops to be sure there's not something else you might prefer. There are heaps of diamond rings out there. It's important not to make a decision you might later regret.'

There then followed a week of intense ring shopping with Mr V marching me into – I do not lie – every single jeweller in the Kent vicinity. But nothing compared to that first ring. In time, I returned to Hatton Garden, this time with my fiancé. The jeweller slid the ring on my finger, and I fell in love with it all over again. And the rest, as they say, is history.

Except Mr V promised me, all those years ago, that come 2012 he would buy me an eternity ring. So once again I found myself back in Hatton Garden, standing outside that first jewellery shop. I knew what I wanted. A bespoke design to match my engagement ring. The jeweller pushed a piece of paper across the glass counter. On it was written a figure. Mr V choked on his complimentary chocolate and nearly fell off his sumptuously upholstered chair.

'Thank you so much,' said my husband, his larynx struggling for normality. 'We'll have a think about it.'

We were meant to be going out for a romantic lunch. Instead I found myself encountering déjà vu as Mr V propelled me along the pavements before randomly diving off into different shops. Once again it was time to suss out the best deal, the biggest bargain, the greatest choice. Except I knew what I wanted. And other jewellers said my design was either beyond their craftsmanship or too intricate for them to attempt. The romantic lunch ended up being a very rushed tuna sandwich in Pret.

Meanwhile we're waiting for a mock-up picture to be emailed over as Mr V can't envisage the design I can see in my head. Patience is required for a little longer. But I really can't wait to get my eternity ring! Which reminds me.

What do men call the three rings of marriage?

Engagement ring, wedding ring, and suffering...

I love to sing in the shower, until I get soap in my mouth.
Then it becomes a soap opera...

There can't be a Brit in the land that hasn't heard of *Coronation Street*. As a child I was brought up on 'Corrie'. When I met Mr V he said, 'You don't watch that rubbish, do you?'

'Moi?' I asked, eyes very wide, 'Good heavens no. Absolute drivel.'

The real truth was that I couldn't WAIT for half seven-thirty on a Monday, Wednesday and Friday to roll around because I absolutely ADORED the programme. Would Bett Lynch divorce Alec Gilroy? Would Rita Fairclough ever find love again? I am reliably informed that she did and is now known as Rita Tanner. And that her name changed several times in between. Rita might be knocking eighty, but she's clearly a goer who has been round *The Kabin*'s block a few times.

It is ironic that I no longer watch the box and my husband is now an avid fan of the programme. However, who needs to tune in to a soap opera when there have been several sensational events unfolding right on my doorstep?

Who is the owner of the drone that has been spotted hovering outside people's windows and... even worse... has a spy-cam fitted to it? Why is the little old lady at Number blah-blah yelling at her neighbour over an overflowing wheelie bin and, even more astonishing, threatening to pick it up and throw it at the offending person (said little old lady is about four feet two inches in height and weighs the sum total of six feathers). Is the rumour true that said little old lady is actually the reincarnation of Super Gran?

But the scenes are about to get darker...

Exactly how old is the skeleton found under the garage foundations of the house down the road when the owners innocently thought it might be fun to do away with the garage and build an extension?

And darker still...

Two weeks ago a young woman was murdered.

Suddenly my village seems to have strayed from the set of *Corrie* to *EastEnders*. Upon hearing about the demise of the nineteen-year-old walking home late one night, my village went into deep shock. This happened right outside the local pub with its frothy hanging baskets, olde-worlde beams and cosy lamplight. Hundreds of floral tributes are still tucked into the hedgerow that borders the narrow lane. Horrified villagers put their hands to their mouths and whispered, 'Things like that don't happen here.' And then earlier on this week, whilst walking Trudy Beagle with a fellow dog walker, my friend told me the windows of her husband's car had been smashed overnight, and apparently our beautiful local meadow is now a popular late-night haunt for a spot of drug dealing.

It has since transpired that two men have been arrested in connection with the murder (thank goodness). Arrests have also been made in connection with the car vandalism. Regarding the latter, lads were driving around with a massive homemade catapult randomly firing large stones at cars, houses and even people. It begs the question why? Boredom? A warped sense of fun? Born with a brain the size of a pea (or rather no brain at all – can't insult peas)?

The folk in my village aren't used to horror. Prior to all this, the most outrageous thing to have happened was somebody swiping the church's lychgate. Heaven knows why (no pun intended).

Hopefully village life will get back on an even keel without any further dreadful dramas. If not, instead of writing novels, I might be scribbling all this stuff down and pitching a new drama to the Beeb. Which reminds me.

Why are men like soap operas?

Because they're wonderful to watch but you mustn't believe everything they say...

What's the difference between an estate agent and a pigeon?
Every pigeon can put a deposit on a Porsche...

For the last eighteen months I've been trying to persuade Mr V to move. Now that we have only one child left at home, we do not need a big house with monster heating bills and a garden that both of us struggle to find time to deal with. I've rebelled slightly in the last couple of months by employing a gardener.

The gardener's skills are impressive. Unlike us, he doesn't hack shrubs about causing them to blend into one another. Oh no. These days our shrubs are *manicured*. Each one is absolutely showcased. The gardener hasn't yet reached the stage of shaping plants into peacocks, but I suspect that might happen soon. After all, our previously wayward holly bush now looks suspiciously like a Christmas pudding.

Anyway, I digress. Project *Moving House* was never destined to be something that would happen overnight. Not with a man like Mr V in the equation. Unlike my hubby, I'm a person who makes swift decisions and acts instantly. Some people might call this impulsive. Others (like me) bluntly call it *not farting about*. I don't know where that expression comes from, but it's very apt, because Mr V is full of hot air when it comes to giving reasons about not rushing into moving. Like:

...parting with our hard-earned money to pay Stamp Duty (don't get him on to that subject unless you have a spare couple of hours);

...forking out to pay estate agents' fees (ditto);

...or stumping up for removal costs (ditto ditto ditto).

I have been using a bit of psychology over the last year and have been gently steering my husband into a viewings, just so he feels he's not been rushed into anything. But now... well now the hunt is on to find our next home. However, this could be tricky. Top of Mr V's criteria is finding a house where the street isn't blocked with cars. Nor must a potential property be by a main road, or out in the back of beyond, or near a telephone mast, or gasworks, or a railway station, or a motorway, or a massive supermarket, or...

Is it any wonder that I feel battle-worn before we even ring the doorbell of a potential property?

Yesterday, we met with three different estate agents to view three different houses. All were newbuilds and all were perfect. I could have lived in every one of them. Right area, right price, and no decorating required. And the amazing thing was – wait for it! – my hubby liked these properties too. And when I say *liked,* I actually mean *blown away.* Unheard of!

The three estate agents were eager to know our thoughts. Mine were unhesitating. I didn't care. Any of them would do. Whereas Mr V stroked his chin pensively.

'All I need to do...' he said, making my heart pound with excitement. What was he going to say? Make an offer? Haggle over the price? Negotiate about fixtures and fittings? Or throw his hands up in the air and cry, "I don't know which one to choose," before stabbing a finger in the direction of all three and chanting, "Eeny meeny miny moe"?

'Yes?' I prompted.

'All I need to do... is think about it.'

This is major progress. Another decade and we just might be on the move. Which reminds me.

Did you hear about the estate agent who sent a complimentary bouquet of flowers to a client? Unfortunately the florist delivered a wreath with a card that read *Rest in Peace.* Furious, the Estate Agent complained to the florist.

'Oh dear,' said the florist, 'somewhere there is a funeral with flowers on the coffin and a message that reads *Wishing you every happiness in your new home...*'

What do you get when you cross a dinosaur with fireworks?
Dino-mite...

It is the first week of November. For the last few days the sound of pops, whizzes and bangs can be heard every evening from neighbouring gardens.

Fireworks don't 'do' it for me. After years of having various dogs cringing at every thunderous explosion, and reading horrific stories in the newspaper about firework accidents, I'd be quite happy to see them banned. However, what Bonfire Night *does* do is remind me that the festive season is edging closer. So, although it's only November, I've been busy doing Christmas shopping.

'Oooh, prezzies,' said Mr V, barging into the bedroom and finding me crouched down on the carpet, huffing and puffing over cellotape that had adhered itself to everything other than the gift I was trying to wrap. My husband immediately began rummaging through all the carrier bags full of gifts that I'd dotted around me. His annual attempts to suss out what presents belong to him tends to drive me slightly potty. What is the point of trying to surprise your loved one if they peek?

'Stop that,' I said.

'What have you bought me?' he said, ignoring me and inspecting a pack of socks covered in reindeer.

Trudy Beagle appeared in the doorway, tail wagging. Her eyes lit up at the sight of wrapping paper. She knows exactly what Christmas is about, from extra turkey dinners to ripping open her very own stocking full of heavenly doggy chews. The tail wagging went into overdrive as she joined Mr V in the inspection of the carrier bags' contents.

'Get her out of here,' I said irritably, inspecting my latest wrapped present. The cellotape was now on the gift paper, but not in a straight line. I pulled it off and promptly ripped the paper in the process. 'Oh for heaven's sake,' I muttered in annoyance.

Crumpling up the paper, I set about re-wrapping the present just as Mr V rocked back on his heels and regarded me with disappointment.

'There are no Pro V1 golf balls.'

'There's no Father Christmas,' I replied, 'but you don't hear me complaining.'

My daughter wandered in.

'No Father Christmas?' said Eleanor, pretending to be outraged. 'Oooh, presents,' she said, rummaging inside a carrier bag. 'What have you bought me?'

'That's IT!' I howled, standing up. 'Out! Now! All of you!' I shooed them out and shut the door. A quick check inside the carrier bags had me opening the door again and whizzing downstairs to the dog's basket. Trudy Beagle looked at me as if to say, 'Spoilsport.' I swiftly removed the pack of chews and squeaky Christmas pudding toy she'd swiped, and took them back upstairs.

Meanwhile, I am now finally wrapped, stacked, beribboned and bowed and feeling tremendously pleased with myself. All that's left to do is the writing of the Christmas cards and buying a silly Christmas jumper. Which reminds me.

How do you know Santa is a man?

Because no woman would wear the same outfit year after year...

What did the bartender say when Shakespeare walked in?
'You can't come in 'ere, you're bard...'

Last Friday I waved good-bye to a very disgruntled Trudy Beagle and set off, with Mr V, to the birthplace of William Shakespeare. We'd booked into a hotel called *The Mercure Stratford-upon-Avon Shakespeare*.

I'd Googled the place earlier and was in awe of this historical building with its Tudor facade, stone floors and open fireplaces. Which is why, when we pulled up outside a small yellow building, I knew without a shred of doubt that Mr V had driven to the wrong place.

'But I thought it was called *The Shakespeare Hotel*,' he said.

Unsurprisingly, there are several hotels in Stratford-upon-Avon that mention the Bard's name. So, after a bit of sat-nav tweaking, we drove through open countryside dotted with thatched cottages that looked like those on the lids of posh chocolate boxes. A little while later, we arrived at our destination.

Now the thing about old places – and let's face it, this one was ancient – is that the minute you walk in there is a switch in 'atmosphere.' Inside, beamed ceilings dared us to bang our heads. Entire walls were lined with pictures of everybody who was anybody back in the sixteenth century. Pious faces sporting pointed goatees or heavily coiled braids stared haughtily down at us. Several faces looked aggrieved. There were lots of ruffles and tight corsets. No wonder those faces looked so pained.

Our room was up two flights of creaking stairs, the second of which was narrow and twisty. Mr V stooped upon entering our room. He flung the suitcases down and immediately reached for the contraption that allows the sixteenth century to collide with the twenty-first. Namely the television's remote control and, more particularly, football.

We were due to meet friends a little later in the bar downstairs.

'You go ahead,' I said to Mr V, 'because I want a quick

shower.'

The moment I was on my own – television now silent – I quickly became aware of the building's sounds. Creaks, gentle groans and tapping abounded. Ignoring it, I walked into the bathroom and got into the tub which combined as a cubicle. Twiddling the shower taps, I frowned. No water. I turned the hot and cold dial to see if that would somehow help. Still no water. I fiddled with the bath taps instead. Hurrah, water! Pressing down the pop-up plug, I added some bubbles and sighed happily as the running water quickly frothed up.

I'd barely lowered myself into the foamy depths when the room's smoke alarm went off. Wrapping a towel around me I fled, dripping, to the landing. The smoke alarm stopped. I ventured back into the bathroom. I'd got as far as lathering myself up when the smoke alarm went off again. For the second time I bolted – towelled and turbaned – to the landing, this time gave a passing elderly couple a bit of a surprise. Once again, the noise stopped. Cautiously, I returned to the bathroom. Settling into the water for a third time, the smoke alarm once again went off with an ear-splitting shriek, but I ignored it. It was only when my ears were literally ringing that the ruddy thing stopped.

Five minutes later, I was just pulling on a sweater when there was the sound of gushing water from the bathroom. Wisps of steam curled from under the door and into the bedroom. I yanked the bathroom door open. The shower was in full flow. Reaching into the cubicle, I turned off the taps. I'd barely exited the bathroom when the water started again. And this time there was a little outbreak of goose bumps on the back of my neck. Should I phone Derek Acorah, or was this a matter for Ghostbusters?

'Okay,' I quavered to no one, as I turned off the taps for a second time. 'I'm going downstairs now.'

That night, I slept badly. Whether this was because of the strange noises that prevailed, or a little matter of the room's extreme sloping floor that impacted upon the bed, I'm not sure. All I know is that I went to sleep with one hand hugging my pillow and the other grimly hanging on to the wooden side lest I shot out the bottom of the bed in the night.

Haunted hotels aside, it was a blissful weekend and I thoroughly recommend a visit to this historical town. Mr V and I enjoyed an open-topped bus ride which departed from the *Pen and Parchment Inn* and rumbled past Shakespeare's birthplace, taking in Anne Hathaway's cottage (Shakespeare's wife), Mary Arden's house (Shakespeare's mother), also Nash's House and Hall's Croft, The Royal Shakespeare Theatre, the Holy Trinity Church and the old fifteenth century grammar school where Shakespeare himself was educated. And did you know it was William Shakespeare who invented the knock-knock joke? It's true! Which reminds me.

Knock-knock!

Who's there?

Iago!

Iago who?

Iago to the store. Do you needa anything?

How to write good
Take the bull by the hand and avoid mixing metaphors...

Having proofread my last novel several times over, I gave the thumbs up for it to be converted into an e-book. The lovely Rebecca Emin is ace at formatting, and a techie twit like me relies heavily upon a clever-clog like her. However, before Rebecca sorted out the paperback version, I decided to run through *Lipstick and Lies* one more time. Seeing your work in a different format can, amazingly, reveal previously unnoticed errors. I downloaded my novel and began to read.

Along came the first howler. My character Cass, mother to a six-month-old baby boy called Eddie, was doing all sorts of wonderfully maternal things... but not to Eddie. Instead she was lugging *Ethan* around on her hip. This wouldn't be quite so catastrophic if Ethan didn't happen to be forty years old and the boss of Cass's husband.

I went screeching over to my computer and whizzed off an email to Rebecca. Minutes later, the MS had been amended and re-uploaded. My heartbeat quietened. Confident that all was now well, I continued reading. But... wait. What was this? The character Jamie had just exchanged a few noisy words with his wife. He was upset. So upset there was a tic going in his cheek. Except for some reason I'd typed *stick*. Since when did hacked-off characters go around with lumps of wood in their faces? I went to pieces. So much so I couldn't think straight. What was the correct word? I began to doubt whether 'tic' was even right. Wasn't it some sort of flea? Perhaps it was *tick*... or weren't those something our teachers used to give us? Howling with frustration, I opted for the word *nerve*. Another hasty email went flying through cyberspace to Rebecca.

Thoroughly unsettled, I returned to the manuscript. What would I find next? I didn't have long to wait. The character Cass was deep in thought. So much so, her mind was whirring. Except Cass was so distressed it was actually her *wind* that was whirring. Cue instant vision of my character staggering about clutching her guts. Once again I raced to my computer and belted off an email to Rebecca.

So all I can do is sincerely apologise to those who downloaded a novel with more clangers than that programme in the early Seventies. Which reminds me.

A lady author died and was given the option of going to Heaven or Hell. She decided to check out both places first. In Hell she viewed a steaming workshop full of writers chained to their desks.

'Oh my,' said the writer, 'let me now see Heaven.'

Moments later she ascended to Heaven. Again, she witnessed a steaming workshop full of authors chained to their desks.

'This is just as bad as Hell,' she gasped.

'Oh no it's not,' boomed a mysterious voice. 'Here your work gets published...'

What kind of cat works at a hospital?
A first-aid kit...

If somebody had told me last Sunday that seven days later I'd be talking about a new addition to the family I'd have said, 'You've lost the plot.' Instead, it turns out to be me who's lost the plot. How else could I otherwise have agreed – on the spur of the moment – to welcoming an eight-week-old scrap of feline fluff? We have a beagle for goodness sake!

Perhaps it was because my daughter caught me unawares. At the time I was deep in thought bashing out some 'misery writing'. I'm currently venturing into unchartered waters and a change of genre with *The Ex Factor*. My mood, as a result, was down. What's the quickest way to elevate the blues? Swap *The Ex Factor* for *The Ah Factor*.

Eleanor walked into my study. 'Look at this,' she said, waving an iPad at me. Filling the screen was a little black and white face with a tiny pink nose.

'Ahh,' I cooed. It would take the hardest heart not to respond similarly. I grabbed the iPad from Eleanor and found my husband. 'Look at this,' I said, parroting my daughter. Whereupon the iPad was batted away

'No, no, no,' said Mr V in annoyance, 'I'm looking at *this*.'

Naturally he was watching the television and refereeing his beloved Manchester United from the sofa. Perhaps I also agreed to this new family member because of my husband's reaction, because in that moment I felt a strange surge of rebellion.

I flounced out of the lounge and back to my study, Eleanor trailing in my wake.

'Can we have it?' said asked, pouncing on my arm and giving it a little shake.

'Of course!' I purred.

Hmm... Eleanor *pouncing*... me *purring*. It was definitely a sign!

Eleanor was in raptures at my response, but also thoroughly confused. How had she managed to pull this off without a major battle of wheedling, begging, tears or sulking? But she didn't stop to analyse the reason why, just in case her mother back-pedalled and changed her mind. Instead my daughter got straight on the phone to the school friend whose cat had produced the litter needing homes.

'My mum has agreed,' I heard her say in excitement. 'Yes, I'm quite sure... I have no idea why... so stick a 'reserved' sign on that one's head because we're coming over... yes, now!'

I abandoned my writing, picked up my purse and the two of us drove to *Pets At Home*, the animal equivalent of Westfield Shopping Centre. Any pet worth its salt would have a field day in there if given free licence with its owner's wallet. Half an hour later we'd picked up a pink pet carrier, pink feeding bowls, pink litter tray, pink collar (yes, it was going to be a girly moggy whether it liked it or not), fluffy basket, scratching post, toys, kitten milk and food. We left clutching a mile-long receipt and an appointment card with the in-house vet for worming, vaccination and micro-chipping. Eleanor gave me an anxious look.

'You're definitely feeling okay, aren't you, Mum?'

'Never better,' I assured, whilst privately thinking that Manchester United had an awful lot to answer for. It was at that moment my husband texted me.

Not sure where you've gone, but good old MU won! I'm popping out for a celebratory pint with my nephew. See you later x

I slipped the phone back in my bag. He would indeed see me later and wouldn't he have a surprise!

When Mr V returned home, Eleanor and I, along with the new family member, had been back a while. My husband was greeted by Trudy Beagle carrying on in a way that can only be described as a gibbering wreck.

'Woof-woof-woof-woof-woof-woof,' she said. Translation: 'Have you any idea what's been going on in this house while you've been out? They've only gone and got a CAT. Do you hear me?'

'Down! Geddoff!' said Mr V, frowning. 'What's got into

the dog? She's behaving like a lunatic,' and with that he frog-marched her into the utility room to make her calm down, and firmly shut the door.

Whereupon my daughter, beaming from ear to ear and clutching the new family member, greeted her stepfather.

'Look!'

Mr V froze. 'What is *that*?' he spluttered.

'Meow-meow-meow-meow-meow-meow,' said the kitten, which I like to think translated as: 'Fancy not recognising what I am. You're clearly low on brain cells. You must be a Manchester United supporter.'

The kitten was then named. Several times over. She started off as *Jingle*, became *Belle*, then *Jingle-Belle*, *Flora*, *Ivy*, *Whisky*, *Brandy*, *Holly*, *Molly* and *Folly*. At one point we liked them all and pondered whether to call her, for short, *JBFIWBHMF*. Except we couldn't pronounce it. *Folly* was probably the most apt name considering the impulsiveness of what we'd done, but then, at exactly the same time, my daughter and I trilled together '*Dolly!*' So hello, Dolly!

Trudy Beagle remains unimpressed. Introductions between the feline and canine family members are progressing according to the internet guide we're following. Dolly has remained cool, calm and collected throughout. Not so Trudy Beagle who initially went to pieces. Day One, she barked herself hoarse. Day Two was better – no bark. Day Three, she just looked browbeaten. Day Four, she walked off in disgust.

So there you have it. We now have a cat. Which reminds me.

What is a cat's favourite movie?

The Sound of Meow-sic...

What do you get if you cross Santa with a detective?
Santa Clues...

Now that we have a big toe in December, I am ready to acknowledge the countdown to Christmas. Behind the scenes I've been preparing (the presents are wrapped, the cards now written) but I don't actually acknowledge the festive season hurtling towards us until the first day of the last month of the year. So up until now, I've steadfastly refused to acknowledge the fairy lights that have been sparkling away in a neighbour's garden since mid-November, or open any early Christmas cards that have plopped on to the doormat by folk who are either trying to prove they're super organised, or maybe they just love the Christmas season so much they want to make it longer. But, as I said, in *this* house, nothing happens until we've waved good-bye to November.

Every year I look forward to Christmas. And every year it fails to live up to my expectations. This is usually because family members (the ones who rub each other up the wrong way) are thrust together and must suffer each other's company for more hours than at any other time of the year. I won't name names, but last year a certain person moaned about everyone and everything. Everybody waded through a very tense lunch, listened to the Queen's Speech – throughout which a heavy atmosphere prevailed – and then gathered around the tree to exchange gifts. I use the word *exchange* loosely, because in all honesty it was a case of policing movements so that presents weren't lobbed like hand grenades.

By four o'clock, one person (who shall remain unnamed) had overstepped the mark and another person (who shall also remain anonymous) finally lost the plot. For five minutes our living room resounded with the noise of two people who'd opted to *exchange* some very noisy words.

At that point I busied myself collecting wrapping paper remnants and discarded ribbon whilst consoling myself that surely we weren't the only ones experiencing a fiasco. I assured myself that other families all over the land were probably deflecting tensions, averting outbursts, biting their tongues, or even drowning their sorrows with the Christmas pudding brandy.

Will *this* year be any different? Hopefully so, because this time around I have refused to entertain anybody on Christmas Day other than immediate family. I'm also seriously thinking about foregoing the traditional turkey and pud to let my eager son do the cooking. He keeps talking very animatedly about vegetarian stews and a chocolate salt tart. I'm happy for the former but will pass on the latter, although Trudy Beagle keeps casting worried looks my way as if to say, '*Vegetarian* stew?'

Meanwhile, first things first. The Christmas tree. My daughter has renounced my tried and tested method of putting away the Christmas tree – namely flinging a vast black sack over the whole thing, baubles and all, before carting it off to the garage where it awaits the passing of eleven months before coming back into the house again. Whip off that black sack and... da-dah! One dressed Christmas tree.

'It's no fun,' Eleanor moaned. 'Part of the enjoyment of Christmas is unpacking each bauble and deciding which branch it should hang on.'

Personally I'm more inclined to call such 'enjoyment' by another name. Like *fannying about*. I can't bear it. I like instant results. Patience is not my virtue. I'm the same when out Christmas shopping. All those shoppers s-t-r-o-l-l-i-n-g along just drive me nuts. What's wrong with power walking? Anyway, I digress.

So to appease my daughter I agreed we would purchase a new, bigger, and better Christmas tree. Did she want to come with me to buy it? Good heavens no. Eleanor was far too busy watching *I'm a Dimwit Get Me Out of Here*. So she could hardly blame me for shopping for a tree that... well... came with few short cuts.

'Where are the fairy lights?' Eleanor asked, rummaging through the shopping bags.

'It doesn't need any,' I said, 'because they're built in.'

My daughter regarded me in horror. She should be

grateful I didn't buy the upgrade – not just fairy lights but also spray-on snow and plastic pinecones.

'What about tinsel?' Eleanor cried.

I shook my head. 'Nope, instead I bought gold beads.'

She frowned and carried on picking up the new decorations. Gold baubles. Gold ribbon. Gold angels. Gold snowflakes. Gold fairy to go on top of the tree.

'Everything is gold,' she said.

My goodness, you have to hand it to my daughter. She knows her colours.

'Is that a problem?' I said, eyebrows raised.

'It's boring,' she replied.

So there we have it. The first bit of Christmas tension. Watch this space. Come Christmas Day, instead of flying presents, there might be a flying Christmas tree complete with airborne angels. Which reminds me.

What did one angel say to the other?

Halo there...

What do you call a letter that makes its reader see red?
A round robin...

Never has my writing been so frenzied. And I'm not talking about the latest novel either. It's getting time to write the annual Round Robin that accompanies those festive good wishes. My daughter hasn't even started writing out her cards yet. She's still on the Christmas shopping bit – as I know to my cost. Earlier this week Eleanor said, 'Can you take me to Bluewater this evening? I need to buy some extra stuff... with your card.'

Now shopping is fun only when you are:

(a) spending someone else's money or

(b) have spare cash to spend.

There is nothing more boring than trailing a teenager going into shops that are as interesting as... say... a football match (sorry Mr V).

Having saved up a bit of her own money, Eleanor promptly blew the lot on her boyfriend.

'What do you think of this?' she asked, holding up a hideously expensive polo shirt.

I'm not being funny, but in Primark I swear to God you can pick up the same polo shirt for a fiver. The one she was holding up was indeed a fiver... plus another fifty, and all because it had a little motif hovering over the wearer's left nipple that signified it was... let me drop my voice an octave to impart a hushed sense of awe... *designer*. The thing that really gets me about *designer* stuff like this, is that it's still made in China, the quality isn't anything to shout about plus it looks incredibly ordinary.

My daughter reverently picked up the garment and went off to the cash till, where a shop assistant grabbed it and stuffed it any old how into a bag.

'Excuse me,' I dared to quaver, 'but that piece of material cost *fifty-five pounds,* so I'd like it folded neatly.'

I tipped the bag upside down and deposited the polo shirt back on the counter. Eleanor looked horrified. Yes, embarrassing parent alert. But frankly if shop assistants want to work in over-the-top shops, they should give an over-the-top service. Never mind folding said garment neatly, what about a bit of bowing and scraping too?

We eventually left the shop – Eleanor with a bright red face, and the shop assistant looking mutinous.

'Are we done?' I asked.

'Not yet,' Eleanor replied, 'because now I need to find something to go with the polo shirt.'

Groan.

An hour later, a second purchase had finally been made. And then, just when I thought we could be on our way, Eleanor dragged me into a card shop. Yes, it was time to buy the most romantic Christmas card in the store.

'What do you think of this one?' said Eleanor, waving a pair of billing turtle doves at me.

'Lovely,' I said, desperate to go home.

'No, it's rubbish.' Eleanor put it back in its slot. 'Ahh. This one is nice. Actually, no it's not. Oh look, this one's better. Um, on second thoughts the words are awful.'

And so it went on. And on and on. Until I swear every Christmas card with the headline *Boyfriend* had been examined and exclaimed over. If I'd known she was going to take so long I'd have sat in the corner and carried on drafting my Round Robin letter. Which reminds me.

What do sheep write in their Christmas cards?

Merry Christmas to ewe…

A man on a tractor was spotted shouting, 'The end of the world is coming!' I think it was Farmer Geddon…

Several thousand years ago, the ancient Maya calendar gave a date predicting the end of the world. Fast-forward to the month of December 2012 and social media and newspapers have been BUZZING with the remote possibility that the world will end on the twenty-first of this month. Eeeeeek!

So the hailed (and possibly feared?) date for this apocalypse came… and went. We're still here. Thank goodness, because I have spent a flipping fortune on this year's Christmas presents.

Between you and me, I never really believed the world was going to end. My understanding was more along the lines of 'new beginnings'. Let's hope so anyway. Our Mother Earth could certainly use nicer human beings living upon her. How wonderful would it be if there were no more wars, or acts of terrorism, or people going barmy with hand guns?

To celebrate the twenty-first day of December, my sister – who is incredibly spiritual – arranged an event with lots of other people who were (unsurprisingly) also very spiritual. I love to dip into this sort of thing, but on my own. Group events always tend to smack of religion which I shy away from. Don't get me wrong. I love God. He's fab. Really. But I like talking to Him on my own. I don't need somebody telling me how to worship, or when to worship, or in what way to worship. But my sister insisted I attend to support her. So I did, and took my parents along too.

My sis sang a number of celebratory songs. Now at this point I'd like to say my sibling should put herself forward for *X-Factor* or *Britain's Got Talent*. For talent she has. In shedloads. So it was something of a rude shock when she stopped her beautiful singing to introduce a lady who was going to treat the audience to a 'sound bath'. Anticipating another round of tuneful vocals, I sat back ready to enjoy. An unearthly wailing hit the microphone and then poured out of the speakers, flooding the small village hall where everyone was congregated. It was at this point I realised what Simon Cowell regularly puts himself through. Except Simon gets an X button to press. And I'll bet he has never listened to a contestant playing the gong. As the gong went bong I had a terrible urge to giggle.

After twenty-five minutes of weird noise where my father and I had exchanged looks and promptly convulsed before hastily turning our snorts into coughs, there was an interval. My mother, doddery on a walking stick, said she needed the Ladies.

'I'll come with you,' I said.

'Don't wait for me,' she said, 'because I'm so slow at walking. You go ahead.'

So I did. Pushing open the door, I was greeted by a row of uniform cubicles. Choosing one, I went in and – not being a *hoverer* – layered the seat in loo paper. Sitting down, I had a shock. A very alarming one. The sound bath had affected the toilet's dimensions. Either that or my backside had tripled in size. If Mr V had been there, I might well have asked, 'Does my bum look big in this toilet seat?'

I leapt off the loo and roared out of the cubicle. I'd have to ask my mother instead. And actually, where was my mother? She'd yet to make an appearance. I found her wandering around a nearby corridor looking bemused.

'Where have you been?' I cried.

'In the Gents.'

'I see.' Actually, I didn't. 'So have you used the loo?'

'No. A man re-directed me. But I ended up in a cupboard full of carpet remnants. Not a toilet in sight.'

I was starting to think the sound bath had sent us both doolally.

'The Ladies is this way,' I said, taking her arm, 'and can I ask you something, Mum? Be honest. Is my backside big?' My mother looked at my denim clad bottom.

'No bigger than when we got here. Why?'

'Because,' I said, dropping my voice to a whisper as we went inside the Ladies and in case anyone was behind one of the cubicle's shut doors, 'my rear doesn't fit the loo seat.'

I pushed open the door to the cubicle I'd vacated earlier and pointed. Behold. It turned out I'd layered up a toddler training seat that somebody had left behind.

So there we have it. A new *Golden Age* has arrived, everybody has survived, and the 'sound bath' didn't shift my backside into an altered dimension. Which reminds me.

Did you hear about the enlightened dyslexic cow?

It kept chanting *ooooM*...

What do ducks do at Christmas?
Pull quackers...

Hot on the heels of the Mayan Calendar's 'End of the World' prediction, the next event on our Gregorian calendar was... Christmas. Did you survive it? Are you still speaking to your cousin whose best friend invited herself along for the day? Are you fully recovered from visitors' children who never behave as well as your own? And did you manage to dodge food poisoning from any undercooked turkey dinners (which has been known to happen in this household)?

As my culinary skills can be iffy, I didn't take any chances regarding Christmas dinner. Aunt Bessie did the cooking. For those who aren't familiar with Aunt Bessie, she stocks many a shelf in a supermarket and never lets the consumer down. My freezer was stuffed to bursting with honey-glazed parsnips, cauliflower cheese, Yorkshire puddings and even her gravy sachets were found nestling amongst packets of frozen peas, carrots and roast potatoes. There was only a slight blip and that was when I burnt Aunt Bessie's Yorkshires, turned her gravy to coloured water and forgot to put her parsnips in the oven. But dinner was edible, and the family were very relieved. Putting their knives and forks together, the family sat expectantly as they awaited the festive season's traditional dessert.

'Ta-dah!' I trilled, and set down on the table a.... treacle sponge. My daughter gaped at in astonishment.

'Where's the Christmas pudding?' she asked.

I tapped the plastic bowl (yes, the sponge was a microwave job) and looked from my husband to daughter to son. Their expressions reminded me of two words. 'Gob' and 'smacked'.

'Don't look like that,' I chided. 'Everybody moaned last year and said they didn't particularly like Christmas pudding, so I made the decision to do something different.'

There was a slurping noise as the plastic bowl unattractively deposited a mound of syrupy stodge on to a plate covered in festive reindeer. The gloop looked slightly more attractive once it was smothered in custard. Yes, Aunt Bessie's.

Boxing Day dinner was a bit of a different matter. This time family were visiting. Mother and Father Bryant, and also my sister and brother-in-law. Including ourselves, there were eight of us squeezing around the table.

'What on earth have you cooked?' asked my sister, peering in pan simmering away on the hob.

'Red Thai curry,' I beamed. 'Don't worry' – I caught her apprehensive expression – 'it's a Loyd Grossman sauce and very nice.'

But my sister – someone who cooks from scratch – was unimpressed.

'I thought we were having a traditional Boxing Day meal. You know, cold meats, baked potato and a big rainbow salad. Haven't you any leftover turkey?' she asked, peering hopefully into my fridge.

'Um... no.'

Regrettably, in my quest to make sure the turkey was not undercooked, it had pretty much been incinerated for yesterday's dinner. Even Trudy Beagle had looked put-upon as she'd dutifully finished it off. My sister turned her attention to some vegetables in another pot.

'Are they organic?'

I should have said yes, but I'm rubbish at lying. My sister is someone who keeps away from any foods potentially covered in pesticide or genetically modified, so ate hardly any of it.

The *pièce de résistance* was my chocolate and coffee cake. It looked amazing. However, the icing was hiding a multitude of sins... burnt sponge, charred coffee granules and an awful lot of bicarbonate of soda due to misreading the recipe. Everybody helped themselves to a generous portion and, for about three seconds, I thought I'd got away with it. Have you ever had a synchronised moment where everybody stops chewing at the same time?

The cake was immediately binned. My mother – always reliable in an emergency – produced an M&S cheesecake from the depths of her suitcase-sized handbag. She has all sorts in there. Need a tissue? A painkiller? A teabag? Something to eat? I kid you not.

As Loyd Grossman had failed to impress with his curry and my cake had proved repulsive, I thanked God that I'd had the foresight to buy a vast cheeseboard and large box of crackers. Setting everything down on the table and urging everyone to tuck in, my sister immediately informed me she "didn't do dairy".

'Oh dear, then have some of Mum's cheesecake,' I said, pushing the plate towards her. Ah. But she wouldn't because... she didn't do dairy. I couldn't even get her drunk to drown her foodie sorrows because her husband had nominated her to be the driver.

So that's it for another twelve months. Perhaps next year I should check out the cost of caterers. Which reminds me.

How does Good King Wenceslas like his pizzas?

Deep pan, crisp and even...

**An optimist stays up to see the New Year in.
A pessimist waits to make sure the old one leaves...**

I'd barely waved off my Boxing Day guests when suddenly it seemed to be time to ring in the New Year. In the past, it would be fair to say that our celebrations of this occasion haven't been very frequent. Usually Mr V and I are on standby picking up our teenagers from various parties. However, this year the kids completely absented themselves by crashing with their friends. I didn't know whether to punch the air and shriek, 'Hurrah!' or weep into a box of man size tissues at the shock discovery of being obsolete. Instead I straightened my spine and, opting for a semi-enthusiastic "Hurrah", telephoned a local restaurant.

'Can you squeeze two more people in this evening?'

They could. Double hurrah.

We later enjoyed a veritable feast (no knackered Yorkshires or watery gravy in *this* place) before going home and welcoming our lovely neighbours who were joining us for the remainder of the night.

The conversation and champagne flowed. My lovely neighbour, as bubbly as the drink and very pretty, pointed to her ample cleavage spilling from her plunging dress and lamented about the regulation New Year Diet when... *ding dong...* family unexpectedly arrived. They wanted to raise a glass with us.

'Come in, come in!' I trilled.

My father and mother came over the threshold followed by my sister and brother-in-law. However, our sofas weren't quite big enough for everybody, so my brother-in-law opted to stand, positioning himself by the fireside. His eyes constantly fell upon my neighbour's ample assets and my sister began to look as though she was chewing a wasp. I offered her a glass of champagne to sweeten her up, but my sis declined on the grounds that alcohol was bad for you. She went off to the kitchen to get a glass of water leaving everyone else to get stuck into the stuff that was bad for us.

It's fair to say that, when Big Ben had chimed the twelfth mournful note indicating the arrival of 2013, I was squiffy. Squiffy enough after Trudy Beagle had had her late-night wee, to go to bed leaving the back door wide open (ah, epiphany... *that's* why alcohol is bad for you!). Still, these things happen. Nobody stole in during the early hours to rob or murder us. If an opportunist had tried, I would simply have pulled one of my burnt, rock-hard Yorkshires from the dustbin and given the intruder a good battering (no pun intended).

Meanwhile, Happy New Year to you all. Which reminds me.

I started my New Year with an IQ test.

The results were negative...

What is a cat's way of keeping law and order?
Claw Enforcement...

I'm currently in possession of two legs that look as though they've been scribbled on with red and brown marker pens. However, upon closer inspection you will see that the red bits are bloody wounds and the brown lines are crusty scabs. Nice. Well not really. It looks rather disgusting actually.

'Look at the state of your legs,' said my husband. 'They look awful.'

And I have to agree. The cause? Our four-month-old kitten, Dolly.

Our darling and rather ancient pooch has reluctantly accepted that a furry feline now shares her home. Trudy Beagle is under no illusions. She might once have been pack leader, but now she's been demoted. When Dolly arrived, there was a power shift. In ancient times cats were worshipped as gods. And it would seem this particular cat hasn't forgotten this little nugget of information.

'Ooooh, naughty Dolly,' said my daughter upon seeing the kitten ensconced in Trudy Beagle's basket.

I have no idea why Dolly wants to laze around on a smelly dog blanket, but she does so almost as if to prove a point... that she is a superior being and therefore she can do what she likes.

The minute Trudy Beagle flops down on the carpet to enjoy a sun puddle, Dolly turns into Karate Kid. Thumps, squeaks and grunts abound as long ears are pulled, and whiskers pounced upon. And heaven help Trudy Beagle if she dares to wag her tail because, in a kitten's head, waggy tails are for patting with pink paddy paws. And if Trudy Beagle goes into hiding and snoozes out of sight under a bed, well there's always human legs for Dolly to play a prank or two upon. It is a rude shock to be busily writing and totally immersed in an entirely different world, only to be yanked back into this one by a kitten hanging off your joggers, sharp claws buried in both fabric and skin. Yowch!

Mr V is a nervous wreck. His days of watching his beloved Manchester United and habitually twitching his toes as he 'runs' (from the sofa) with his team, are over – otherwise those little piggies are pounced upon and shredded by tiny sharp claws. These days I'm never sure whether it's Wayne Rooney causing my husband to howl, or Dolly.

Meanwhile, as I write this piece, our kitten is checking out the tap in the utility room. Water is Dolly's latest fascination. Which reminds me.

Did you hear about the cat that drank five bowls of water?

It set a new lap record...

Teens are at that awkward stage. They know how to make phone calls.
They just don't know how to end them...

I think I've turned a corner with my teenage daughter. You know, the corner you metaphorically take on two wheels as you flee from stroppy moods, scowls, huffs, puffs, and general whines of, 'It's not fair,' or (drop a gear and hit the accelerator for this one), 'Can I have some money?'

So what's the reason for this shift in direction? Well, I'll tell you. It's because earlier this week my daughter asked a question which, quite frankly, was astounding. I see it as a milestone.

We'd just finished dinner. The table was covered in dirty plates and glasses, and the worktop littered with paraphernalia. As I put my knife and fork together, my daughter stood up and said, 'Do you need any help?'

I've waited fifteen years for this question. It's nothing short of a miracle. In fact, I was so gobsmacked I couldn't speak. So Eleanor took it as her cue that help was not required – and swiftly fled.

I think the real reason behind this sudden thoughtfulness is due to her lack of input being flagged up whilst visiting her boyfriend's family. Eleanor's boyfriend is very practical. Unlike his girlfriend. So when he knocked upon Eleanor's bedroom door with a full English breakfast, my daughter was thrilled to bits and tucked in. However, downstairs there was a small matter of a kitchen now looking as though a cooking bomb had gone off. Greasy pan. Congealed saucepan. Fat splattered cooker. You get the picture. Being a teenager who has, up until now, not lifted a finger at home, it simply didn't dawn on my daughter to lift that finger while away. And boys are boys, so naturally this boy forgot all about the mess. Out of sight, out of mind. Consequently, minutes later, the two of them had hopped on a bus and tootled off to do a bit of shopping.

When the boyfriend's mother returned home from work – tired and looking to cook dinner – she wasn't too chuffed at having to roll up her sleeves and get scouring before she could even pick up a potato and get peeling. When Eleanor and her boyfriend returned, the pair of them were taken to task. And rightly so. But I've been flabbergasted at the change in my daughter since this event. Her bed has been made, clothes have been folded and put away, washing has been taken to the laundry bin, and even her desk has been tidied.

So the secret to training your teenager is clear. Forget nagging. Forget pleading. Forget shouting, or bribing, or acting all depressed and downtrodden and miserable. It's simple. Get somebody else to put the verbal rocket up your teenager's backside. It is quite apparent your teenager might not listen to you, but they definitely listen to someone else. I reckon that David Cameron should take this on board and offer it as a public service to all harassed mothers of teenagers. Which reminds me.

What is adolescence?

That period in life when parents become more difficult...

What's the definition of an actor?
Somebody who tries to be everybody other than himself...

I was lucky enough to attend the *National Television Awards* on Wednesday as a 'seat filler'. I took my daughter and her boyfriend along. They are both avid telly fans and couldn't wait for the opportunity of doing some serious shoulder rubbing with celebrities.

I don't watch the box. Consequently, I'm a bit clueless about what name goes with which face. Nonetheless, I love the thrill of being backstage with glamorous people and scores of television crew barking orders into their headsets. The atmosphere is always electric, and it's a little bit daunting avoiding all the cameramen trailing thick, snaking cable in their wake.

I was a bit anxious about the journey to the venue. The weather has recently been awful with lots of ice and snow, so I booked a cab making sure there was plenty of time to spare. My daughter emerged from the house wearing both ultra-long false eyelashes and a stunning evening gown. She looked like a cross between a movie star and Daisy Duck fluttering her lashes at Donald.

Our taxi driver bucketed along frozen country lanes at hairy-miles-per-hour. He casually guided the vehicle with one hand resting across the top of his steering wheel. His style of driving was far too laid back for me. I was as tense as a coiled spring, and as the car swung from left to right and left again over patches of ice, motion sickness set in. There was only one thing for it. I needed to man up and ask the driver to please put both hands on the steering wheel.

Just I opened my mouth to speak, I spotted our driver only had one arm. Yes, really. Too late, he'd noticed I'd been about to say something.

'Everything all right?' he asked.

'Yes thanks,' I chirruped, and instead rummaged in my bag for a peppermint. 'Er, would you like a sweet?'

As soon as the words were out, I realised the foolishness of my question. The driver couldn't take his one hand off the steering wheel to take the mint, and I didn't feel on close enough terms to say, 'Open wide and I'll pop it in.'

Fortunately he looked at the proffered packet of sweets and declined.

When we eventually arrived at London's O2 Arena, a strong wind was blowing across the Thames and nearly knocked us over. Normally my daughter would clutch her flowing locks and lament about her hair-do getting wrecked, but on this occasion she was hanging on to her eyelids and shrieking about her lashes taking off.

Inside the O2's VIP area, Eleanor and I whipped into a unisex restroom to attend to wind-damaged eyelashes and severely ruffled tresses. Suddenly a gentleman burst in, gave us both a cheery hello, and then disappeared into a cubicle. As I stood in front of a mirror applying lipstick, the sound of the man relieving himself was very audible.

'Mum,' my daughter whispered, 'that's—'

She broke off as the man dashed out doing up his flies.

'See ya,' he said, giving a cheeky grin.

I paused in mid-lippy application to briefly smile back. The moment the man had left the restroom, Eleanor turned back to me and gleefully said, 'That was—'

I will spare his blushes and not name him.

'Oh my God,' Eleanor cried, 'I've just seen my first celebrity!'

'I don't care who he is,' I sniffed, 'he didn't wash his hands!'

But my daughter was already hitting her iPhone and accessing social media to announce not only had she seen *Mr Famous*, but she'd heard him peeing too.

In due course we filed into the celebrity section. I peeled away from my daughter and her boyfriend, and found a seat. For the first thirty minutes I was left undisturbed and happily watched a stream of unfamiliar actors collecting their awards. However, then somebody in my row had to go up on stage. Musical chairs then took place. I jumped up, went to the wing and waited for direction on where to next sit.

'Over there,' said one of the crew, giving me a little

107

prod, 'front row, and make it quick because the cameras are about to do a sweep.'

I took off at a sprint – not easy in mega high-heels – and nearly went flying. I was aware of my stilettos connecting with something soft and squidgy. I flung myself into the empty seat, then dared to look back at what I'd trodden on. A cameraman, lying on his tummy and dressed head-to-toe in black to blend in with the shadows, was clutching his calves and quietly swearing. The woman on my left gave me a disdainful look. I shrugged apologetically before concentrating on Dermot O'Leary, the presenter, who had burst into his next round of patter.

Glancing sideways at the woman sitting next to me, I couldn't help but think she looked awfully familiar. Was she by any chance...? Oh what *was* her name? Definitely well-known. Even an ignorant non-telly-watching person like me knew that. I attempted looking discreetly at her again and instead... oh WOW!... now *there* was somebody I *did* know and sitting only TWO SEATS away. I gaped openly (and probably lustfully) at the heavenly Gary Barlow from "Take That". And who was that sitting on his left? I was sure I'd seen her face splashed across the newspapers quite recently, and that she'd caused a bit of an uproar. Yes...it was coming back to me... the media had branded her a cradle-snatcher. This was the woman who had *sooo* upset my daughter by allegedly taking teenage-sensation Harry Styles (Eleanor's crush) to her bed. She was called – I mentally clicked my fingers while waiting for my brain to deliver the info – got it! Caroline Flack! And good heavens, if she was thirty-two then I was twenty-one.

Suddenly there was an interval break. Julian Fellowes, English actor, novelist, film director and screenwriter, and a Conservative peer of the House of Lords, came over to talk to the gorgeous Mr Barlow. The woman next to me looked mildly irritated, and I suddenly felt very sorry for her. I gave her a nudge and whispered chummily, 'I guess you have to get used to Gary being monopolised when you're married to him.'

'I'm not his wife,' she said haughtily.

Oh Lord. She was probably somebody really famous who I'd clearly offended by not recognising. Rule number one: don't try and chat to celebrities when you are a nobody. Rule number two: practice your own haughty looks so you can toss a few back. I later found out she was Karen Brady, current vice-chairman of West Ham United and Lord Sugar's sidekick on *The Apprentice*. Okayyy. Definitely not married to Gary Barlow.

I managed to stay seated in my front row's coveted spot until Nicole Scherzinger came off stage and wanted to sit next to Gary, which meant more musical chairs.

My next spot was sitting behind Pudsey the dancing dog, who won this year's *Britain's Got Talent* alongside owner Ashleigh Butler. Now, as a long-time dog owner and lover of anything furry, I couldn't resist leaning forward and asking Ashleigh if I could stroke her pooch. Pudsey – who was as soft as a cotton wool ball – gave me a doggy smile accompanied by a couple of woofs before high-fiving me. Definitely much friendlier than Karen Brady.

I sat back down and chatted with another seat filler who'd slipped in alongside me. We both agreed Pudsey was very obedient.

'I wish my dog behaved like that,' I said wistfully.

'I wish my children behaved like that,' she replied.

But the moment where I *really* experienced a crazy frisson of excitement was when Marie and Donny Osmond went up on stage. What teenager of the Seventies didn't want to look like Marie? Or didn't have a mega crush on Donny? Back then it was either David Cassidy or Donny Osmond who screaming girls swooned over. My own bedroom bore testament to my teenage crushes. One wall was covered in pony posters, the other with a grinning Donny. Those teeth! And he still had them! And later, backstage, they both walked straight past me. I couldn't help myself. To hell with not talking to celebrities. Nervously I stammered out a hello.

'Hiiiii, I love your dress!' Marie gushed.

And she was off, chatting to me like I was a long-lost

friend. What did she say? I haven't a clue. Afterwards, I was far too dazed to remember. And then she took my hand in farewell. *Took my hand!*

'Who were they?' asked my daughter, face blank.

'In my day,' I said, eyes pumping out cartoon love hearts, 'those two were the male and female equivalent of your idols, Harry Styles and Demi Lovato.'

Which reminds me.

Why do actors enjoy their work so much?

Because it's all play...

I have a black belt in cooking.
One chop and you're dead...

In the last three weeks something very weird has happened. I've had an urge to cook. Now, anybody who knows me on a day-to-day basis would be astonished to hear this. First, they might wonder exactly what I'd cooked. Second, they'd excuse themselves from eating any of my cuisine saying it wasn't their sort of dish (in other words, yuck). I am no Gordon Ramsey, although I do a fab impression of him when staring into the depths of a charred saucepan while the smoke alarm shrieks in the background.

Due to having a hungry family who can only eat so many plates of beans on toast, for years I've resorted to convenience meals which rack up the supermarket bill.

'The weekly shop came to *how* much?' my husband is frequently heard to cry.

So is it guilt that's finally got to me? Up until this week I didn't give a tossed pancake about being a cooking goddess. But the desire to turn my kitchen worktop into a heaving mass of chopped herbs and fresh produce prevailed. There was also a little voice in my head asking, 'Perhaps you want to try home cooking because your Christmas efforts in front of family were so shaming?'

You only have to scroll through social media to see how people delight in posting pics of dishes they've created. I've always refrained from doing the same. I mean, what's the point of posting a picture of a plastic tray sporting synthetic-looking mash? But then I gave in to the urge to cook a simple Shepherd's Pie (the equivalent of a dinner party recipe in this house), AND it turned out to be not only edible but delicious, so suddenly I found myself joining the masses... in other words, whipping out my mobile and uploading a photograph to the whole wide world. The response from friends and family was so overwhelming and uplifting that I felt as elated as someone who'd won lottery. Mr V kept saying, 'Did you *really* cook this or did your mother do it?'

A macaroni cheese came next, followed by cannelloni,

lasagne and then... wait for it... the giddy realms of *experimentation*. Stir fries with chilli jam and mouthwatering chicken in red wine. And then I tried a risotto. Which was absolutely disgusting and tasted like socks. Unwashed socks at that. Never mind. Two steps forward, one back. But the point is, I seem to have found myself on an adventure and – I never thought I'd say this – it's been quite exciting! However, I'm not getting carried away. For example, I won't be attempting homemade cereals. Which reminds me.

Did you hear about the man who drowned while making his breakfast muesli?

He was pulled in by a strong currant...

What is a vampire's sweetheart called?
His ghoul-friend...

I've been alive for... ooh, quite a while now, and have never, ever, received a Valentine card from a mystery admirer. Okay, I'm probably too long in the tooth these days, but my point is that even when I was a teenager with smooth skin and everything pointing North as opposed to heading South, nobody ever secretly fancied me.

Hearing my teenage daughter chatting excitedly about this commercialised day of romance mentally sent me hurtling back through time where, every fourteenth day of February, I could be found hanging around my parents' hallway by the letterbox. Would a rush of red envelopes with the coveted '*SWALK*' written on the licked-down seals slither enticingly through the brass flap before they all plopped down to the hall carpet? As the postman came up the garden path, the sense of anticipation was almost unbearable.

'What *are* you doing?' my mother would enquire to my lurking self as she appeared, kitten heels clicking, dressing gown swishing, to scoop up the newly deposited envelopes. There would then follow muttered oaths about too many brown envelopes, and why hadn't *Interflora* delivered? Oh yes, even though she was married, she expected Father Bryant to have organised an annual bouquet in exchange for ironing his shirts three hundred and sixty-five days of the year.

Women are hopeless romantics. And men are... well, they're not. They aren't programmed like women. They don't pass a shop window and melt at the sight of a teddy bear holding a velvety rose in paws embroidered with red hearts. They don't stop and gaze at a brightly lit window of sparkly earrings or necklaces and think, 'Wow, I have a sudden urge to splurge on the wife/girlfriend/fiancée/partner/earth mother to my beautiful child. Nor do they pause outside *Thornton's* and deliberate whether to spoil the missus with some lush chocolate complete with professionally iced personal message.

My first Valentine's Day with Mr V was amazing. He organised a hugely extravagant, mind-blowingly beautiful and vast bouquet of flowers. It took several vases to accommodate all the stems.

'Oh! My! God!' I kept shrieking as I floated around the house in a state of euphoria. 'There IS a romantic man who dwells upon this planet – and he's all mine!' followed by gleeful cackling. What Mr V didn't tell me was that those flowers were to last for every subsequent Valentine's Day that has rolled around ever since.

'Do you know how much that bouquet cost me?' he said afterwards, which admittedly took the edge of that long ago exhilaration.

Never mind, ladies. With a bit of luck, a last-minute bunch of roses will be thrust before our noses, in which case we will ignore the fact that they're supermarket flowers with a half price sticker on the cellophane. Which reminds me.

A man (who shall remain unnamed) was asked by his friend if he'd bought his wife anything for Valentine's Day.

'Yes,' said the man. 'I've bought her a belt and a bag.'

'That was very kind of you,' said the friend. 'I hope she appreciates it.'

'So do I,' said the man, 'and hopefully the vacuum cleaner will work better now…'

What do you call a vegetarian who goes back to eating meat?
Someone who has lost their veg-inity...

Having finally decided that maybe, just maybe, I might like cooking after all (albeit simple recipes you understand) yesterday I was all revved up to give it another enthusiastic whirl. Pausing briefly to suck on a pencil and think about what, exactly, to cook, I then scribbled out a shopping list. Mr V watched.

'What's that?' he said, pointing at a word on my notepad.

'Mince,' I replied.

'Oh no, not mince. I don't want you to make anything with mince. I'm never eating mince again. I like to know where my food comes from,' — Mr V skirted around the notepad as if it was a dangerous animal — 'I don't care what it says on the package label, I'm not eating it.'

I frowned. 'What are you talking about? The label has always said *100% beef*.'

'But *is* it?' questioned Mr V, waggling a finger. '*Where* does it come from? Can you answer me that, eh?'

What was this? Twenty questions? Mastermind? I put my hands on my hips and addressed my husband in the tone one might reserve for a pre-school child.

'Beef mince comes from a cow.'

'That's the trouble with you, Debbie. You spend all your time on Facebook or writing. You don't watch the news or any sort of current affairs programme. Nor do you read the newspapers.'

True, true and true. News at Ten (if it's still even on) was THE most depressing programme ever. War. Poverty. Murder. Rape. Corruption. Famine. Hurricanes. Tsunamis. Child abuse. Animal cruelty. Lying two-faced politicians playing God to humanity. And the newspapers are no better. I can't stand it. So, rightly or wrongly, I've withdrawn and now live in my own rosy bubble. And it's great. In my world I say hello to locals, walk my dog with a neighbour, spend time with my parents, rejoice when the sun shines, put my umbrella up when it rains and marvel at the shapes and colours of storm clouds, and love to write fluffy nonsense in a bid to spread some cheer and hopefully make a few readers smile. Okay, it's a cop out. I don't know whether it's iffy hormones or just a bad dose of over-sensitivity, but I've reached a point where reading newspapers makes me bawl.

'There is currently a lot of hoo-ha about horsemeat in our food chain,' said my husband.

Ah. Yes. Unfortunately some bits of news do filter into my brain via the car radio (you can't totally fail to hear some of the misery going on in the world no matter how hard you try). I've been a vegetarian for decades, so having the screaming heebie-jeebies at possibly consuming horsemeat hasn't been a personal issue.

'I don't know why you're making such a fuss,' I said. 'After all, you're quite happy eating cute ducklings, and dear little pigs that wag their tails like dogs, or a darling little calf, not forgetting sweet little lambs that go *baa* and skip around —'

'Yes, thank you very much,' — Mr V put up a hand to halt my diatribe — 'I'd rather not be reminded that my dinner once had legs and bleated.'

'Right. So your main concern is that your dinner never said *neigh*.'

'Absolutely. So beef is off the menu.'

'That's fine by me. So, tonight, lentil stew all right?'

'Ah, the only trouble is, I don't like lentils. Tell you what, fancy going out for a curry?'

Does he even need to ask? Yum!

Indians don't eat cows for religious reasons, so there is never any danger of consuming something that once said *moo*. So we had a curry. Mr V chose chicken korma. I gave him an impish look.

'What?' he said, fork suspended in mid-air.

'Cluck cluck cluck,' I said, taking mischievous pleasure in the horror on his face.

Which reminds me.

What did one vegetarian spy say to the other vegetarian spy?

We'll have to stop meating like this...

Fashion?
It's something that goes in one year and out the other...

The school half-term is almost over. Yesterday my daughter nagged me for some last-minute quality time together. In other words, shopping. Thankfully I've had some spare cash this month, so tagged along with Eleanor as she trotted around Bluewater shopping mall. First stop was a popular place that, for the purposes of this chapter, I'll refer to as *Always 22*.

Now the last time we visited this store, we came out with several shopping bags. On that occasion there had been a lot of oohing and aahing about their reasonable prices and delightful fashion. But not so this time. Well, to be fair the prices were still good – but the fashion was dire. Nylon this and crimplene that. Half the stuff looked like gear my granny used to wear. They say fashion goes in cycles, but I'm not sure Eleanor's ready to look like a 1950's housewife. There was also a lot of monochrome stuff very similar to what's languishing in the back of my wardrobe from the last time black and white was trending (surely not *that* long ago?!).

After two hours of trekking about, our purchases had amounted to zilch. Previous fizzy anticipation of a good splurge had all but sputtered out. Why is it that when you mustn't spend money, everything in the shops looks fab, but when you have a few quid in your pocket, everything in the brightly lit windows is dire? Presumably it's something to do with the Law of Sod.

Walking past another store, I perked up when spotting a sweater sporting some pretty gems. I've always been a sucker for sparkly stuff, be it in jewellery or on jumpers, so dragged Eleanor into the shop with me.

'Good afternoon,' simpered the shop assistant. 'Can I help you?'

'Yes, please. I can't find the price tag on this sweater. How much is it?'

'Gorgeous, isn't it?' the shop assistant purred, 'and very good value at just one hundred and forty-nine pounds.'

I gasped and tried not to clutch my chest.

'Would you like to try it on?'

'No thank you,' I spluttered, and did a hasty about-turn.

'*Mum!*' Eleanor reprimanded, catching up with me. 'You sounded really narky just then.'

'No I didn't!'

'Yes, you did.'

'Well I didn't mean to sound rude but, honestly, what a ridiculous price to pay for a jumper. And I'll bet all those gems would fall off the moment they were shown the washing machine. Ooh, look.' I skidded to a halt outside another popular (and considerably cheaper) store. 'Let's try in here.'

We sailed through the doors and I instantly found another sparkly sweater for thirty quid. Yayyy! Which reminds me.

What do you get if you cross a kangaroo with a sheep?

A woolly jumper...

What two levels of maintenance do teenage daughters desire?
'High' and 'Ultra High'...

Yesterday evening left me feeling somewhat bemused. Why? Because I found myself on a double date with my daughter and her boyfriend. This all came about because last week Eleanor informed me it was her *anniversary*.

'Anniversary?' I repeated, looking blank. Had she, at some point, secretly married? Given that she's not quite sixteen years old, surely not. 'What anniversary?'

'It's been a whole year since I started dating M.'

Well congratulations. But in my day if you had a boyfriend you didn't celebrate *going-out-together-anniversaries*. But apparently I'm way behind the times – as always. These days teenagers celebrate not just going out together for an entire year, but in some cases going out together for a full month. Particularly when some of them chop and change boyfriends at a phenomenal rate.

'So,' I said, furrowing my brow, 'hypothetically speaking, you could even have a *weekiversary*?'

My teen rolled her eyes by way of response.

'Can you give me a lift?' she asked.

'A lift? When? And where to?'

'To the restaurant. It's this Saturday that we'll be celebrating our anniversary!'

'But I'm going out myself on Saturday.'

'Can't you forfeit?'

'No!'

'But it's my ANNIVERSARY!'

Geez. I have always tried to compromise where my children are concerned. A little bit of what they want, and a little bit of what I want. In this case we both wanted to go out. And on a Saturday.

'Okay. In that case you'll have to go to the same restaurant as us.'

My daughter looked horrified. 'You're joking.'

I wasn't.

My daughter prepared for the event like a bride. A trip to the beautician where eyebrows were shaped, and various parts of the body waxed. Then off to the hairdresser where her hair was curled into a waterfall of tumbling waves. Next was a visit to a local nail bar for a manicure and polish. Finally, she slithered into a new dress with perfectly accessorised shoes and clutch bag. She walked into the restaurant looking a million dollars. Which was only right considering she'd practically spent that amount getting ready for the occasion.

Mr V and I followed Eleanor and M into the restaurant.

'Your family table is here,' said a waiter, bowing and scraping.

'No, no, no,' said my daughter, protesting. 'M and I must have a table somewhere else. Preferably a good mile away from the parents.'

And so it was that Mr V and myself found ourselves at one end of the restaurant while my daughter and her boyfriend sat at the other. I stared myopically at them. They were holding hands across the candlelit table, billing and cooing like a pair of turtle doves.

How lovely, I thought. How romantic. I looked at my husband.

'Do you remember when you used to look at me like that?'

'Ooh, beef medallions,' said my husband by way of response.

I sighed. 'I thought you were worried about beef being horse meat in disguise?'

'Not here,' he murmured, stroking the menu lovingly. At one point I thought he was going to kiss it.

My eyes flit across the restaurant. Eleanor and M were still holding hands and apparently in deep in conversation. I tried and failed to lip read. Where was *my* husband's hand? Why wasn't he staring into *my* eyes like he'd found Mecca?

'How about some romantic conversation?' I suggested.

Mr V put down his menu. 'Manchester United won against Norwich today. Four nil. Cracking. And I'm warning you now, Debbie, next Tuesday the boys are up against Real Madrid, so absolutely no interruptions, okay?'

'You once told me my eyes were like limpid green pools.'

'Rooney scored a brilliant fourth goal. And Van Persie's back injury seems okay now.'

'Do you like my dress?'

'United hardly broke sweat re-establishing their fifteen-point cushion at the top of the Premier League.'

'That's so thrilling. Now can we talk about something else?'

So my husband talked to me about mortgages instead. Offset ones. And money. And how to save it. He's very good with money. So am I, but more so at spending it... like when I recently bought a new car. In my defence, I demonstrated impressive money-saving sense by purchasing a little Micra. Very economic. Does umpteen miles to the gallon. And thanks to technology and carbon footprint whatsits and clean emission thingies, the road tax is only thirty pounds a year. Yes, *thirty pounds a year*. The fact that I forgot to renew the road tax and was fined forty quid is neither here nor there. Which reminds me.

A man was driving behind a lorry. Suddenly he had to swerve to avoid a falling box full of nails and tacks. Seconds later a policeman pulled him over for reckless driving and tacks evasion...

How do you cure Insomnia?
It's a case of mind over mattress...

My husband hasn't had a particularly good week. He's had a lot of driving around the country, extra-long working hours, a hotel's hard bed, and a definite lack of sleep. As is so often the way when life is super busy, he's hit the pillow only to find his brain in overdrive. Sleep – even when exhausted – doesn't always happen.

Mr V needs noise in order to nod off, whereas I'm the opposite. I need silence that is so thick and heavy you might hear the proverbial pin drop – which doesn't make for a restful night with my husband.

In order to solve this conflict of noise versus silence, my husband goes to bed with a mini-radio and headphones. He plugs himself into *Talk Sport* and, within seconds, has usually drifted off. At some point during the night the earphones and Mr V's head part company, and the wretched things somehow end up on my pillow emitting a tinny racket. This disturbs my sleep and drives me slightly nuts. To say I'm a crosspatch in the morning is an understatement.

Over the years, Mr V and I have attempted to resolve our respective sleep issues by getting bigger beds. Married life started out in a standard 4' 6" double bed. One year later it had been shelved for a king-size jobbie.

'Isn't it lovely having extra room,' said Mr V, stretching out like a starfish.

'What extra room?' I retorted, hugging the edge of the mattress.

The next house move provided a large master bedroom, and I wasted no time in sourcing a bed of epic proportions.

'Ooooh, look!' I said, drooling at on-line pictures of bespoke seven footers.

'Don't be daft,' said my husband. 'Queen-size will suffice.'

The downside of a big bed is fighting with all the linen when it comes to laundering. Shaking a vast duvet into its cover single-handed is a task that leaves me hot, bothered, and muttering silent oaths.

Meanwhile, Mr V persists in star-fishing leaving me perched precariously on the edge. And as for my husband's bedtime radio, I can honestly say I hate the contraption with a passion. Take last night. Mr V's headphones had gone AWOL and for once they weren't on my pillow. I would point at, here, that I was asleep when he discovered they were missing (the "silence" had woken him up!). It was the early hours of the morning when he patted one hand across the bed but couldn't find the elusive headphones. Giving up, Mr V settled back against his pillows to listen to the radio *without* headphones. But being that he needs NOISE to go to sleep, he turned the volume right up. So as my husband tumbled blissfully down the corridors of sleep, on the other side of the bed I was rising to the surface of wakefulness in panic listening to men with gruff voices talking to each other.

My eyes stared into the darkness as my heart began to unpleasantly pump. Oh. My. God. We'd been broken into. Burglars were downstairs or... possibly upstairs? Could they even – I gulped – be in our bedroom? I didn't hang around to find out. Flicking on the bedside lamp, I grabbed the lamp by the base and sprang to my feet ready to bash Mr Burglar's brains out. Mr V promptly sat up, squinting, and demanded to know why his wife was looking wild-eyed and brandishing a B & Q lamp.

This tale has a happy ending. Firstly, I didn't kill my husband. Secondly, the 'lost' headphones were found at the bottom of the bed. The wire was in a complete tangle. I left Mr V unravelling the jumble and grumpily took myself off to the spare room. Is this the way forward for a decent night's sleep? Which reminds me.

Did you hear about the insomniac who went to the doctor?

'Doctor, doctor,' he said, 'I haven't slept for days!'

The doctor looked at his patient and said, 'Try sleeping at night...'

What do you do if your old boiler explodes?
Buy her some flowers...

Every year our boiler packs up. It is the *Law of Sod* that this always happens in the winter. If our boiler had a personality, I'd describe it as bloody-minded. Why else would we be layering up with woollies to stave off the shivers from snow on the ground, or gale force winds, or minus-something temperatures? Because – and excuse me for saying this – our boiler is a bitch, that's why.

Over the years Bitch Boiler has played up, cut out, only heated the hot water, then only heated the radiators, and then finally refused to heat anything at all. Last time around the engineer gave BB a new circuit board which coaxed her back into life. But was she happy? No. Instead, BB heated the house to warm, then hot, then boiling hot, and finally meltdown. Twiddles to her thermostat brought zero response until, in desperation, I took to the fuse board.

BB's most recent trick was to make a sound like a jumbo jet taking off in the utility room. This sent the pipes in the overhead airing cupboard into a noisy tailspin and had the hot water tank emitting sounds like an out of tune orchestra.

British Gas are always ace at sorting out BB's problems (until next time around), so much so that we're on first name terms with the local engineers. There's Joe who likes tea with no sugar, and Barry ("Call me Baz") who likes coffee with three sugars. Trudy Beagle particularly likes Baz because he always absent-mindedly places his coffee cup on the floor not realising that beagles will not only eat anything, but drink everything too – especially coffees with three sugars. But now we have a new family member to also watch out for. Dolly, the cat.

'Ah, what a sweet kitty,' said Baz, until Dolly pounced on his ankle and clamped down hard. 'Aww, look how much fun she's having,' he said through clenched teeth. Whereupon Dolly turned her back on Baz, dived into her litter tray next to his toolbox and did the biggest—

Well, I won't go into detail.

Suffice to say BB is once again doing her stuff and Baz managed not to faint from the pong of Dolly's doings. Which reminds me.

A boiler engineer was called out by Buckingham Palace to heat the Queen's kennels. The boiler engineer was halfway through the job when the police arrested him. Why? Because he wasn't Corgi registered...

Boyfriend: 'Darling, if we get married will you be able to live on my income?'
Girlfriend: 'Of course. But what will you live on?'

My daughter has been dating her boyfriend for a little over a year. Personally, I think she's too young to be so serious about a lad, but there you go. The two of them are currently "Love's Young Dream" and can't wait for the weekends to roll around so they can see each other.

Things were very different in my day. When I was fifteen I, too, was madly in love with a boy. Although this particular male had four legs, a mane and tail, and when we kissed no tongues were involved. Also, my daughter is very attractive, whereas I just wasn't, which is probably why she has a boyfriend at fifteen and I didn't. In fact, Eleanor is never short of admirers. Indeed, only a couple of nights ago a lad popped up on Facebook Chat from two summers ago.

''Ello, zis is Antoine 'ere.' Okay, he didn't type it quite like that, but he's French so I'm trying to set the scene. ''Ow are you?'

My daughter said she was fine, thanks, and politely asked how he was doing. Which brought forth gushing chat about how much he missed my daughter, how he couldn't stop thinking about her, she was the sun, the moon and *les étoiles* and any chance of popping over and staying during the summer holidays so they could have a fine romance? Eleanor was aghast.

'Mum?' she called out.

'Yes?' I replied.

'How do you politely tell someone to go away?'

'I have absolutely no idea.'

'Well what did you do when you were dating somebody you weren't bothered about?'

Was she kidding? I just never had this problem! It was hard enough trying to bag someone I could refer to as *my boyfriend* never mind tell him to bog off.

Of course the cynics might say that Antoine was merely trying to butter my daughter up in order to have a free jolly in England for the summer.

Meanwhile, there is a small matter of GCSEs coming up and I really would prefer my teenager to focus on passing a few of them. Which reminds me.

A mother said to her daughter, 'How did the exam go today?' The daughter replied, 'The questions didn't give me any trouble at all, but the answers did...'

**Did you know old skiers never die?
They just go downhill...**

Yippee! This Easter Sunday Eleanor and I will be hooking up with a couple of cousins and flying off to Les Arcs in France for a fabulous week of skiing. Mr V is opting out (again) on the grounds that he's lost interest. He is adamant this loss of interest is nothing to do with a preference for being a couch potato and being left alone to watch, in peace, Manchester United on the telly.

'So what would you like me to fill the freezer with?' I asked. 'Steak and kidney pie? Lasagne? Some cod and chips?'

'Nope,' said Mr V, shaking his head. 'I'm going to be eating super healthy stuff while you're away.'

'Okay,' I said, my pencil hovering over a shopping list, 'so we're talking salads? Tins of tuna? Brown bread with grains and seeds? And lots of fresh fruit?'

'Buy me a carton of milk and a large box of crunchy nut cornflakes.'

'Cornflakes?'

'Yep.'

'And what else?'

'Nothing.'

'You're going to spend an entire week eating cornflakes?'

'Yes.'

'What, as in breakfast... lunch... dinner... absolutely nothing but cornflakes?'

Mr V frowned. 'Actually, make that two boxes.'

I rolled my eyes and chucked my pencil down.

Meanwhile the family moggy, Dolly, will be staying at the local cattery. Likewise, Trudy Beagle will go to a nearby kennel. I can tell Dolly knows change is in the air because she keeps looking at the suitcases with wary eyes. The family pooch is an old hand at reading the signs. The moment she spotted the open lids and half-packed suitcases, she jammed her tail between her legs and gave a sigh of resignation. Why can't Mr V look after the cat and dog? Well, would you entrust the care of your precious fur babies to a man all set to survive on cornflakes for a week?!

The boarding tickets are printed and have been placed with the passports in hand luggage. All that Eleanor and I need to do now is start our snowy adventure. That said, I hope it will be without mishaps and definitely no *iffy* moments... like the time I fell down a crevasse and hysterically demanded a helicopter rescue before my husband risked life and limb trying to pull me out – only to fall down another crevasse himself. Or the time we went skiing in Italy, did *one last run* before the chairlifts closed, ended up in France and had to take a three-hour taxi ride back to our hotel at a cost of two hundred euros. Or the time we again got lost, ended up doing an off-piste black run which resulted in legs like jelly and an overwhelming need to consume a stiff drink or six for shock. That's the only time in my life I've ever been hopelessly drunk. I can still remember watching the road going up and down and thoughtfully warning pedestrians to wait for the big waves to pass. But I'm ninety-nine per cent sure nothing is going to go wrong on this trip. Which reminds me.

Spotted in a skier's Dictionary:

Bindings – automatic mechanisms that protect skiers from serious injury during a fall by releasing skis from boots, sending the skis skittering across the slope where they then trip up two other skiers...

Why is age a very high price to pay for maturity? Because, after forty-five, your *get up and go* gets up and goes...

So my cuzzie and I survived a week's skiing in Les Arcs with our daughters. Being husband-free, there had been an unspoken pact to let our hair down and have *a jolly good time.*

'Shall I pack the Scrabble?' I'd asked Anita (yes, I'm a sad person thinking that staying up late hunched over a Scrabble board constitutes a "jolly good time").

'Certainly not. There's a big après ski scene in Les Arcs and we are going to check it out.'

'Right-oh,' I'd warbled, and the Scrabble board had remained at home.

We arrived in Les Arcs with a sense of anticipation. We might be middle-aged...*very* middle-aged on my part due to being the eldest by five years... but, hey! Age is just a number and it's all about mental attitude. They say you are as young as the man you're feeling, so when we took a coffee break after a morning's skiing and had a couple of French guys making eyes at us, we were secretly thrilled to bits. The fact that the chaps in question were older than us and dressed as women were neither here nor there – these days you have to take your thrills where you can.

After coffee, we returned to the slopes – and oh what slopes these were! To put those skis together and just hurtle off... except... hang on... why was I being left behind? Why were my legs constantly applying the brakes every time a bit of speed kicked in?

'Stop it!' I mentally hissed at my leg muscles.

'Bugger off!' they retorted. 'You think we're letting you bust one of us? Not likely!'

And so a pattern was set. The others would whizz off with me lagging further and further behind. Since when had I become so cautious? Was it an age thing? A sense of self-preservation? And what was going on with my co-ordination? My body was covered in bruises, but not from falls, rather instead from clumsily bashing myself against turnstiles, chairlifts, metal poles and steel bars. Never mind, a different sort of bar was awaiting and offering consolation.

'Try a mojito,' said Anita. 'It will loosen you up.'

It certainly loosened my tongue up. I couldn't stop talking. And as I gazed up at the mountains from our prime view on the wooden veranda, I silently declared war on those peaks. *Tomorrow I will ski you like a devil possessed.*

The following day I stood at the top of what looked like a lumpy sheer drop and tried to ignore my heart beating in my throat. Anita furtively produced a hip flask.

'A drop of Dutch Courage?'

When I'd consumed more drops of Dutch Courage than was probably sensible, I set off. Ah, right, *this* was the way to ski! Easy peasy Jack Daniels squeezy. Thrilled to bits, when we later stopped for coffee, I instructed the waiter to stick in a shot of rum. Anita looked alarmed.

'You don't want to lose control of your legs, Debbie.'

'Nothing wrong with my legs,' I beamed. Until the following morning when I tried to get out of bed. They were as stiff as a couple of ironing boards. Unfolding them, I gingerly stood up.

'Perhaps we could make today an easy one?' I asked Anita, as I creaked over to my skis in the locker room.

'Good idea. Let's focus on après ski instead.'

Ah yes. The après ski. My cousin and I hadn't yet done anything wild on account of being absolutely knackered at the end of the day, whereas our daughters had no problem keeping their eyes open throughout an entire evening. Anita and I found ourselves walking into a bar, gamely ordering a drink, and five minutes later yawning into our glasses. What was wrong with us? Surely it wasn't because we were *a certain age* was it?

'Oooh look!' said Anita, pointing to a shelving system in one corner of the hotel's recreation room. 'A Scrabble board!'

So while our daughters listened to the thumpity-thump of party music, my cuzzie and I argued whether "euoi" was truly a word and, if so, what the heck did it mean? Not exactly painting the town red.

By Day Five we were so pooped from all the mountain air and exercise, we didn't even try to do the après ski thing. We left our daughters holed up with their iPads, mobile phones and music and took ourselves off to bed. Just as I was snuggling under the duvet, Mr V rang.

'How are you?' he asked.

'Good,' I replied, stifling a yawn.

'What are you up to this evening? Bar crawl? Night club?'

'Er, neither. I'm in bed.'

'In bed? But it's only quarter to eight!'

In my defence, France was one whole hour ahead. Okay, not much of a defence.

So there you have it. Footloose and fancy free for a week and in bed at silly o'clock. So much for middle-aged rebellion. Which reminds me.

Somebody once told me that the good thing about middle-age is that your glass is half full. The not-so-good-thing is that in a few more years your teeth will be floating in it...

Nobody can fix the economy. Nobody can be trusted. Nobody's perfect so...
VOTE FOR NOBODY!

You know, I'd have liked to have written a few words about Mrs Thatcher's death which happened earlier this week. However, I'm all too aware that this could set off a vitriolic tirade of comments. Sadly, freedom of speech doesn't seem applicable these days when it comes to politics. I read about Spice Girl Geri Halliwell saluting Mrs Thatcher on Twitter, calling her the first woman of 'girl power'. The resulting wrath was such that she was forced to delete the tweet. In a country like Great Britain? Come again? Geez...

When the news first broke of Mrs Thatcher's death, the thing that struck me the most was that it was impossible to scroll through Facebook's newsfeed without spotting comments like 'yippee' or 'how wonderful' or 'if you liked Thatcher, unfriend me now'. Currently the newspapers are full of photographs of endless riots, looters, and arsonists supposedly "letting off steam" about a Prime Minister whose policies they didn't agree with. Erm, the only thing is, she's not led this country for over twenty years. So, actually, those people were simply looking for an excuse to go out and make trouble without a thought for wrecking others' means of making an honest living.

I'm no political animal and quite honestly think many of the politicians in this country are a bunch of muppets. But whether you liked or loathed Margaret Thatcher, I cannot rejoice in her death or that of ANY politician, past, present, or future. She was a human being, a wife and a mother – same as me and every other woman out there on Planet Earth. Since when did so many people fail to recognise that we should all stop this simmering hatred and start being nice to each other – REGARDLESS OF OUR POLITICAL PERSUASION, RELIGION, GENDER, RACE? The bottom line is, we're all in this together, so for God's sake let's start by being kind to each other, because THAT is what will make this world a much nicer place.

Right, that's me off my soap box. Which reminds me.

A little girl asked her father, 'Do all fairy tales begin with *Once upon a time*?

Her father replied, 'No. Some begin with *When I am elected...*'

My daughter bet I couldn't make a car out of spaghetti.
You should have seen her face as I drove pasta...

Last Saturday Mr V wanted to go looking at cars. Now it must be said that I'm not a fan of hanging around car show rooms. All that standing about in a vast space occupied by hugely expensive shiny objects. Spotlights in the ceiling positioned *just so*. Paintwork gleaming. Bonnets protruding like women sticking their chests out. Men trying not to drool too obviously.

Over the last few weeks Mr V has carted me around various dealerships. Audi. BMW. Back to Audi. Back to BMW. And then Mercedes. My husband is a man who likes to *think things over*. And I am a woman who doesn't. If you want a car, get on and buy it. Don't "um" and "ah" and ponder, then scratch your chin as you pace backwards and forwards. It's a waste of time and energy. Apart from anything else, I have a low boredom threshold. Last weekend my boredom threshold hit rock bottom. Which is possibly why, as we arrived at yet another Mercedes dealership, I decided to play a game... which car would I buy if I were car shopping? Except I got a bit carried away.

While Mr V ambled into the show room to um, ah, ponder, scratch his chin, and pace backwards and forwards, I was sprinting across the parking lot to admire rows of shiny cars. Oooh, that one was nice – big sporty wheels. But what about this one? An M Class. Blimey, it only did *how much* to the gallon? I swiftly moved on. This one was more like it. But wrong colour. See? Instant processing of brain, immediate acceptance or dismissal of what the eyes are seeing. None of this fannying about and pacing up and down whilst deliberating over a model with a horrific insurance group. I ground to a halt. There, before me, was the car of my dreams. Well, no, actually I lie. The *real* car of my dreams was the M Class, but I was more than happy to settle for this one. The B Class. Very elegant. Silver. Which also meant it didn't need to go through the car wash every two minutes like other colours (never buy black, looks great until it rains, which is virtually every day in the UK).

I peered in through the driver's window. Automatic. Sat-Nav. And several other buttons and controls – way beyond my immediate understanding on account I've never driven anything so swish before (thanks to owning a moulting dog and kids who drop sweet wrappers everywhere). But as I stood there, totally enthralled, my mind was made up. I was having this car. I strode off to the show room.

'So what sort of deal would you give me?' Mr V was asking a young salesman. So young that surely, he shouldn't be driving, never mind selling cars. I'd heard all these questions before along with the haggling and weighted silences aimed to tease the salesman. I stood there and waited for the next pause – which wasn't long as my husband loves to stretch a salesman's nerves to breaking point. I jumped in.

'That car over there,' I said, pointing beyond the showroom's vast glass windows. 'I'd like to buy it, please.'

Mr V's jaw hit the spotless tiled floor and I thought the salesman was going to faint. Never before had he experienced such a fast deal. And he hadn't even had to seek me out!

'If you'll excuse me for one moment,' said Mr V to the salesman before propelling me away by the elbow. 'What the devil are you doing?' hissed my husband.

'I want to buy a new car.'

'But you bought a new car only a few months ago.'

This is true. But it was a Micra. There is a world of difference between a Micra that bashes my front passenger's knees every time I change gear, and a Mercedes. The only thing they have in common is that they both begin with M.

'I know, but this time I'm going to be utterly selfish and buy what I want.'

And so I did.

In the meantime Mr V is thinking about checking out a convertible sports car. Another ten years and he might even buy one. Meanwhile I'm off for a little drive. Which reminds me.

A woman told her husband she wanted a new car. 'I want something that goes from nought to one-hundred and forty in three seconds.'

The husband produced some weighing scales and said, 'Stand on that...'

What happens when a frog parks in a no-parking space?
It gets toad away...

I'm loving my new car. And so are my kids. Now that I have a car with more legroom, taxi duties have doubled.

Earlier on this week my children went to see the popstar Pink at London's O2. I was pushed for time and unable to do the taxi run in to the City, so nervously put my daughter on a train instead. Rob, my student son who is currently living at digs in Stepney Green, was under strict instructions to meet his sister promptly at Victoria Station. However, as the concert finished late and I didn't want Eleanor travelling home alone, I later drove to Greenwich to meet both kids, telling Rob I'd drop him back to Stepney. He was grateful for the lift, especially as he's currently a bit twitchy about living in *The Black Hole* (a pet name for his awful student flat which looks even more dreadful since being burgled and having the door smashed in, but that's another story).

Now I don't know if you've ever tried parking at the O2, but it's a nightmare. Well, it's not so much a problem *prior* to a concert, it's afterwards when twenty thousand people come pouring out with half of them heading off to the car parking area. I've been caught out before, but this time knew what to expect and opted to park and wait at the nearby Sainsbury's. Rob said he'd use his mobile's maps app to guide him and Eleanor to Sainsbury's. I gave him the supermarket's postcode and waited. The minutes ticked by. After half an hour I rang my son.

'Where are you?'

'Going round in circles. We've just crossed the same roundabout three times and nearly been flattened by traffic – it's manic.'

'What the heck are you doing on a roundabout, and why aren't you using your map app?' I squawked.

'Because my phone's battery is dangerously low, and I don't want it to die on me. I'd rather be able to stay in contact. Text me some landmarks.'

The line went dead. A part of me wanted to abandon the car and look for them on foot – they couldn't be that far away. However, like a million other late-night taxiing parents, I'd set off from home wearing my pyjamas and didn't want to get arrested for being an oddball. Instead I looked around me for some handy landmarks. Thankfully, there were quite a few. I was opposite *Prezzo* with its brightly lit neon sign. Next to this was *Nandos* and a main bus stop. I picked up my phone and tapped out a message.

Thank God for mobiles! Where would we be without them? Unfortunately, still lost in the case of my children, for whilst mobiles are a fantastic invention, I cannot say the same for predictive text.

My phone rang.

'Hello?'

'Mum! Where the heck are you?'

'I've just texted you my location!'

'It was utter nonsense. Try again.'

I hung up and retrieved my text message.

Important opposite Prezzo, directly opposite hands and a bus stop.

Ah, I could see that wasn't very helpful. Almost as bad as another time I'd texted my son who was waiting at a different venue and had also asked me to give some friends a lift home:

Give me a time for Santa to pick you up. And if your arrows are drunk, they won't be allowed in the car.

I still haven't worked out why Father Christmas came into the text or why "friends" was substituted for sharp spears. All very odd.

Anyway, there was a happy ending to this tale. My children, frozen and wet through from a sudden and impromptu cloud burst, eventually found their pyjama-clad mother and the three of us finally set off. Which reminds me.

A blonde (*ahem*) was driving down a one-way street when she was pulled over by a traffic policeman.

'Lady, do you have any idea where you're going?' asked the cop.

'No,' said the blonde, 'but it must be pretty unpopular. Everyone else is leaving...'

Apparently there are plans to install a clock in the Leaning Tower of Pisa.
If it goes ahead the tower will have both the time and the inclination...

This time last week I was Italy with Mr V. We enjoyed a long weekend exploring Florence and Pisa. Time goes nowhere, and already those days seem like a beautiful dream, although we have lots of wonderful photographs to look back upon.

Our long weekend began with the alarm shrieking at three forty-five in the morning. There was a moment of wanting to ignore it, but then we switched into wannabe-a-tourist mode. Flinging back the bed covers, in no time at all we were off to Gatwick Airport. As the car sped along the motorway, I had a nagging feeling I'd overlooked something. I did a mental check. Dog in kennel – yes. Cat being looked after by daughter – yes. Passports – yes. Tickets – yes. What *had* I forgotten? It would come to me. Eventually.

EasyJet now have a bag drop system rather than traditional check-in. Initially I couldn't determine what difference that made until the nice lady weighing our suitcases told us we'd apparently booked "Speedy Boarding". Good heavens, had Mr V and I unwittingly splurged in order to get to the front of the boarding queue? Apparently yes... along with everybody else on our flight.

Half an hour later we were on the plane. Mr V sat back in the cramped bucket seat and skimmed through the Duty Free shopping magazine. Thirty seconds later, he put the mag down.

'I'm bored,' he said, fidgeting like one of the children on the seat in front of us. 'How shall we pass the flight time?'

'I'm good, thanks,' I murmured, eyes not leaving my kindle.

'Shall we have a chat?'

I nearly dropped my kindle from shock. Take away the

television with all its sports channels, and my husband is a lost soul.

'Okay,' I said, snapping my kindle shut. 'What shall we talk about?'

'Oooh, let me think.' Mr V rubbed his chin thoughtfully. 'What about work?'

'Work? But the whole purpose of this trip is to forget about work for the next few days.'

'Well it's hard to think of anything else to talk about. After all, I work very hard.'

'So do I.'

'Not as hard as me.'

'Rubbish! When you come home from work, that's it. Your day is done. Mine, like many women out there,' I flapped a hand in the direction of the airport, 'is still going. I work from the minute I get up to the moment my head hits the pillow. I not only do the day job, my writing means I'm also doing an evening job, AND I run the family home, which is a 24/7 job.'

Mr V adjusted his seating position. Body language conveyed he was on the defensive.

'Making a few meals here and there does not mean you're working flat out.'

I picked up the Duty Free magazine and privately wondered if EasyJet had ever witnessed a passenger being whacked with it. Hard.

Taking deep breaths to stop me committing murder in front of two hundred passengers, I distracted myself with a bit of people watching. Some folks on board were wearing a very strange combination of clothing. Take him over there. A blue and white striped shirt, pink jeans and orange socks tucked into bright green shoes. Interesting. My eyes flicked down to my own footwear. Boring flip-flops, which had been kicked off in order to accommodate in-flight socks that looked like something my granny used to wear. So cool. Not.

When we arrived in Pisa, a glorious golden sun greeted us. The temperature was twenty-seven degrees. I groaned. Oh no, I'd forgotten to pack shorts. Was that what had bothered me so much on the journey to

143

Gatwick? But... no... no, it was something much more important. I just couldn't quite put my finger on it.

Checking in at the hotel, we dumped our suitcases and immediately set off to see the famous Leaning Tower of Pisa. Unfortunately our sense of direction is appalling, and we ended up at the train station. Turning around, we retraced our footsteps, and walked along narrow streets lined with quaint trattorias, their brickwork smothered in hanging baskets bursting with flowers. Open doorways wafted smells guaranteed to make the tummy rumble. But not even the delicious aroma of garlic, tomato and basil could distract us, for there, peeking over the rooftops, was the tip of the tower.

I can't properly describe the effect this sight had on me. It was literally like a magnet, pulling me forwards. I found myself breaking into a jog, hastily dodging other tourists as this iconic structure came fully into view. And suddenly it was revealed in all its glory. A vast cylindrical building, partially sunken and seemingly tilting precariously, but incredibly not toppling over. All around us sightseers were doing the "holding it up" pose. The architecture was stunning and the stonework glorious, but not just on the tower, but elsewhere too. To the left of the bell tower was the cathedral and baptistery, both of which were grandiose masterpieces.

Florence was another incredibly place to explore with its stunning palaces, vast cathedrals and spectacular museums. My camera was working flat out that day.

But all good things come to an end, and suddenly it was time to go home. With a sense of satisfaction, I carefully wedged a souvenir bottle of bubble-wrapped olive oil into one of the suitcases.

When we landed at Gatwick Airport, I remembered what it was I'd forgotten to do. Completely failed to book travel insurance. This small but important detail came to light when the bottle of olive oil shattered in transit turning everything within the suitcase to a glistening mess.

'Never mind,' Mr V trilled, 'we can claim on the insurance.'

Or not, in this case. Which reminds me.

If olive oil comes from olives, where does baby oil come from...?

Who invented algebra?
A clever *x*-pert...

This week my daughter started her GCSE examinations. There was much muttering prior to the first exam, with complaints of feeling stressed. By the end of the first week Eleanor was frequently wailing comments like, 'I'm going to fail. It's all *Miss*'s fault. She hates me.'

I have no idea why Eleanor thinks her tutor – out of a vast class of pupils – dislikes just *her*. I suspect most of the teachers dislike *all* their pupils, which is hardly surprising considering some of the "leaver pranks" that have been going on in the last week. Eleanor has been secretly delighting in the pranks that a notorious clique of girls have been playing on certain teachers this week, reducing the usually stern detention-wielding lecturers to gibbering wrecks. Stink bombs have been detonated in the canteen, bags of flour have erupted upon doors opening, and all classroom clock hands have been put on back to front. The group went a bit far tipping red ink over hundreds of sanitary towels before creeping into the staff room and wallpapering all the windows.

'I hope you aren't taking part in these pranks,' I said sternly to Eleanor.

'Of course not,' she replied.

I believed her. Why? Because she didn't blink. Years ago, I saw the amazing Derren Brown live. He told the audience that he wasn't telepathic or psychic, and that his incredible showman skills came about from learning how to read body language. Tip Number One. If you want to lie, don't blink while telling your porky pie. It's a total giveaway. Tip Number Two. I think Derren Brown may well be telepathic or psychic because he blinked while denying it!

Anyway, I digress. Eleanor came home from school after sitting the first GCSE exam and she was totally euphoric. I sighed with relief.

'Your smile tells me it went well,' I beamed.

'No, it just means that I can now put all this' — she pointed to a stack of revision paperwork — 'in the bin because I never have to study this subject again.'

Unless she ends up doing re-sits of course. Which reminds me.

The following questions were set in last year's GCSE examinations and are claimed to be genuine answers from sixteen-year olds. Ready for a giggle?

Q. Name the four seasons.

A. Salt, pepper, mustard and vinegar.

Q. Explain one of the processes by which water can be made safe to drink.

A. Filtration makes water safe to drink because it removes large pollutants like grit, sand, dead sheep and canoeists.

Q. How is dew formed?

A. The sun shines down on the leaves and makes them perspire.

Q. What guarantees may a mortgage company insist on?

A. If you are buying a house they will insist that you are well endowed.

Q. In a democratic society, how important are elections?

A. Very important. Sex can only happen when a male gets an election.

Q. What are steroids?

A. Things for keeping carpets fixed to stairs.

Q. What happens to a boy when he reaches puberty?

A. He says goodbye to his boyhood and looks forward to his adultery.

Q. Name a major disease associated with cigarettes.

A. Premature death.

Q. What is artificial insemination?

A. When the farmer does it to the bull instead of the cow.

Q. How can you delay milk turning sour?

A. Keep it in the cow.

Q. What is the fibula?

A. A small lie.

Q. What is the most common form of birth control?

A. A condominium.

Q. Give the meaning of the term "Caesarean section".

A. It's a district in Rome.

Q. What is a seizure?

A. A Roman Emperor.

Q. What is a terminal illness?

A. When you are sick at the airport.

Q. Use the word "judicious" in a sentence to show you understand its meaning.

A. Hands that judicious can be soft as your face with Mild Green Fairy Liquid.

Q. Who was King Solomon?

A. A man who had three hundred wives and seven hundred porcupines...

What did the vampire order at the bar?
A bloody Mary...

It's been a bit of a week as I continue to recover from an operation on my head. There were some complications for some reason with blood clotting problems and several sizeable haematomas.

Being a parent trains you to deal with pretty much any crisis. Feeling ill? Mum's here. Want to throw up? Mum's here. Missed the bowl puking? Never mind, Mum will clear it up. Funny tummy? Mum will help.

From the moment a woman gives birth Mother Nature programs her to deal with dirty nappies and puked upon clothing. Unfortunately, Mother Nature forgot to program me to deal with blood. Scraped knees were okay, but their frequent nosebleeds when little took a lot of effort not to faint. I can't do blood. So when my daughter gave me a concerned look and said, 'Er, Mum, are you aware that your hair has gone very red?' it's fair to say that I nearly passed out on the spot.

Going from blonde to redhead without a trip to the hairdresser is not something I ever want to deal with again. In the last seven days I've had eighty-something mils of blood syringed out of my scalp and, in the process, endured heart palpitations, rubbery legs and an upper lip covered in beads of sweat. What *is* it about blood that sends some of us keeling over?

The first time I was aware of a problem in this area was w-a-a-y back in my school days. I can still remember sitting, cross-legged, in the assembly hall listening to the headmistress excitedly telling us about a visitor who'd come to talk to us.

A gentleman then stood up, introduced himself and said he wanted to have *a little chat*. The guy was a scientist exploring heartbeat patterns and was after some volunteers. He had a huge reel-to-reel tape recorder that he then used to demonstrate some of his findings. I can still remember him smiling at us all and saying, 'THIS is what a beating heart sounds like!' as he pressed the *play* button.

The hall was instantly filled with the roaring sound of BOOM-BOOM... BOOM-BOOM. *Wow, that's interesting*, I thought as I listened to beat of an anonymous person's heart. Except... what was that? A duet was going on with another more persistent noise. A sort of... squelchy gumboot-stuck-in-sticky-mud noise. And as I sat there in my pale blue cotton uniform, I suddenly felt most peculiar. A teacher tapped me on the shoulder.

'Deborah,' she whispered (nobody called me 'Deborah' other than the teachers and, to this day, anyone calling me 'Deborah' immediately has me thinking I'm in BIG trouble!). 'Deborah, come with me. You're not feeling well.'

'How do you know that?' I asked in astonishment. Was Miss Bellamy a secret mind reader?

I stood up, swaying, and Miss Bellamy grabbed me. To my embarrassment the top half of my cotton dress was wringing wet and had completely stuck to my body. Yes, I'd been on the verge of fainting. And all because of some boom-booms and squelches. Pathetic, I know. And no, I didn't put myself forward as a volunteer for the heartbeats project. Nor have I ever been able to bring myself to be a blood donor, even though I admire every single person who has ever donated a pint of blood (bleurgh, I'm feeling peculiar just typing that). *Pause to take a deep breath...*

My mother, a retired nurse, had always hoped that my sister and I would follow her footsteps into the nursing profession (she also harboured hopes of us bagging eminent surgeons as husbands and having a real-life *Mills & Boon* happy-ever-after). She couldn't understand why the thought of being gowned and masked and assisting a handsome doctor in surgery would have me swooning for all the wrong reasons. To this day I have no idea what makes some of us cope so brilliantly at the sight of blood, while others are reduced to the screaming heebie jeebies. Which reminds me.

What do vampires use to sail cross the sea?

Blood vessels...

What is a "concert"?
A place where people gather to cough and sneeze...

Last night I saw the amazing Barbra Streisand live at London's O2 Arena. The concert had been much anticipated for months by my father, sister and I who had bagged our tickets the moment they came out. We'd gone overdrawn at the bank for those tickets which had cost *mumble mumble* pounds. It didn't matter that they weren't front row, or middle row (in fact they weren't even back row, they were in what is known as 'the vertigo row'). But none of that mattered. This woman was a legend. A superstar. And we were going to see her!

As a teenager I devoured all La Streisand's films and had all her records. While my friends tried to emulate supermodel Cindy Crawford, I wanted to look like Barbra. I did manage to grow a fairly impressive nose in my teens, but that was where any similarity ended.

The big day rolled around and, just as we were leaving, a drama contact got in touch saying she had two free places in front of the stage. Would I like them? Although this sounds amazing, sometimes such freebies can be a let-down. The reality is that you are a 'seat filler' so that – when the television cameras sweep over the auditorium – there are no audience gaps (stars want to show the world they are popular, after all!). But going along as a seat filler is risky business. You might get yourself settled all ready to enjoy the night ahead, only to find a celebrity asking you to shift because they'd only popped to the loo. If that happens, you have to go behind stage, totally out of sight and consequently can't see bugger all. I wasn't prepared to take that chance. I wanted to watch every moment of my heroine – even if it did mean using binoculars to see her.

However, I didn't want to waste the seat filler tickets and knew my son would probably appreciate a give-away, so gave him a ring. As a London student, he wasn't far away.

'If you want to see an icon, get yourself over to the O2

151

right now.'

Thirty minutes later Rob and a mate were there, just seven rows from the edge of the stage and sitting next to Graham Norton and other famous faces. My sister, upon finding out, was absolutely livid.

'Fancy not letting *us* sit there.'

She was still grumbling about it when we puffed up the steep steps to Level Four.

'How much further?' Janice asked.

'Keep going,' I said grimly.

'How much further now?'

'Almost there.'

'But we're practically touching the ruddy roof of the dome!'

'Er, yes. That's our seat. Up there.'

'The very top row?'

'Yes.'

'We paid all this money for the highest row in the O2?'

'Yes.'

'And to think we could have been on the ground floor. Un-*believ*-able. I can't see a thing up here. Did you bring the binoculars?'

Now wasn't the time to tell her that I'd forgotten them, because suddenly I was experiencing a head rush. You see, I'd made the massive mistake of looking down. As I slowly made my way along the very narrow platform towards my seat, the O2 seemed to tilt on its axis. Forget experiencing a menopausal hot flush. At that moment my entire body went into meltdown. I clung on to the back of plastic seats as I edged, inch by inch, along the wafer-thin platform. My palms were so sweaty, they'd have failed to grip anything if I'd tripped or fallen. And then, ahead, another nightmare loomed. A little gathering of people were standing up, pressed back against the wall so that we could squeeze past them. My father seemed to think this was all terribly funny and laughed his head off as I shuffled along the ledge at a snail's pace. My sister was still fuming which was doing wonders for averting any vertigo of her own. I finally reached the little group of people, but was unable to shimmy around them.

'I'm terribly sorry,' I croaked, 'but I don't think I can move another step.'

'Yes you can, dear,' said a sweet old lady of about ninety. She took my hand and helped me along the ledge, all the while giving me calm words of assurance. 'You won't fall, dear, but, if you do, I'll catch you.' The thought of me falling and inadvertently taking her with me had a rallying effect. Angels come in many guises and I reckon that little old lady was one of them. Thanking her from the bottom of my heart, I took a deep breath and sidled past everyone before collapsing into my seat. I clung on tightly to the sides until the O2 stopped rocking about.

When Barbra Streisand came on stage, the vertigo instantly subsided. I was in my own private bubble. Despite the distance, I could see her perfectly because I had my specs on! What a voice. And how fabulous did she look? The audience was introduced to both her sister and son who sang duets with her, and there was a guest spotlight on a trumpet player and young violinist whose talent went off the radar. There were songs from musicals, and of course classics like *Evergreen* plus the bouncy beat of *No More Tears* which, back in 1979, Barbra sang with disco queen Donna Summer. Which reminds me.

What do cars do at a disco?

Brake dance...

I love British summertime.
It's the one day of the year I look forward to the most...

Our summer holiday is FINALLY booked. Talk about *lastminute.com*, but at least we can now tell ourselves that in ten days' time Mr V, Eleanor and I will be basking in the sunshine on the beautiful island of Crete.

The last time I visited Rethymnon was twenty-four years ago with my first husband. I still have a clear memory of walking the Samaria Gorge, an amazing ten-mile landscape of stones, stones, even more stones, with a meandering river intersecting various parts of the guided walk.

'I can't wait to be back in Crete,' I enthused to Mr V. 'We can hike the Samaria Gorge together. It's absolutely breathtaking. We mustn't forget to pack our walking boots.'

My husband looked horrified. 'You can do what you like,' he said, palms up in a back-off gesture, 'but the only walk I'll be doing is the one that takes me to a sun lounger.'

Oh. What a shame. But perhaps I'll persuade him to go for a jog along the beach instead. It is, after all, the longest in Crete and stretches nearly three miles. There is something blissfully peaceful about leaving footprints in wet sand and listening to the ocean's gentle *shushing*.

Hopefully this year's holiday will be free from any drama. I'll never forget when my (then younger) son went back to the apartment to use the loo, left the keys on the hall table, and then, in an absent-minded moment, shut the front door after him. Cue hysterics of the unfunny kind as Robbie realised he'd locked us out.

One hour later my husband was clinging to knotted sheets and dangling off the balcony directly over ours. The occupant of that apartment, a Spanish lady who spoke broken English, thankfully understood our dilemma and gamely helped us 'break in' to our apartment. She and I sat on our bottoms, feet pushed against her balcony wall, our weedy arm muscles popping as we provided the ballast against Mr V's weight.

'I've run out of sheet,' Mr V's panicked voice had floated up.

'You'll have to jump,' I'd called back.

There was a pause as my husband had digested this information. A second later the knotted sheets went slack, followed by a terrific crash and resounding silence. The Spanish lady and I had stared at each other in horror.

'Er, I'm a bit squeamish about bl-blood,' I'd stuttered, paling to the colour of the knotted sheets. 'Pl-please would you l-look and see if my h-husband is still alive?'

'No, no,' the Spanish lady protested, 'or I might vomit.' Terrific.

'We do it together,' she instructed, hauling me upright where I stood on shaking legs.

Slowly, we peered over the balcony to find Mr V staring back up at us, star-fished out on a demolished plastic table. He was winded and couldn't immediately speak, but when he did it came out in a gibbering jumble of, 'Never again,' and 'Whisky.' But thankfully he did live to see another day...

...or the time our children took it upon themselves to rescue a frog that a group of Spanish children were tormenting. This resulted in an almighty ding-dong between me and the Spanish children's mother, even though neither of us could understand a word the other was saying...

...or the time my daughter had a ten foot wave crash down on her and I dramatically flung down my book to run into the sea and save her – doing breaststroke...

...or the time we took our hired car to a Spanish village for a meal but spent hours trying to leave the place, driving over and over down the same street until I was convinced we'd stumbled upon the set of *The Prisoner*. We got back to our apartment at four in the morning.

Meanwhile I'm embracing what appears to be the start of British summertime. Later today I shall wheel out the barbecue from the garage and cremate a few bangers and burgers. The fact that we will still be wearing jeans and sweaters is neither here nor there. The main thing is we won't be wearing added layers of coats, scarves and woolly gloves. Which reminds me.

What is the definition of an English summer?

Three hot days and a thunderstorm...

What is a child's experience of Father's Day?
If Mum is laughing at Dad's jokes, it means they have guests...

Today, in the UK, it is Father's Day. This is a time of celebrating the love we have for our fathers and – if we have kids – also making it a memorable day for our husbands and partners. However, a day like this one can sometimes be a bit of a double-edged sword. I'm talking about if your father, or the father of your children, is no longer in this world.

Whilst I'm very lucky to still have my father, my children are not so fortunate. Today they will remember their dad with some tears. That said, they are blessed to have a stepfather who has treated them with kindness and love. To show their own love and appreciation, this afternoon my father and Mr V will be treated to an excellent lunch at a local Italian restaurant.

Have you noticed that shops now sell cards that say *Happy Father's Day from the cat*? Likewise, pooches...

Dear Dad
Here is your pipe
Here are your slippers
Sorry one is chewed
And the other resembles a shredded flipper
Love from your faithful hound xx

Mr V isn't really a 'pet person'. It took a while for Trudy Beagle to win his heart. When our cat joined the family a few months ago, Dolly was very much on the starting line for endearing herself to him. Not that she hasn't tried. It's just that her idea of what is a demonstration of love isn't quite shared by Mr V... like curling up in the suit he'd failed to hang up and covering it with a liberal layer of hair... or pouncing on his socks – while his feet are still inside... or shimmying up his legs – whilst bare.

I'm not one to watch television, but last Thursday the newspaper headlined an experiment with cats who would be wearing tiny cameras and trackers on their collars and recording the findings. The idea was to monitor where a moggy went after jumping through the cat flap. As Dolly has just started venturing outside, I was quite keen to watch the programme. Mr V reluctantly paused *The Sopranos* for a full five minutes in order for me to watch some feline behaviour. Just when it got to a really interesting bit, he pressed the remote-control button and a man with a freaky hair-do (dark brown with silver side panels) filled the screen. Anyway, I digress.

What I *did* learn from my five-minute viewing is that the average female cat only strays fifty metres from her home. This was pleasing to know because I've been quite anxious about Dolly (a) getting lost or (b) finding the road and getting... well, let's not go there. Suffice to say Dolly hasn't yet ventured out of the garden, preferring instead to spy on sparrows or chase gnats, pat leaves, and pounce on the Trudy Beagle's tail but not, necessarily, in that order. I will be one of the people who buy a card from both the dog and cat for Father's Day, although Mr V will strenuously deny he is their father. Which reminds me.

Teacher (on phone): You say Michael has a cold and can't come to school today?

Voice: Yes.

Teacher: And to whom am I speaking?

Voice: This is my father...

Teacher: Simon, can you spell your name backwards?
Pupil: No, Mis...

I rarely watch television, and I hardly ever pay attention to newspapers or the dramatic headlines that pop up on my computer's news feed. It's all too depressing. However, I do sometimes skim bylines about celebrities. Such was the case last Friday when I paused to admire the photograph of a reality star by the name of Kim Kardashian. Apparently she'd given birth to her first child, a darling little girl. News of a birth always gives me a warm, fuzzy feeling, whether the baby belongs to celebrities, or Mr and Mrs Smith down the road. Whenever somebody has a new arrival, the first thing we do is congratulate them. This is usually followed with a question.

'Does the baby have a name yet?'

And, upon being told, we respond with delight.

'Oh, what a *fabulous* name, I love it!'

And we'll say that even if we privately think "bleurgh". But, you know, even names that are a bit bleurgh are surely more preferable to names that are simply plain ridiculous. When I read that proud parents Kim Kardashian and Kanye West had called their baby "North", I found myself re-reading the byline. Surely that was a misprint? Perhaps they meant "Nora"? Or "Norma"? But, no, it was definitely "North". So, coupled with Kanye's surname, that meant the new arrival was called "North West". A compass point. Well isn't she going to have fun time being teased at school... not!

I'm not quite sure what planet some celebrities are on when their newborn arrives. Are the mothers, perchance, still hormonal and not thinking straight? Hollywood actress Gwyneth Paltrow called her baby girl "Apple". Perhaps, after labour, Gwyneth flopped back against the pillows, replete and content, and thought, 'My daughter is the apple of my eye.' Unfortunately, many of us can only visualise a giant green Granny Smith. Actor Sylvester Stallone and his wife named their son "Sage

Moonblood" – which, for me, conjures up a red moon covered in leaves. Michael Jackson called his son "Blanket" – cue an instant vision of a woollen bedcover. And possibly Bob Geldof and the late Paula Yates mistook their three gorgeous daughters for poodles hence "Little Pixie", "Peaches Honeyblossom", and "Fifi Trixibelle".

I'm just waiting for some wag (or should I say "WAG"?) to name their child "Banana", "Duvet", "Happy-Clappy Sunbeam" or "Sat Nav". Frankly, nothing would surprise me. Occasionally we come across strange surnames, but there's not much we can do about those. I can still remember somebody reading my last name upside down and then calling me "Mrs Viagra". Which reminds me.

Have you tried the new beverage called "Viagraccino"? One cup and you're up all night...

What do you call a movie about eating healthily? My Big Fat Greek Yoghurt…

Having just returned from ten nights in Crete, I cannot believe how quickly this holiday came and went. It was a joy from start to finish. Oh, apart from my ankles. For some strange reason they kept swelling up. Actually, they've been doing this for a while, but it's probably due to the menopause, or something. But enough of that.

A joyful holiday mood is always heightened knowing there will be guaranteed sunshine and a beach on the hotel's doorstep. Factor in having all meals prepared and cooked, no washing up, a maid changing the sheets and towels every day, and the bedroom and ensuite constantly sparkling, it's fair to say I was in a constant state of bliss!

My only complaint – if you can even call it that – was the size of the bathroom. It was on the small side. It was something of a squeeze when the three of us were in it all together and vying for the mirror. The wall-mounted hairdryer – right by the sink – had a habit of bursting into life every time someone's shoulder accidentally nudged it. There was also an iffy moment when the whole thing fell off the wall and splashed into the washbasin which, at the time, contained Mr V's shaving water. Fortunately no lights fused and nothing went *bang*.

Guests were entertained every other evening. I loved Monday night DJ who played non-stop music from the late seventies. Suddenly I was transported back to my college days and, much to my daughter's horror, danced in my flip-flops to Chic's *Le Freak*, the iconic Gloria Gaynor's *I Will Survive*, and Donna Summer's *Hot Stuff*. Spot the teenager slinking down in her seat, totally disowning her mother. On the "quiet" nights, we entertained ourselves. This usually involved a pack of cards and a chess board. Mr V regards himself as a potential World Class chess champion. Sitting down on a backless chair, he proceeded to teach me how to play. By the sixth game I'd cottoned on and had his queen screaming for mercy. It was at this point my husband had a sudden loss of interest in the game.

'You're a bad loser,' I said.

'Rubbish. I let you win,' he replied, leaning back and quite forgetting his chair didn't have one. Oops...

Sharing a family room did have its disadvantages. Each night Eleanor and I would do our utmost to get to sleep before Mr V. Although my husband will strenuously deny it, the fact remains that he has a snoring problem. One night it was me to hit the pillow and instantly zonk out. Hurrah! My victory was short-lived. I was awoken by Eleanor touching my arm. Pat-pat... pat-pat.

'What?' I said, opening bleary eyes and trying to focus in the gloom.

'He's snoring,' she said, jerking her head at the mound next to me. 'Give him a shove.'

'Why can't you give him a shove?' I grumbled.

'Because you're the nearest,' she said sweetly.

Eleanor then turned over and instantly zonked out, leaving me to stare at the ceiling for the next three hours whilst listening to my husband making sounds comparable to a farrowing pig.

No holiday is complete without an excursion. Ours was a trip on a beautiful catamaran. The boat made its way out to sea, then started heaving itself over some rather big waves. For the first time ever I experienced seasickness. I wasn't alone. Several people were at the back of the boat standing within the shade of an awning. I took myself off to join them thinking that perhaps a little less sun might help me feel better. Upon getting to the back of the boat, I discovered that these people weren't just enjoying some shade, they were actually, er, you know, in the process of *being* poorly. Oh, yuck! I went swiftly into reverse – straight into the captain.

'You okay?' he asked in his heavy accent. 'You wanna puke?'

'No thanks,' I trilled, as if declining an invitation.

'Happy fish today!' he laughed, nodding at the sea. I followed his gaze. There was a lot of nasty stuff floating on the water. Oh yuckity-yuckity-yuck!

Fluttering a hand to my mouth, I hastily returned to the front of the catamaran. Fortunately, after another hour or so, my seafaring legs kicked in and my stomach settled down. Thank goodness, because it wasn't a short boat trip. Seven hours to be precise.

Two swim stops meant lots of snorkelling for some, whereas others like me simply preferred bobbing about in the crystal clear waters. Lunch was taken in a traditional taverna overlooking the harbour. It was here that everyone spotted a huge turtle gracefully swimming on the water's surface. What an amazing sight! Which reminds me.

What do turtles use to communicate?
A shell-ephone...

Did you know that half of all marriages end in divorce?
It's not as bad as it sounds, because the other half end in death...

I have a new book out. It's called *The Ex Factor* and it's like nothing I've written before.

They say being a parent is the hardest job in the world. Well, I also think being a stepparent falls within that category. It's one thing to discipline your own child, but it's something else to try and gently guide a child that isn't biologically yours. Equally, it's one thing to love your own child, but can be a tricky matter wanting to lavish love on your stepchild. Firstly, they might be full of resentment and not want you to love them! Secondly, that child's parent might be twitchy about your affection for their offspring, making them feel threatened in the belief that you are trying to compete with them.

My first husband was a bit older than me and had been married before. At a very young age, I became stepmum to a delightful little boy. His mum was lovely, and I was extremely fortunate to have a good relationship with her. Indeed, we spent many a Christmas and New Year celebrating together. The happiness of that little boy and making sure he was surrounded by people who were friendly with each other was all that mattered.

My first husband had health issues and eventually passed away. When I re-married, I once again became a stepparent, but this time the experience was very different. For diplomatic and privacy reasons I will leave it there.

It is shocking how many fathers are denied access to their children by ex-wives and partners. Sometimes there are valid reasons, like violence. But in many cases, it is simply down to an ex-partner wishing to punish, and the most common reason appears to be due to a partner leaving.

It is, no doubt, a heady experience to be in the driving seat controlling someone you think has wronged you. But who is benefitting from this emotional war? There are no winners. Only casualties.

Trawling through forums, I read chat-thread after chat-thread from distressed men – and women – who were being denied access to their kids. There were also tales of ex-partners doing their best to wreck second and even third marriages. There were children at war with their new stepbrothers and stepsisters who, they felt, had been thrust upon them. One thing became clear. This needed writing about!

I ended up furiously penning a gritty family drama about a fictitious family going through issues that many blended families 'out there' will identify with. If you are one of them, hang in there! And if you go on to download *The Ex Factor* then I hope it provides some comfort knowing you are not alone. Which reminds me.

A wife said to her husband, 'If I were to die first, would you remarry?'

'Well,' said the husband, 'I'm in good health, so why not?'

'Would she live in my house?'

'It's all paid up, so yes.'

'Would she drive my car?'

'It's new, so yes.'

'Would she use my golf clubs?'

'No. She's left-handed...'

Doctor to patient: I have some bad news and worse news.
Patient: What is it, doctor?
Doctor: The test results show you have just twenty-four hours to live.
Patient: Oh my God! What's the worse news?
Doctor: That I tried telling you this yesterday, but your mobile phone was switched off...

I have just returned home from a stint in hospital. In recent months some odd things have been going on with my body. I ignored them and put it down to 'being a certain age.' Little did I know that I had been failing to recognise some life-threatening symptoms.

Earlier on this year I had a perfectly straightforward operation but, afterwards, encountered complications. There were blood clotting problems. Then huge haematomas appeared. A massive infection followed. What should have been a straightforward and swift recovery became a protracted period of months with numerous prescriptions of antibiotics. I didn't ever stop to wonder why I wasn't healing, and neither did the doctor dishing out all those antibiotics. Instead, I told myself that I'd feel much, much better once I was on holiday in Crete.

I'd only been on the outward flight for thirty minutes when my ankles swelled up. I regarded them in dismay but, again, put it down to getting older, even if "old lady" ankles at fifty-two seemed a bit unfair.

The holiday was wonderful, and although the ankles continued to swell, I wasn't concerned and blamed the heat.

On arriving at Chania Airport for the return flight home, a holiday rep noticed my swollen feet and insisted I see a doctor at the airport. I had to have a 'safe to fly' certificate as, by this point, my puffy feet had extended right the way up to my knees. The lower half of my limbs looked like they belonged to a person three times my weight.

Once back in England, I simply kept my feet elevated

and got back to work. I was far too busy to trouble doctors. However, one week later, both my legs – from thighs to toes – had morphed into tree trunks. I finally took myself off to a different GP.

This doctor suggested a blood test. And that, I thought, was that.

Twenty-four hours later, the GP telephoned trying – and failing – not to sound frantic.

'Whatever you are doing, you must stop right now and immediately go to A&E.'

'What?' I quavered. 'Why?'

'Because you have an abnormally high white cell count.'

'Do I have leukaemia?' I whispered, clutching the edge of my desk.

'I'm not at liberty to tell you,' said the GP.

Gee, thanks. But in my heart of hearts, I already knew the answer.

Hours later, I'd been officially diagnosed with *Chronic Myeloid Leukaemia* and was put into isolation because something as simple as the common cold could turn into pneumonia and become life threatening. My immune system was shot to pieces, hence the blood clotting and slow healing issues. For the first forty-eight hours I couldn't stop crying and fear had me metaphorically stuck on the ceiling. All I kept thinking of was that long-ago film, *Love Story,* where the main character dies of leukaemia. However, medicine has come a long way since then and, thank God, treatment is now available.

Although the condition cannot be cured, with lifelong drug therapy it can be 'put to sleep'. Words cannot express the joy of knowing that I'm not yet due a one-way ticket for the tunnel of light.

Whilst in hospital awaiting test results, my sister suggested I keep calm by meditating. I gave it a whirl and, despite being sceptical, had some mind-blowing experiences. They simply had to be written down. I'm currently working on a charity book about this period in my life, days that saw me plunged in an abyss of despair to reaching indescribable heights of joy. The book will simply be called *100* because that is a number that kept cropping up again and again as I frenziedly wrote about the experience. Which reminds me.

A schoolboy told his parents, 'I got 100 in my maths test and still didn't pass.'

'Oh dear, why ever not?' asked his mum.

'Because the answer was 200...'

What is colic?
A reminder for new parents to use birth control...

Kate and William have now registered the birth of their beautiful baby boy, His Royal Highness Prince George Alexander Louis of Cambridge.

I was one of the millions who rejoiced at the birth of the royal arrival, third in line to the throne. However, I was amazed at some of the sour comments on Facebook and Twitter. How can anybody *not* celebrate a new life? Yes, one in three children are born into poverty, and certainly this little chap should never know paucity. But I believe the royal family work extremely hard and are fantastic ambassadors for our country. The United Kingdom is envied by many other countries for our royals, everything they stand for, and the sheer history that is steeped behind the House of Windsor.

My own husband is anti-royal – something that never fails to amaze me considering how very pro-royal his parents are. I have no doubt that my mother-in-law is, right now, placing her order for a Prince George china plate to adorn her living room wall. When it arrives, it will proudly sit next to her other royal plates, including that of our lovely Diana. But for all those anti-royalists out there moaning about the cost of the royal family and say the money would be better off going to, say, the National Health, let's take a closer look at the statistics – because I've been doing some digging.

The royal family costs forty million pounds per annum to maintain, BUT the revenue paid to the United Kingdom from the royal lands is a breathtaking TWO HUNDRED MILLION. Now I'm not brilliant at maths, but even I can work out that the royal family brings a profit of one hundred and sixty million pounds. And it is THEIR land that generates that income so, no, you cannot boot them off it any more than you would snatch away the measly acre belonging to that horse-mad couple in my village.

Quite apart from this staggering amount of money, the royal family are a huge tourist attraction. Twelve million people come from all over the world to stand outside the gates of Buckingham Palace and visit The Tower of London generating a revenue of... wait for it... seven BILLION pounds.

So people like my husband should perhaps pause and think again before throwing out ignorant comments. Who would honestly want to be Queen Elizabeth? She's eighty-seven years old, STILL working, and STILL throwing open her doors to the public with a smile on her face. I wouldn't want her job for all the tea in China, even if it did mean parking my bottom on a gilded chair at the end of the day. So long live the Queen and long live new arrival Prince George. Which reminds me.

Why did the Republican cross the road?

To get to the other bribe...

Changing address.
It's a moving story...

After several months of having our house on the market, we have achieved several viewings, one buyer, then a collapsed property chain, followed by a drought of interest. Sigh. Mind you, trying to find a property that Mr V and I *both* like is far from plain sailing, so if a buyer with a completed chain were to make an offer on our home, we'd be in a bit of a pickle because currently we have nowhere to go.

Originally we were keen to move to leafy Penshurst. However, daughter Eleanor is adamant about enrolling at a local college, which means a move to this area would see me zipping up and down the A21 four times a day.

I've since found a Grade II conversion in Wrotham, a small oasis of quaintness but not a million miles away. Delighted, I shooed Mr V away from the sports channel and drove him to the show home.

'What do you think?' I asked hopefully.

'Hmm,' he replied.

I found myself holding my breath as we walked on beautiful golden planks of flooring, through a state-of-the-art kitchen, light and airy lounge, pretty bedrooms and a gorgeous bathroom. *Please like it,* I silently willed my husband.

'So, what do you think?' I asked again, as my husband stared out of an upstairs window at the view below.

'It's promising.'

This is tantamount to an amber traffic light. Not a yes but, equally, not a no. I have to play things *very* cool in order to get my husband to shift that amber light to green. Any hint of a pressure and he'll go swiftly into reverse. Why can't he be like me? Make a decision and go for it! Instead, there's all this prevaricating. Thinking about it. Thinking about it again. Holding the idea up like a picture and studying it intently. Trying to get my husband to move – even when he says he wants to – is always like trying to uproot an oak tree.

'Let's go for a walk around the village,' he said, 'and get

171

a feel of what it might be like living here.'

Oh my God! The amber light was flickering. Still not green, but quite possibly on the verge of change. I tucked a strand of hair behind one ear.

'If you like,' I said nonchalantly.

We set out through the gated entrance. I had a terrible urge to skip off down the road, gallop past the ancient church, zigzag across the high street and shout, "Whoopee!" However, I restrained myself, taking care that my walk along the pavement was that of a person oozing indifference. Rounding a corner, we came across a narrow road lined with twee clapboard buildings that dated right back to seventeen-something-or-other. I lost control.

'Oh, isn't it pretty,' I gushed, and promptly went into raptures about the village's tiny hair salon, its attractive pub smothered in hanging baskets that were positively bursting with blooms, a tiny flintstone Post Office, and charming old-fashioned grocery shop – perfect for nipping in if you'd run out of milk but didn't want to do a big supermarket shop.

'It's okay,' said Mr V on the walk back to the car. 'But I'm not yet convinced it's for us.'

And as is always the case, I felt my hope wobble. Still, you never know. The amber light didn't entirely swing back to red. He had said *not yet*. So fingers crossed. Which reminds me.

A woman complained to a colleague that her back was sore after moving furniture to a new house.

'Why didn't you get your husband to help?' the colleague asked.

'Yes, I should have,' said the woman, 'although the couch would have been easier to move if he hadn't been sitting on it watching football...'

Changing address.
Yet another moving story...

At the time of writing this, I'm in a state of excitement. Not only have we had an offer on our house (a bit on the low side), we've had a second viewing by a very eager couple who have four children. I'm crossing my fingers, toes, and legs that they make a decent offer that will make my quest to downsize a reality.

I always get into a terrible tizzy when a viewer is due. Firstly, the house must be spotless because first impressions are everything. Secondly, any 'clutter' must be well and truly hidden. This means that everything the kids leave scattered over bedroom floors gets hastily shoved into wardrobes. Finally, the house must smell nice... which means Trudy Beagle is put out the back door. The last thing I want is an elderly dog trailing visitors around and parping every thirty seconds. Dolly the cat is also consigned to the garden in order to stop her doing a guaranteed poop in her litter tray just as a viewer rings the doorbell.

However, I suspect that yesterday's viewers might not have noticed our pets letting us down. I'll call them Mr and Mrs Haggard. They staggered through the front door, clutching a two-year-old tot apiece. Twins! Double trouble.

'I'm so sorry,' said Mrs Haggard, debating whether to put her charge down, 'but—'

'Yes?'

'On the journey over—' she trailed off awkwardly.

'What is it?'

'The children were making... um... lots of bottom noises. They might interrupt our viewing by wanting a poo.'

Hurrah, it wasn't just my dog and cat who had an urge to produce a poo on a viewing. Excellent news.

'Absolutely no problem,' I beamed, 'your twins can take their pick because there are four loos in this house.'

Never miss a sales opportunity!

'This is the lounge and, as you can see, there are wonderful French doors issuing forth (I lurve saying *issuing forth*) on to a large decked area.'

The family looked dutifully at the French doors. Their gaze was met by Trudy Beagle staring mournfully from the other side.

'Doggy,' said one of the twins.

'Woof,' said Trudy Beagle wagging her tail optimistically. Little people usually had sweeties.

'Woof-woof!' shrieked the twins, bounding up to the glass panes.

'Woof-woof-woof-woof-woof-WOOF,' answered Trudy Beagle, tail wagging like a metronome.

There then followed a duet of barking from both sides as Mr and Mrs Haggard's twins and my beagle got down to the serious business of making an absolute din.

'The next room,' I said, raising my voice and sweeping them out of the lounge and into the kitchen, 'is the hub of the household.'

Never miss a sales opportunity!

'Note the large sliding doors *issuing forth* on to a patio.'

Mr and Mrs Haggard obediently looked at the sliding doors. Once again, a beagle stared back at them from the other side of the glass.

'Oh, another dog!' said Mrs Haggard.

'Er, it's the same—'

'Woof-WOOF!'

'Woof-woof-woof-woof-WOOF-WOOF!'

'FOLLOW ME!' I shouted over the din of both children and dog barking at each other.

'This next room is the teenagers' den, but it seems like only yesterday it was their playroom. Note yet another set of French doors *issuing forth* (sorry, can't resist it) on to a Mediterranean terrace.'

Never miss a sales opportunity!

Mr and Mrs Haggard's eyes once again fell upon Trudy Beagle, nose pressed up against the glass.

'Oh, wow, a third dog!' said Mrs Haggard.

'Um, it's still the same—'

'WOOF-WOOF!' yelled the twins.

'WOOF-WOOF-WOOF-WOOF-WOOF-WOOF!' shouted Trudy Beagle, which roughly translated as, "When are you going to give me sweeties?" As if to underline her point, she spotted some bird poo on the glass, stopped barking, and began licking the glass. Dolly then minced into view, spotted Trudy Beagle apparently having a treat and decided to join in. *Bleurrrgghhh*!

I swung round to face Mr and Mrs Haggard thus blocking their view of my dog and cat behaving, it has to be said, worse than their two-year-olds.

'Let me show you the study,' I said, relieved that this room had no doors *issuing forth* on to anything at all and no pets tucking into bird crap.

Moving upstairs, I began showing the bedrooms but was interrupted by Twin Number One wanting to do a poo and absolutely adamant this take place in the family bathroom which had a fun toilet seat decorated in mermaids. Twin Number Two then also wanted to do a poo but threatened to throw a tantrum if made to use the same toilet, preferring instead to use my son's bathroom which had a loo seat as blue as the sea and decorated in goldfish.

Within minutes both bathrooms stank to high heaven transporting me back to the days where, as a young mother, I'd marvelled at how something so small could produce so much poop.

'This is our youngest daughter's room,' I said, finally leading them into Eleanor's bedroom.

'Ooh, built in wardrobes,' said Mr Haggard in delight.

'Indeed,' I smiled, 'you can never have too many of these, eh!'

Never miss a sales opportunity!

'May I?' said Mrs Haggard, fingers coiling round the handle.

'Oh, um, well, I'm not sure—'

Too late. Mrs Haggard was already yanking open the door. Seconds later a guitar had landed on her foot causing her to hop about in pain (memo to self: sometimes you need to reign back on the sales opportunities). Which reminds me.

What do you call a dinosaur that has a sore foot?

An Ankle-oh-*sore*-us...

Why are conveyancing solicitors like rhinoceroses?
Because they're thick-skinned, short-sighted, and always ready to charge...

It's official. Mr and Mrs Haggard want to buy our house. They've put in an offer, higher than the last two viewers and, rightly or wrongly, I've taken it upon myself to accept it. I want to move. I want to get on with it. I'm fed up trying to keep our home looking like a showhouse twenty-four-seven in case a last-minute viewer turns up on the doorstep. However, I had to pick my moment to tell Mr V. As expected, upon hearing we had a definite buyer, his mouth did a fair impersonation of Trudy Beagle's bum.

'We'll talk about it over dinner,' he said.

'What, with the kids around?'

'No. We'll go out tomorrow, Saturday, without teenagers squabbling and interrupting us.'

'Lovely,' I beamed. Usually it's *me* clamouring to be taken out to dinner.

'There are some things we need to discuss, Debbie,' he said, looking grim.

Oh. Right.

So the following evening we sat huddled over an extremely tiny table for two, where a single candle and solitary flower in a bud vase jostled for space with cutlery and napkins. At the table next to us was a guy I initially mistook for one of Katie Price's ex-husbands. Alex Reid. For those not in the know, Alex Reid is a cage fighter with big biceps and a crooked nose. Anyway, it wasn't Alex Reid. I know that for sure because our table was, like, four point five inches in distance from this chap's table, and his girlfriend was calling him *Jason*.

'Are you listening to me?' said Mr V.

'Of course.' Not.

'So, Mandy, what did yer dad say when yer told 'im you woz goin' out wiv a bloke of thir'y-one?' asked Jason.

Cue screech of laughter from Mandy, followed by a mega flick of hair. I was nearly whiplashed by blonde extensions. ''E don't know, does 'e! I don't fink 'e would approve much, me bein' so much younger an' all that.'

Mr V: 'What would you like to eat?'

Me: (perusing menu) 'I'll have...'

Jason: (perusing menu) 'What d'yer fancy?'

Mandy: (peering over menu) 'You!'

Mr V: 'I'm going to have a salad.'

Me: 'I'll have the wilted spinach.'

Jason: 'I'm starvin'. I'm so starvin' I could eat a bleedin' 'orse.'

Mandy: 'Do they do 'orse in 'ere? Where's it got 'orse on the menu?'

Mr V: 'I'll have the medallions for mains.'

Me: 'I'll go for the fish.'

Jason: 'I'll 'ave 'alf a cow instead. I need to keep up me protein.'

Mandy: 'And I'll 'ave... wot are those smelly pink fings called?'

I had an overwhelming urge to lean across and reply, 'Feet.'

Mr V: '...selling the house at a price I'm not happy about.'

Me: 'Mmm.'

Jason: 'I go to the jimmm every mornin'. I like doin' press ups.'

Mandy: 'You 'ave luvly mussolls.'

Mr V: '...tell the estate agent...'

Me: 'Mmm.'

Jason: 'Would yer like to feel 'em?'

Mandy: (a bit breathless) 'Wot, in 'ere?'

Mr V: '...buyer's market, did you know prices are on the up....'

Me. 'Mmm.'

Jason: (starting to look very perky) 'Which bit d'yer wanna touch?'

Mandy: (arching back, chest out, flicking hair all over place) 'Ooooh!'

Mr V: 'Ah, starters!'

Me: (lifting neighbour's hair extensions off my spinach) 'Ah, starters!'

178

Jason: 'Well ain't this a good start!'

Mandy: 'Ow dear, there's some green stuff in me hair.'

Okay, yes, I made that last line up, but she really did have some spinach in her hair.

Meanwhile Mr V thinks I've undersold the house. This is quite a staggering opinion given that he wants top dollar for our property but is quite happy to make ridiculous offers on other people's homes at thousands and thousands of pounds less than the asking price. However, the conveyancing wheels have been set in motion and I, for one, am keeping my fingers tightly crossed for a smooth and successful house move. Which reminds me.

A prominent young conveyancing solicitor was on his way to work when he was hit by a bus. Suddenly he found himself at the Pearly Gates facing Saint Peter.

'This has to be a mistake,' spluttered the solicitor. 'I'm only thirty-five and much too young to die.'

'That's odd,' said Saint Peter, 'because based on the number of hours you've billed clients, we thought you had to be at least one hundred and five...'

How do cats end a fight?
They hiss and make up...

Over the years I've had the pleasure of being 'mum' to several fur babies. These have mostly been dogs, but there have been a smattering of moggies too, albeit many years ago. After a feline absence of nearly seventeen years, Dolly came into our lives last November. She's a very beautiful black and white long-haired diva. If Dolly were human, she'd probably be something glamorous, like a popstar, or super model.

Like all pets, at some point it's necessary to take them to the vet. I'm not talking about neutering, or vaccines. Rather, when they get poorly. Last week Dolly went off her food. I spent a small fortune on chicken and turkey breast, also some ham in order to tempt her into eating.

'Do not touch!' I said, slapping Mr V's wrist as he reached for the ham.

'Why not?'

'It's for Dolly.'

'Dolly? But she's a *cat*! What's wrong with her eating *cat food*?'

'Because she's not feeling fab.'

'She told you this, did she?'

'Yes,' I said defiantly.

'Well I'm sure Dolly won't mind me pinching a bit of ham.'

'Dolly might not, but I do. Now leave the ham alone.'

My poorly girl was then presented with a bowl of freshly chopped meat which she devoured in a matter of seconds.

'There's nothing wrong with that cat!' said Mr V. 'She's faking!'

The following day, I kept Dolly in to monitor her. She seemed fine, other than refusing her normal cat food, so more fresh meat was offered and instantly polished off.

'That cat has got you sussed,' said Mr V.

Dolly used her litter tray and produced so much wee that at one point I thought I was listening to a horse rather than a cat. At least there was nothing wrong with her bladder. But she didn't produce a poo. I decided to keep her in for a second day but, again, no number two was forthcoming. On the third day I telephoned the vet.

'Yes, Mrs Viggiano, you'd better bring Dolly in to see me.'

Alarmed, I bundled Dolly into her carrier, and headed off to the surgery.

'Hmm,' said the vet, pressing Dolly's tummy.

I gulped, anxiety making my stomach church.

'What's wrong with her?' I quavered.

The vet regarded me over half-moon spectacles.

'Nothing. You simply have a constipated cat.'

'Oh dear. What does she need then?' I had visions of sprinkling crushed-up laxative over her chicken, turkey and ham.

'She's a fluffy girl. Might have a furball in there. I'll give her an enema.'

In the moments that followed, I was very glad I wasn't Dolly.

After much swearing — the cat, not the vet — Dolly went back into her carrier.

'Don't take too long to get home, Mrs Viggiano, because the enema will start working in about thirty minutes.'

In fact, I'd only travelled thirty *seconds* down the road when the car was filled with an obnoxious smell. I was transported back in time to when the children were babies, in nappies, and strapped into their car seat. Inevitably a wail would go up until the infant child was home, topped, tailed, and in a fresh nappy. In this case a wail did go up, but regrettably my cat wasn't in a nappy.

'Meow,' said Dolly plaintively. '*Meowwwwwwww.*'

Oh God.

'We'll soon be home, darling,' I soothed, as if I was once again talking to a distressed infant instead of a distressed cat.

Belting in through the front door, I left Dolly — still in her carrier — in the utility room, then dashed upstairs and ran a warm bath. No, not for me. For the cat. Well, sorry, but if you'd seen the state of her fur... actually, let's not go there.

Dolly was then swaddled in an old towel, and both she and the towel went in to the bath together so she couldn't scratch. Two bulging eyes angrily regarded me as I swished her up and down, up and down, very much like one would handwash a delicate woollen garment. This action was accompanied by more feline swearing. As the water changed to brown, the air turned blue.

I was astonished at just how tiny Dolly is under all that long fluffy hair. A bedraggled sparrow with baleful eyes emerged a few minutes later. As I attempted to towel her dry, she raked her claws down my arm. Gratitude! She then stalked off to vent the remainder of her fury on poor old Trudy Beagle. Which reminds me.

What is it called when a cat wins a dog show?

A cat-has-trophy...

Soon I will be decorating, so I've bought a step ladder.
I don't get on with my real ladder...

The weather is gently changing, which is no surprise given that summer is drawing to an end. All over the country, the kids have returned to school. My youngest child, Eleanor, is now sixteen. Next Monday she starts college and will be studying Performing Arts. Time — like the birds now gathering for migration — flies.

I do believe Mr V and I are what is known as 'empty nesters'. Just like those migrating birds, we are preparing to leave this nest. A downsize is imminent and it won't be long before boxes and crates, rather than belongings and furniture, fill these rooms.

Will I miss this family house? No. One way or another, it's a place that's seen an awful lot of drama, not all of it good. Will I miss the people around here? Yes. I have lovely neighbours and have made some smashing friends. Hopefully we will keep in touch, although I will miss my dog walks with Trudy Beagle at the local meadow with fellow pooch pals.

They say that change is as good as a rest and, wow, do I feel like I need a rest. Mentally, that is. The last twelve months have been... well, to put it lightly, both challenging and emotionally exhausting. So it is with great hope and a sense of joyful anticipation that I will be embracing our new abode (if all runs to plan, please God!) at the end of next month or very shortly thereafter.

We are buying a brand new house. I keep popping over there to peek at progress. Last time around, I was excited to see the kitchen had been fitted, tiling to all the bathrooms was complete and everything just looked so amazing and fresh. A fresh start in every way! Next week we will choose the carpets, which wardrobes we want, and even the size of the garden shed. Yes, it's true, size matters! So does colour. Mr V has been happy to leave me to oversee much of this, although Eleanor has been keen to give some input. Together we have pored over soft furnishings and colour charts, favouring pastels and light tones. It's been exciting and uplifting. We've leafed through furniture directories and trawled on-line websites for ideas, and already tempted fate by purchasing two things for the house before exchange of contracts! Eleanor is also keen to join me on some of my site visits. We stopped by at dusk earlier in the week and, as the car rolled to a standstill outside 'our house', my daughter gave a gasp of delight.

'This place looks almost magical,' she sighed happily.

And it's true, it did. We gazed, spellbound, at some of the completed dwellings crouched at the base of the main building – a dominant and very striking Grade II listed conversion. Soft white lights twinkled in the blue-grey dusk giving an almost Christmassy feel to the moment. As the sky darkened and shadows lengthened, the setting before us looked very like Hogwarts in the Harry Potter films.

Meanwhile I'm ear-marking time to 'upcycle' an unwanted and ancient bureau that my sister gave me. I'm thinking *Farrow and Ball* posh paint and jewelled handles. Which reminds me.

A blonde decided to impress her husband by redecorating the lounge while he was at work. When the husband came home, the tell-tale smell of new paint hung in the air. He walked into the lounge to find his wife busily working away, but very hot and bothered. This was hardly surprising because she was wearing a ski jacket *and* a fur coat, both at the same time.

'Why are you decorating dressed like that?' he asked incredulously.

'Because' — said the blonde, putting down her paintbrush — 'the instructions on the tin said, "For best results, put on two coats..."'

I had an EasyJet curry.
It tasted a bit plane...

Last night Mr V took me out for an Indian. As we sat there dipping our poppadums into spicy chutney, we couldn't help but reflect over the last twelve months. In a nutshell, it's been awful. So much has happened. Mostly cr*p stuff. But you know, I'm not really a negative sort of person and always try to look for the silver lining in every dark cloud that comes along. It's just that there have been so many dark clouds in such a short period, I feel like I've not been given enough time to seek out those silver linings.

For the first time in my life I am truly aware of my own mortality. Life is short. It is also extremely precious. Last year, like so many of us, I took everything for granted, particularly my health. It's only when your life is threatened that you actually stop and take a good, hard, very long look at everything – and at this point, if it happens to you, you will find yourself viewing your life from a totally different perspective as previously.

For example, if somebody used to hack me off, or wind me up, or upset me, I'd silently rant, "Don't rise because one hundred years from now it won't matter, because we'll all be dead!" Which is true enough. But the important thing is, while our two feet are still firmly planted on Earth's surface, the things that get on top of us *do* matter. And it matters how we deal with these things. We shouldn't let these things fester inside us, otherwise it can make us ill. I have a feeling that silent ranting might not be very good for one's health. So my advice is... let it out. Shout a bit!

Today I'm going to come face to face with something that I've been reluctant to do until now. I've put this moment off for many reasons. But the important thing is, I'm doing it. Not for me, you understand, but for a person I love. And also, far more significantly, because I don't want this otherwise unaddressed situation to remain 'inside' me, silently festering. It's not healthy. So despite my reservations, I'm regarding it as a therapy of sorts — regardless of the outcome.

Meanwhile, on a lighter note, I need to jump in the shower because the smell of last night's curry is lingering in my hair. Which reminds me.

Have you seen the Top Ten Curry Charts? Get ready to groan!

1. Poppadum Preach — Madonna
2. Korma Chameleon — Culture Club
3. Dansak Queen — Abba
4. Tikka Chance On Me — Abba
5. Tears On My Pilau — Kylie Minogue
6. It's Bhuna Hard Day's Night — The Beatles
7. Brothers in Naans — Dire Straits
8. I'm a Bhaji Girl — Aqua
9. Dansak on the Ceiling — Lionel Richie
10. Love me Tandoor — Elvis Presley...

What did the tree wear to the pool party? Swimming trunks...

I'm trying to persuade my husband to be as enthusiastic about our impending new home as Eleanor and me. In an effort to instil a sense of excitement, I took him along to see how the house was progressing. As we drove through the electric gates (well, they will be when the electricians do their magic), I felt a thrill ripple through me. I sneaked a sideways glance at my husband. His mouth was set in a grim line.

'Doesn't the setting look fab!' I trilled.

No response.

I parked the car and had barely opened the driver's door when Mr V was out and striding off, head rotating three hundred and sixty degrees as he took in the surroundings. A ferocious looking builder with a Polish accent materialised from nowhere and demanded to know what we wanted.

'Um, we're buying Plot 129,' I said nervously. 'Any chance of looking inside?'

The builder was instantly all smiles. 'In you go,' he gestured with one hand, 'and ignore mess. Soon it be perfect. No worries.'

'I'm sure it will be,' I gushed, resisting an urge to bow and scrape. After all, I didn't want him doing a dodgy job on the place. No wonky light switches or leaking showers, thank you very much.

Mr V stepped over the threshold, into a hallway littered with paint pots and strode straight through to the lounge. A pile of workmen's paraphernalia was positioned roughly where I was envisaging a coffee table.

'It's certainly coming along,' I said and gave my husband an encouraging smile. His mouth remained in the same grim line. 'And look at the kitchen!' I waved a hand expansively at bubble-wrapped units. 'Quartz worktops! And a built-in microwave. And a fridge where the door shuts properly. And a decent sized freezer, and-'

But I'd lost my audience. My husband was taking the bare wooden stairs two at a time. I scampered after him.

On the first floor a sink was in my son's future bedroom. In the master bedroom lay the emersion heater. I poked my head around the ensuite bathroom.

'Tiling looks beautiful,' I purred. But Mr V was off again up the next flight of stairs and ducking under a precariously placed ladder. The loft room is the biggest bedroom and will be ours. The skylights look out upon nearby Grade II listed buildings, recently renovated and displaying a skyline of chimney pots, roof terraces, wrought iron balconies and gables. 'When I've finished revamping my bureau, it's going to be placed just here so I can look out on all that,' I gestured, 'while I'm writing.'

Mr V gazed at me, his face expressionless. Suddenly he was off again, clattering down the two flights of stairs and out into the newly landscaped grounds. Dismayed, I drooped after him. My husband has been the same every time we've upped sticks. Even when moving to our current house — a property he was far more enthusiastic about than me —the moment the removal men turned up he'd have the jitters.

'Have we done the right thing, Debbie? Have we made a massive financial mistake? What if we hate it?' These are questions I've heard every time we've exchanged contracts.

When my husband moves into a house, he's like a sapling putting down roots. And when it's time to move on, it's like trying to fell a flipping great tree. I caught up with him and, together, we got back in the car.

'You really don't want to move here, do you?' I said, gazing ahead at all the beautiful mews houses behind an avenue of freshly planted trees. Trees that, even as I stared, were no doubt putting down their roots. Finding their new home.

My husband gave a huge sigh. 'I'm moving here for you.'

'It's a stop gap,' I shrugged. 'Two or three years. As soon as Eleanor has finished at North Kent College we will move again.. To your beloved Penshurst.'

Mr V nodded. 'Come on. Let's drive to John Lewis. We'll look at house stuff.'

I put the key in the ignition and started the engine up. I have no doubt that when the time comes to move to Penshurst my husband will be resisting all over again. Established trees are difficult to shift. Which reminds me.

What's the difference between an oak tree and a tight shoe?

One gives acorns, the other gives corns...

What does the richest person in the world make for dinner every night?
Reservations...

Moving Day is looming closer. I know our cat, Dolly, is going to miss the garden pond. This morning I spotted her hovering on the bricked edge, bottom wiggling, all set to try and pat one of the goldfish nibling something on the water's surface. Her eyes were full of mischief, tail swishing but, as always, the goldfish swam to the bottom and joined his family. There are only about a dozen fish left after a visiting heron stopped by and helped himself. I inherited the pond from the previous occupant of our house, and was a bit naïve about such birds filling their bellies in a matter of seconds.

When we move to the new house, Dolly will have to content herself with a much smaller garden and her mischief will be limited to pouncing on Trudy Beagle. As the one who always did the gardening, I am overjoyed that, soon, I will no longer need to lug a sizeable and hefty lawnmower down a series of stone steps to the grass or spend hours bent like a cotton picker whisking out weeds and cutting back shrubs.

Meanwhile I'm slowly taking *this* house apart, selling surplus furniture and bric-a-brac in preparation for the imminent downsize. This week a wardrobe and desk have gone under the *eBay* auction hammer. Getting the wardrobe down the stairs wasn't too bad. The desk was another matter. I remember my father originally assembling the desk within the bedroom that it has spent the last eight years in. I assumed it would fit through the door when the buyer came to collect. Wrong! As my buyer and I huffed and puffed, turning the desk this way and that to get it through the doorframe, it became apparent this wasn't going to happen.

'Do you have a screwdriver?' asked the gentleman.

'A screwdriver?' I repeated moronically.

In this house that is a bit like asking if we have a spaceship tucked under one of the beds.

'Yes, a screwdriver. Perhaps I could borrow one from

your husband's toolbox?'

My husband doesn't have a toolbox. A lunchbox, yes, but not a toolbox. The last time my husband was armed with items from a toolbox (my father's) he destroyed some flat packed furniture we'd bought only hours earlier.

Instead, my buyer had to resort to selecting a knife from the cutlery drawer in order to loosen the desk's screws. When, finally, we got the blasted thing through the door and out on the driveway, the next problem was trying to get it into the gentleman's car. I felt like a contestant on The Krypton Factor as, together, we tried to fit a rectangle into a square. This time a kitchen knife from the cutlery drawer wasn't going to do it. We definitely needed a screwdriver.

Fortunately my kind neighbour came to the rescue and removed another panel from the desk. I heaved a huge sigh of relief when the damn thing was finally shoved into the buyer's boot.

Meanwhile I have more two more desks to shift and also some beds plus kitchen cupboards full of blenders, juicers, electric whisks, and all manner of paraphernalia bought in a very mad moment when I decided to emulate Nigella Lawson. And I need to get my *eBay* skates on, because the clock is ticking. Which reminds me.

How did I get Trudy Beagle to stop begging at the table?

I let her taste my cooking...

What happened when the bomb-sniffing dog wrote his autobiography?
It made the Best Smeller list...

When I was in hospital being treated for leukaemia, mentally I was in a dark place. My sister recognised this and loaned me a book. It was full of spiritual teachings. When life screeches to a standstill and we are full of fear, it isn't surprising that so many of us turn to God, or the universe, or a greater energy — call it what you will.

This book became my lifeline and it went everywhere with me. Down to X-Ray. Into Ultrasound. In the queue at Phlebotomy. When I was back in my hospital room, totally isolated because of a rubbish immune system, the book stayed on my lap. I delved into these teachings at every opportunity, desperately trying to understand what was written on the pages within. And finally, when the wonderful day came where I was allowed to go home, the book came too, squashed into the depths of my handbag.

My first husband was absolutely fanatical about the care and condition of any book he read. Indeed, by the time he'd finished reading a book, you'd have been forgiven for thinking it had never been read at all. It would be pristine. Not one folded page. Not one crinkle in the cover. Quite how he managed to pull off such a feat was beyond me. Unfortunately, I am the opposite. I open the book, flatten the page, turn corners down by way of a bookmark and, by the time I've finished reading it, the book's spine has more wrinkles than a crone.

Reading is such a pleasure. I always think the enjoyment is heightened when the devouring of words is twinned with a snack. So regrettably my current read also sports greasy fingerprints from buttery toast and smudged marks from melted chocolate. Indeed, when the annual summer holiday rolls around, my paperbacks end up covered in a different sort of muck — that of sand, sunscreen and seawater. Sometimes it's so bad the pages become unglued. If you spot a sunburnt blonde chasing paper along a beach, that's me. In short, I may be an avid reader but I'm not a very good carer.

'Why are your books so scruffy?' my sister once complained. 'Anybody would think you are a total slob.'

I'm not a slob. Not by any stretch of the imagination. But for some bizarre reason I do slide into Slob Mode when it comes to books. So when my sister leant me this particular book, I was wary of accepting it.

'Oh, but it's brand new,' I said in horror.

'That's okay,' she replied.

I opened the first page and was horrified to see it had been inscribed with a personal message by the author. And not to my sister either. It was addressed to her husband.

'Oh, but this is *Richard's* book,' I gasped. 'Does he know you've given it to me to read?'

'No, but don't worry about it. He's had it for years and years and never read it, and it's very unlikely he ever will. In fact, I think he's forgotten about its existence so you might as well keep it.'

'Keep it? Wow, thanks,' I beamed.

And with that I treated the book as if it was my own. Fatal.

This morning I had a telephone call. It was my brother-in-law.

'Hi, Debbie. I just wondered if you'd finished reading my book?'

'Er, not quite,' I said nervously. *His* book. Not *Debbie's* book. 'Did Janice tell you she'd given it to me?'

'She did, but it wasn't hers to give.'

'Y-yes,' I stammered, 'I see.'

'So, the thing is, I'd like it back.'

There was a pause while I did the sort of gulp you hear in cartoons.

'Ah. Right. Um, well obviously it's not as, er, *pristine*, as it was. So, oh, I know!' I said, having a lightbulb moment. 'What about I buy you a brand new book to replace this one?'

'No, no, no. That's nice of you to offer, but I'd like the original back. It has a personal message in it, you see, from the author.'

'Yes,' I whispered while all sorts of words fired off in

193

my brain which are far too rude to write here. There is a lot to be said for the invention of Kindle. Indeed, why the devil hadn't I just downloaded the same book in the first place? But it was too late for that now. A rescue operation had to be done. And quickly.

So the book in question has been wiped clean, polished with a soft duster and, as I currently write, is being flattened under the weight of umpteen other books in order to restore the jacket and internal pages to some sort of decent condition, rather than curly edges with fluffy corners. When I hand it over, it will be swathed in bubble wrap so my brother-in-law can't see the second-hand condition until I've put some distance between us. About twenty miles to be precise. Which reminds me.

What sort of people make the best bookkeepers?

The people who borrow your books and never return them...

What happened to the leopard that fell in the washing machine?
He came out spotless...

Yesterday I spent three hours alternating between washing machine, tumble drier and ironing board. However, after my 'wake up' health call earlier this summer, I no longer obsess about my house looking like a show home, or wet laundry untidily strewn over radiators, or trying to keep an immaculate garden whilst juggling the day job and then writing long into the night. Something had to give. So these days the house is tidy, but cleaned when I get a moment rather than a twice weekly blitz. I've also taken on the services of a gardener to do the heavy stuff, like chopping back branches and shrubs and manicuring flowerbeds. Laundry is done once a week in one hit, rather than keeping on top of it throughout the week.

Help from family members is still rather scant on the ground. My son, home from uni for a rare weekend visit, immediately disappeared into his room insisting he had to revise for his finals. My daughter took that as her cue to barricade herself into her bedroom claiming she had to deal with coursework. Mr V did what he always does when the weather is fair and fine. He disappeared off to a golf course with a client. Apparently a lot of business gets done on a golf course. A few pints get sunk too, but hey ho.

With everyone out of the way, I was quite happy to get on with the chores uninterrupted. Except...

'We're hungry,' came the call down the stairs.

A huge time-consuming brunch then took place followed by a major clear-up of greasy pans and saucy saucepans. Returning to the ironing board, I'd only removed two garments from the ironing basket when along came the next interruption. My son needed a lift to the barber. Currently we're not on the bus route. Indeed, we're not on any route at all due to being stuck out in a village with no street lighting, no pavements, and not even a corner shop. As my son is not yet a driver, taxi services fall to whichever parent is available.

Leaving my son at the barber's, I charged home and plugged the iron in again. It had barely heated up when Mr V rang from his car.

'I'm five minutes away and absolutely knackered. Get a bath on.'

'You seriously want me to put on a bath?'

'Yes.'

'Where?'

'Eh?'

'Should I put it on my head, like a hat? Or perhaps wear it like a cape around my shoulders?'

'Are you in a funny mood?'

'Yes, can't you hear me laughing?'

Actually, I wasn't.

I carried on ironing. But not for long. *Brrrring-brrring*. This time it was my son.

'I'm done, but I bumped into a mate and he's giving me a lift home, so you don't need to collect me.'

'Great,' I said, as hot steam spat over the shirt I was ironing.

'But I'm covered in little itchy bits of hair, so can you draw me a bath?'

'*Draw* a bath?'

'Yeah.'

'What with? A pencil or a biro?'

Needless to say, neither Mr V nor my son had steaming bubble baths awaiting them. Both wore hurt expressions at their requests not having been carried out which, for a moment, I felt a bit guilty about. But only for a moment, you understand.

In my next life I'm going to be a man. I think it must be a hell of a lot more fun than being a woman. A man can walk into a bar on his own without eyebrows being raised. A man is a lot safer than a woman walking the streets after dark. A man can have as many partners as he likes without being called a tart. And a man can collapse in front of the telly, while the only thing the wife can collapse is the ironing board.

Oh I know there are a few men out there who mow the

196

lawn, wield a power drill and aren't afraid to don an apron or plug in a vacuum cleaner, but sadly I haven't personally come across one. Which reminds me.

A woman went shopping. At the check-out, she opened her purse to pay. The cashier noticed a TV remote control in her purse.

'Do you always carry the remote with you?' he asked.

'No,' the woman replied, 'not usually. But my husband refused to come shopping with me today.'

The cashier laughed and scanned the woman's purchases. She handed over a credit card.

'Oh dear,' said the cashier, a moment later. 'It appears your husband has blocked your credit card.'

'What?' screeched the woman.

'I guess there's a moral,' grinned the cashier, 'and that is to respect your hubby's hobby...'

How much fun is it doing your laundry? Loads...

Ah, you've found me immersed in another thrilling episode of washing and ironing.

Some people find these chores therapeutic. Yes, it's true. I can remember a friend, many years ago, telling me that — after a busy day in the office — she enjoyed nothing more than going home to run a hot iron over crumpled clothes. She said that listening to the hiss and spit of the iron as it whooshed backwards and forwards over her beloved husband's shirts was calming. Apparently, if the iron happened to give a little splutter that engulfed her in steam, well, that was the ironing equivalent of Nirvana. This, of course, was before she went on to have several children, ended up with her nerves frazzled by juggling the office job with a family, and finally told them all to iron their own wretched shirts before taking off with the window cleaner. Okay, he wasn't the window cleaner. But he was somebody like that. The milkman. Or the postman. And no, I don't know if she found bliss with her new man. I lost touch with her after that, although I rather suspect the danger of finding a new love is that you simply exchange one load of domestic drudge for another.

Anyway, I digress. My old friend's words of finding the task of ironing to be a therapeutic one remained lodged in my memory. I suppose it's because — when standing over an ironing board at midnight — I've tried to con myself into believing that I'm doing something soothing. A bit of respite. Something that makes my shoulders droop with relaxation and my mind uncoil from tension.

However, as my fingers fight to pull apart tightly balled-up socks and unpick a crop of buttons from shirts and blouses (my husband and daughter only undo the top two buttons before bending, head over feet, to pull the garment over their heads so that not only does the shirt remain securely fastened, but it's also inside-out), I have to confess that wearing a serene expression and thinking tranquil thoughts doesn't come easily. And when I've

198

finally put those garments the right way round, unpicked all those buttons and ironed everything to perfection, I don't appreciate Dolly mincing over when my back is turned to make an impromptu bed out of everything and smothering it all in hair. Argh! Which reminds me.

A guy walks into a laundry run by cats.

'Excuse me,' he said to the cat in charge. 'Can you get milk stains out?'

'Sure,' said the cat. 'We'll soon have that stain licked...'

My friend and her bestie thought about buying a tree house.
But they were worried they'd fall out...

British Summertime is officially over. We are now into Daylight Savings Time which means the United Kingdom reverts to Greenwich Mean Time. Thanks to someone having this bright idea (no pun intended), today we all get a little more light *plus* an extra hour. How will you use yours?

I know what I'll be doing. These precious additional sixty minutes means more time to pack a few more boxes. Moving Day is next Thursday. It coincides with Halloween. Potentially this means that two lots of trick-and-treaters will be ringing the doorbell – the first lot as we leave this house, the second as we arrive at the new abode.

Our current home no longer looks like a place where the heart it. The warmth, like a snatched away blanket, has been withdrawn. There are now bare rooms devoid of personal belongings. There is something very forlorn about the house. It's really quite sad.

Yesterday was a day of marathon telephone calls trying to contact everybody before they all naffed off home early to enjoy the weekend. EDF Energy had such a long telephone wait time (fifty minutes) that the battery on my handset died. On the third attempt — using an old-fashioned telephone with a twirly cord — contact was finally made. Currently it is only the Halifax Bank who remain officially uninformed about our new address.

'Hello? Hello! I'd like to notify you of a change of address.'

'Okay, let me get your details up on my screen. Ah, here you are. Right, I see you have a joint account.'

'Yes, that's right. The account is in the name of both me and my husband.'

'Is your husband there?'

'No. He's been dispatched to do some chores relating to the house move. Although I suspect he's standing inside a television shop watching Manchester United on twenty different screens.'

'Right. The thing is, I need to speak to him too.'

'Shall I get him on his mobile? Perhaps I could press my mobile to this handset and you can speak to each other?'

'That might be difficult. I know! Tell me your pin number and I'll override my computer security.'

'What pin number?'

'You should have a six-digit security number.'

'No, sorry I don't.'

'Okay. No worries. I'll send you one in the post.'

'Fine. But I'm moving. So, you'll need my new address.'

'Ah. We're not allowed to send it to the new address. It must go to the old address.'

'Okay. Well I'm at the old address until next Thursday.'

'Oh dear. The pin number will take seven working days to get to you.'

'By which point we won't be here.'

'Yes. I quite understand. Um, what about you pop into the Halifax in person?'

'Yes, I could come in on Monday.'

'With your husband?'

'Er, no. He'll be at work.'

'Ah.'

'What about you ask me a million security questions. You know, my mother's maiden name, how many dogs I've had, and what colour toilet paper I use.' Okay, I didn't really say that last bit about toilet paper, although I was tempted to.

'I could in normal circumstances, but not for an address change.'

I mean, seriously, who invented so much red tape that you can't even update your new address? Meanwhile I've resorted to the good old-fashioned practice of getting the Post Office to redirect all our mail. Which reminds me.

Last week God visited Noah, who was now living in the North of England.

'Once again,' said God, 'mankind has become wicked. Build an ark. Save two of every living thing along with a few good humans. You have six months before I start torrential rain for forty days and forty nights.'

Six months later God returned. He saw Noah weeping, and there was no sign of an ark.

'Noah! I'm about to start the torrential rain. Where is the ark?'

'Forgive me,' Noah sobbed, 'but things have changed. I needed Building Regulations approval and I've been arguing with the Fire Brigade about a sprinkler system. Getting the wood was a problem because all the trees have Preservation Orders on them, and I live in an area of Outstanding Natural Beauty owned by The Woodland Trust which was set up to protect the spotted owl. And when I started gathering the animals together, the RSPCA sued me for confining wild animals against their will. And then the County Council, the Environment Agency and the Rivers Authority ruled that I couldn't build an ark until they'd conducted an Environmental Impact Study on your flood proposal. The Trade Union said I couldn't employ my sons and that I can only hire accredited workers with ark building experience. And to make matters worse, Customs & Excise seized all my assets claiming I was trying to leave the country illegally with endangered species. So forgive me, Lord, but it's going to take at least ten years to build this ark.'

Suddenly the sky cleared and the sun shone down. A vast rainbow stretched across the sky. Noah looked up in wonder.

'Does this mean you are no longer going to destroy the world?'

'No,' boomed God, 'because it seems the Government has beaten me to it...'

'Why?'
'Because I said so!'
(The most common conversation between a mother and child — of any age!)

Hurrah! We've finally moved into our new house!

The thing about settling into a newbuild, is everything looks so shiny and beautiful. This gives a desire to buy things that match. For example, leaving behind kitchen units that looked not just 'tired' but totally exhausted, meant I wasn't keen on packing up our plastic toaster that cost a fiver from *Asda*, nor twenty mismatched tumblers. Now that I have a gorgeous kitchen with glossy cupboards and quartz worktops, it would be fitting to have a bit of 'boast' to our toast and 'class' to our glass. So I've splurged and bought some new stuff. It's true, retail therapy makes you glow! It's even nicer to prolong that glow by telling your friends and family what you've been buying — although, perhaps not in the case of my mother.

My mother is a bit like a female version of Uncle Albert from *Only Fools and Horses*. She begins a lot of sentences with, "When I lived through the war." Let me just say here, I have total admiration for war babies — my mother in particular — for not just surviving horrendous circumstances, but also enduring the poverty and hardship that went with it. I do understand where my mother is coming from when she berates modern society for 'waste'. In my country, kids are fortunate not to grow up in a war zone. We are all blessed not to know famine. We are lucky to have jobs and be able to sometimes buy nice things. However, a line must be drawn somewhere underneath the subject, especially when the joy of buying something new is soured by another lecture on 'waste'.

Last weekend I had my parents over for Sunday lunch — the last Sunday lunch in our old house. As I dished up dinner, I was fizzing with excitement. Why? Because I'd bought new cutlery. And no, it wasn't a gorgeous satin-lined boxed jobbie from *John Lewis* reduced from hundreds and hundreds of pounds to ninety-nine quid in a sale (although I must confess I was sorely tempted), *this* purchase came from *Next* and cost twelve pounds. Actually, I lie. It cost double that because I bought two sets!

'We're eating off these knives and forks for the last time' — I beamed at everyone — 'because I've bought new cutlery!'

My mother's fork, en route to her mouth, froze mid-air. It wobbled alarmingly as her eyes swivelled in my direction. Suddenly I was caught in the glare of two blue headlamps.

'You've bought new cutlery?'

Damn.

'Yes.'

'But there's nothing wrong with *this* cutlery!'

There then followed a need to justify myself. To explain, with excuses and great power of reasoning, why I'd spent twenty-four pounds on new knives, forks and spoons.

'I've had this old set for over twenty years and so much of the silver has spoilt. I mean, look at this' — I picked up a dessert spoon and showed my mother its underside — 'almost black!'

'There's nothing wrong with this cutlery, my girl. It just needs a good clean.'

'It *is* clean, Mum. It gets cleaned every day.'

'How?'

'In the dishwasher. Anybody want another potato?' I asked, desperately trying to get off the subject of cutlery and talk about something else. The latest Government disaster. The increase in the cost of fuel. The weather. Anything. Just *not* my cutlery.

'I'm not talking about cleaning cutlery in a dishwasher,' said my mother indignantly. She'd downed her fork and knife and was clearly intent on making a speech. 'I'm talking about cleaning it *properly*. With elbow grease.'

My father was then dispatched to the sink, dinner abandoned, holding aloft the blackened spoon to demonstrate to us all — and particularly me — the art of cleaning cutlery 'properly'. Five minutes later he'd rubbed the dessert spoon so aggressively the scourer had a hole in it. He then finished by polishing the spoon with a dry cloth for a full minute.

'Look at that!' said my mother triumphantly. 'You can see your face in that spoon.'

Marvellous. Except I haven't the time nor the inclination to spend five minutes apiece on my ancient canteen of cutlery.

'Well I've bought new cutlery now,' I said, somewhat defiantly. 'I shall put this old set into the local charity shop and let somebody else have the pleasure of cleaning it.'

'What a waste. When I was in the war, we were lucky if we had enough utensils to go around. Sometimes my brothers and I had to eat with our fingers — and that was if there was food to eat. Sometimes we went hungry.' My mother then turned to her granddaughter sitting opposite. 'Are you going to waste those carrots, Eleanor?'

'Nothing will go to waste' — I interrupted with a sigh — 'because Trudy Beagle will have any leftovers.'

But my mother wasn't going to be easily deflected.

'What else have you bought?' she asked.

I considered. Should I tell her, or not? She smiled encouragingly. Oh, thank goodness. A truce.

'Well,' I said cosily, 'I've also bought new bedding.'

The smile instantly vanished.

'You've bought new bedding?' she said, her tone so shocked you'd have thought I'd told her that I'd robbed a bank.

'Y-Yes,' I quaked. 'New bedding.'

'And what is wrong with the old bedding?'

'Well, exactly that. It's old.'

'It's not old!' my mother exclaimed. 'Your bedding isn't as old as *my* bedding, and we've had ours for years' — she glanced at my father — 'haven't we, Tony? *Decades*!'

In that moment I had an overwhelming urge to excuse myself from the dinner table and hasten off to the local church for confession.

"Forgive me Father, for I have sinned. I've bought new bedding."

"This is terrible, child. You must confess to the Lord to be forgiven. Is there anything else you've bought?"

"Yes. Cutlery. And table mats... scatter cushions... a state-of-the-art toaster... a matching kettle and—" sounding hysterical now — "new wardrobes."

"Outrageous. Do you know how wasteful you are?"

"Yes. My mother tells me every week. Especially when I burn food, knacker saucepans and end up going to the local chippy for emergency sustenance for my family."

"You are sinner. You must say six Hail Mary's then go to that chippy and get me some crispy cod for my dinner."

Much as I love my mum, she does have a knack of taking the joy out of things. I hope I never turn into my mother. Which reminds me.

Recently, on our way to my parents' house, I glanced at my sixteen-year-old daughter and said, "Isn't that skirt a bit short?" Eleanor had immediately rolled her eyes and given me one of those *Oh, Mum!* looks. When we'd arrived at my folks' place, my mother had come to the door and immediately said, "Debbie! Don't you think your top is awfully low cut?"

H-e-l-p...

Traffic cop: 'Didn't you hear my whistle, madam?'
Woman driver: 'Yes, but I don't like flirting when I'm driving.'

I like to think of myself as a friendly sort of person. It's not unheard of for me to strike up conversation with, say, another shopper who happens to be standing in the same check-out queue as me.

'Oh dear. Looks like somebody has lost their purse,' I might say to the woman in front of me who, exasperated with the woman in front of *her* has huffed and puffed loudly before treating the rest of the queue to some extravagant eye rolling.

'Yeah, but I just wish she wasn't in *my* queue, I'm in such a rush.'

'Ah well, these things happen. Are you rushing off anywhere nice?'

'I'm babysitting my little granddaughter.'

And so on. My own daughter has always been somewhat embarrassed at my talking to strangers. I don't know why. Maybe it's an age thing. Now in my early fifties, I don't care who I talk to, and my daughter — at sixteen — is of an age where paranoia is normal, and firmly of the opinion that parents should be seen and not heard. I find most women in the same age bracket to be the same as me. One minute you are strangers, the next you're discussing intimate details.

For example, earlier this week I had a lady visit from a well-known curtain company. She staggered into the hallway with five heavy swatch books and, pushing her specs up her nose, sat down to do business. Mulling over fabrics requires a cup of tea. Ten minutes later we were settled, at the table, me poring over textiles and my sales lady sipping her cuppa. Somewhere along the way our conversation strayed from thread counts and prices to the menopause, the pros and cons of HRT, and whether to have a boob job. All rather personal stuff. However, whilst it is marvellous to hit it off with someone, sometimes I suppose I do need reminding of *who* I'm striking up conversation with. Like the time I was with Eleanor, in *River Island*, paying for shopping.

Young Man: 'That will be umpteen pounds and twenty-two pence.' *Broad grin.*

Me: 'Thank you.' *Proffers MasterCard and returns smile.*

Eleanor: *Scowls. Her mother is in the shop to pay for goods, not indulge in making smiley faces.*

Young Man: *Takes MasterCard and shoves it in machine.* 'Very nice weather we're enjoying at the moment.'

Me: 'And I see you're dressed accordingly.' *Gives another smile whilst waiting for machine to prompt for pin number.* 'That's a lovely t-shirt you're wearing. Looks nice and cool.'

Eleanor: *Rolls eyes at me being an embarrassing parent making chitchat.*

Young Man: *Beams.* 'Thanks. It's my favourite.'

Me: 'It showcases your wonderful biceps.'

Eleanor: *Looks astonished.*

Young Man: *Also looks astonished.*

Me: *Enters pin number blissfully oblivious to the fact that this is not my son I'm talking to.*

Young Man: *Leans across counter.* 'I'm very proud of my muscles.' *Lowers voice.* 'I'm a gym addict.' *Waggles eyebrows.*

Me: 'I always admire anybody who has the dedication to work out.' *Waggles eyebrows back, just to show there is a tiny part of me that can move without breaking out in a muck sweat.*

Eleanor: *Mouth drops open.*

Young Man: 'Do you want to feel them?'

Me: *Retrieves MasterCard from terminal.* 'Okay.' *Snaps purse shut and leans across counter.*

Eleanor: *Mouth open so wide there is danger of tripping over bottom lip.*

Young Man: 'Rock hard.'

Me: 'Gosh, yes you are, aren't you!'

Eleanor: *Eyes flicking backwards and forwards from Young Man to Mother.*

Young Man: *Whispering.* 'I could take you to the gym.'
Me: 'Do you think?'
Eleanor: *Eyes in danger of crossing.*
Young Man: 'Have a think about it.'
Me: 'I will.' *Picks up shopping.* 'That's awfully kind of you.'
Eleanor: *Snatches shopping from me and flounces off.*
Young Man: 'Bye. For now.'
Me: 'Thanks again.' *Dashes off after daughter.*
Eleanor: 'Oh. My. God! I've never been so embarrassed in my life.'
Me: 'What? Why?'
Eleanor: 'You were giving him the come-on.'
Me: *Spluttering.* 'Don't be ridiculous.'
Eleanor: 'And then he flirted with you. With *you*! You're old enough to be his mother.'
Me: 'He was just being friendly.'
Eleanor: *Doing a silly voice.* 'Oooh, do you like my muscles? Oooh, yes I'd love to feel them.' *Dropping the silly voice.* 'It was outrageous.'
Me: 'Oh don't be so absurd.'

However, being friendly or, as my daughter thinks, *over* friendly, could perhaps be misconstrued as flirting. Earlier on this week there was possibly such a misunderstanding by a man living a few doors down from me. I was sitting in my car, having just pulled into our parking bay, when there was a knock on the window. So I buzzed it down.

Another Young Man: 'Er, hi. You're in my parking bay.'
Me: *Giving a dazzling smile to diffuse a potentially iffy situation.* 'I do believe this is *my* parking bay.'
Another Young Man: 'No, it's definitely mine.'
Me: *Smiling so widely my lips are in danger of meeting at the back of my head.* 'No, it's definitely mine. When my husband and I bought this house, the marketing suite showed us a map, and this bay belongs to Plot 129. That's me. I'm Plot 129. Well, not literally. Obviously. I'm Debbie.' *Smile still firmly in place — after all, person is a new neighbour.*
Another Young Man: *Not introducing himself back.*

209

'Right, well I'll go and query this with the marketing suite myself and we will soon find out who *really* owns this parking bay.'

Me: 'Sure,' *getting out of car*. 'I'll come with you.'

Another Young Man: *Looking alarmed*. 'That fine. I can go by myself.'

Me: 'It's no problem. Let me join you.'

Another Young Man: *Backing away*. 'Really, there's no need.'

Me: 'Truly, I insist.' *All set to be jolly good neighbours.* 'So, as I said, I'm Debbie, and you are?'

Another Young Man: *Gone in a cloud of dust*.

So, did that particular young man get the wrong end of the stick and, far from thinking I was just being a friendly neighbour, believe that I was... you know... *after him*? Surely not. Which reminds me.

My next writing project is a telephone book.

So, can I have your number?

What is the one thing you can't get rid of by losing it?
Temper...

As a teenager, I used to be a bit of a hothead. You know... strop about if I couldn't get my own way over something. Get a bit shouty. Pout a lot — sulkily, not seductively. And if a temper tantrum reached boiling point, I'd wave my arms like windmills. My parents lost count how many times I'd yell, "It's not fair." Those words must surely be every teenager's catchphrase.

But as the years pass and we walk through life, inevitably we grow out of saying, "It's not fair." We also find our tolerance levels get better, so we react differently to the way we did when a teen. I remember reaching a defining point somewhere in my forties where I was only a fraction of the hothead I'd been in my teens. Possibly this was helped by the fact that I now had two teenagers of my own frequently yelling, 'It's not fair,' whilst windmilling their own arms as they proclaimed their misfortune... plus I was also too knackered or browbeaten to retaliate.

'Aren't you calm,' my mother said to me last week. 'You're nothing like the feisty woman you used to be.'

Actually that's not true. Deep down, I am still feisty. It's just that I've put a lid on it. After my spell in hospital this summer, everything was put in perspective. If a day is full of sh*t hitting fans, rather than retaliate, I've simply learnt to duck. Avoiding cr*p may be tedious, but it's much more preferable to bone marrow tests and unappetising hospital food. Anyway, I digress.

'Aren't you calm,' said my father, when the brand new hot water tank in our brand new house began leaking everywhere on the day we moved in.

'Aren't you calm,' said my husband, when his bathwater failed to flow out to the main drain and instead erupted out of the downstairs loo and flooded the hallway and kitchen.

'Aren't you calm,' said my daughter, when a random painter misread his address sheet and painted our new garden shed bright green.

'Aren't you calm,' everyone chorused as the kerb on our parking bay collapsed damaging my car... and I put out my shoulder wrestling with the back door that refused to lock... and an over-enthusiastic doorbell ringer cornered me in my own hallway before offering to save my soul. Calmness reigned. *Serenity* had become my middle name.

But I suppose everybody has a line they are finally pushed up to. Mine came last Tuesday when a well-known bedroom company were due to fit our bespoke wardrobes. Oh, how I'd waited for this moment! Soon I would be able to unpack the remaining packing boxes and put all our clothes away! We'd paid a lot of money for these wardrobes. The designer and I had spent hours poring over graph paper. The surveyor had checked and double-checked the measurements. There was then a two week wait while everything was cut and made-to-measure at the factory. Finally the fitter turned up to put it all together. Yessssss!

'Hello,' said Mr Fitter.

'Good morning,' I said politely. No beaming or smiling. After all, I didn't want him thinking I was flirting. Too many misunderstandings have occurred regarding harmless smiles in the last few weeks.

'Where are we doing it?'

'In the bedroom.'

There was an uneasy silence as we both contemplated the misfortunate innuendo behind our words.

'Follow me,' I said hastily, desperate to regain employer/employee status.

There are two flights of stairs in our new home. By the time we'd reached the bedroom, the fitter was panting for all the wrong reasons.

'I smoke forty a day,' he wheezed. 'I can't say I'm too happy about having to lug all the material up to the top floor.'

'I'm an ex-smoker,' I said, with all the dispassion of the reformed.

Mr Fitter gave me a sour look. Nothing worse than

being around an ex-smoker!

'Right, well you're going to have to clear this bedroom,' he said, planting his feet wide and sticking a pencil behind his ear, 'because I have no space to get my big tool out.'

There was another weighty silence as we both digested his unfortunate wording.

'How big?' I said.

'Vast. It's my workbench.'

'Workbench?'

'Yes. I use it to jigsaw.'

I immediately gathered his jigsaw wasn't of the toyshop variety.

'You're not cutting materials in here!' I protested.

'I will be if you want me to make your wardrobes,' said Mr Fitter looking mutinous.

'Make my wardrobes? What do you mean *make* my wardrobes? My wardrobes have already been made! They just need putting together!'

'No. They need making. And I'm making them.'

'I'm terribly sorry,' I said, squaring my shoulders, 'but there seems to have been a monumental misunderstanding. My daughter is asthmatic. No way would I have signed a contract with your company if your designer had explained you'd be making my wardrobes *in* my house! I can't possibly have wood dust filling the air.'

There then followed an awful lot of chuntering. Mr Fitter was extremely put out at having his job cancelled. Time was money, didn't I understand? He had a wife and family to feed. And a forty-a-day cigarette habit to fund, I nearly added.

Minutes later the designer was on the phone full of apologies at *forgetting* to mention that the wardrobes hadn't been cut to size at the factory.

'Are you sure we can't cut them in your house?' he wheedled. 'What if we put down a dust sheet?'

'A dust sheet,' I said calmly. Oh yes, I was oh-so-calm. The sort of calm where you enunciate everything slowly and quietly before spectacularly losing the plot. And suddenly I was whizzing back through time to my sixteen-year-old self fighting an urge not to windmill my arms and shriek, "*It's not fair!*"

To cut this tale short, Mr Fitter has gone and Mr Designer has probably had his knuckles rapped. Meanwhile, I've appropriated a number of portable hanging rails, unpacked our clothes and binned all the boxes. A new wardrobe fitter has been employed —one that makes the wardrobes in a factory, then later pieces it all together *like* a jigsaw, rather than actually *using* a jigsaw. And I'm almost back to feeling calm. Which reminds me.

A woman waiting to have her new wardrobes fitted... no, no, no... let's change that. Two hunters were out in the jungle, when an elephant appeared from nowhere and squashed flat one of the hunters. The remaining hunter was horrified. He whipped out his mobile phone and called the Emergency Services.

'Help,' he gasped. 'My friend is dead. What can I do?'

'Calm down,' the operator soothed. 'I can help, but you *must* keep calm. First, let's make sure he's definitely dead.'

There was silence, then a gunshot was heard.

'Okay,' said the hunter. 'Now what...?'

What did one toilet say to the other?
You look a bit flushed...

We've now been living in our brand-new house for precisely one calendar month. It's been challenging to say the least. The most traumatic bit was three floods in as many days thanks to a split water cylinder, an unconnected water pipe and a broken drain.

I pitied the poor young man sent to deal with the latter. Somebody had parked their car over the drain's cover and gone off to work. Consequently the problem couldn't be resolved until that person was home again and able to move their car. By this point it was gone eight in the evening and bitterly cold.

The young man, collar up against the elements and head wrapped in a woolly balaclava, finally got to work. He wasn't much older than my son. Due to the fiddly nature of the repair, he couldn't wear gloves, and I kept worrying about his hands being cold.

'Offer him a cup of tea,' said Mr V.

'Good idea,' I replied.

We then ate our dinner while the young man laboured away outside. Every now and again I'd glance at the window and see, on the other side of the glass, small pockets of mist. It was the young man's hot breath causing vapour in the cold night air. My heart squeezed with concern.

'I'll offer him some dinner,' I said.

'Yes, he must be starving,' my husband agreed.

We then spent the next thirty minutes interrupting the young man's work with various offerings.

'Egg and chips?'

'No, thanks.'

'What about a chip butty?'

'No, ta.'

'Hot buttery toast?'

'I'm good, thanks.'

'What about some hot soup?'

Eventually the young man stopped what he was doing and gave us a frank look.

'Um, I have absolutely no appetite right now. I'm dealing with a soil pipe.'

'Ah.'

Say no more.

'But I'll have another cup of tea,' he said, giving a wan smile.

Since then, the young man has had several other drains to repair on this development. It is suspected that a workman with a grudge against the building company made mischief. Certainly it has been far too coincidental that a number of other neighbours have also had problems with soil pipes.

An immediate neighbour had an awful experience upon stepping into her much-anticipated 'rainfall' shower. Seconds later her screams were like that from the Hitchcock movie *Psycho*. But as her husband crashed into the bathroom, he was horrified to find her not covered in blood but, rather, something truly unspeakable. *Ewwww*...

Suffice to say I have since met another new neighbour who moved in last Friday.

'Hi,' he said, sounding anxious. 'Can I ask if you've had any problems since moving in?'

Shall I tell him, or will you? Which reminds me.

Somebody broke into our local police station and stole every single toilet. The cops are working on the case, but right now have nothing to go on...

What is a ghost's favourite Christmas entertainment?
A phantomine...

Last Friday evening, my daughter roped the family into "supporting" the theatre where she studies Performing Arts. The Christmas show was about to kick off.

Eleanor wasn't in the show, so I will confess that none of us were chomping at the bit to sit and watch a bit of am-dram. However, she gave Mr V and I a rousing speech about the theatre struggling for funds and that we should all do our bit for the community. In other words, she bullied us into going. So, like all good victims, we drooped off to watch the Christmas show dragging four other family members with us.

For the purposes of this chapter, both her theatre and the show shall remain nameless!

At a cost of ten pounds per ticket, you don't have to be a mathematical genius to work out that a total of sixty quid was spent. That's quite a lot of money, especially at this time of year.

My mother is disabled. As we filed into the dark auditorium, I was unimpressed to discover absolutely no disabled seating. I gave Eleanor a look of anguish.

'Where are we sitting?' I asked.

'Er—' she paused to study the tickets — 'Row J. That's—'

'Right at the top! Didn't you tell your director that your grandmother was disabled?'

'Yes, but they said there was nothing they could do about it.'

'The director could at least have reserved a seat at the front,' I chuntered.

As my mother gazed up the flight of stairs before her, she looked like a woman about to climb Everest.

'Don't worry,' — Father Bryant assured Mother Bryant — 'we will help you.'

With that he supported my mother's left side while I supported her right. And off we set. One step. Two steps. But as we went up to the third step, unable to see properly in the dimly lit auditorium, my mother stumbled and broke away from me. Off-balance, she crashed into my father who, in turn, lost his footing and promptly nose-dived into somebody's lap. Mother Bryant tottered precariously. My hand shot out and encountered a bit of woolly cardigan. Clinging on to it, I thought a fall had been averted. Regrettably her cardi wasn't zipped up and I was left holding a fluffy garment while Mother Bryant landed on top of my father —who was still nose down in someone's crotch. Not a good start.

By the time we'd re-assembled and limped to our seats, the show had kicked off. We flopped into our seats next to Eleanor who was paying attention the play's every detail. She had to review the performance as part of her coursework.

'I hope you're going to complain about your grandparents falling over,' I hissed.

'I can't. The director will get the hump.'

'Oh will she now?' my voice rose an octave.

'Shh,' said a person in front of me.

'Sorry,' I whispered, 'but we had a bit of an accident and—'

'Shh!'

'I'm only trying to explain—'

'Mum!' Eleanor implored. 'I have to review this. Can I watch it, please?'

'Yes, of course, I'm not stopping you from watching it. All I'm saying—'

'SHH!'

So I shushed. Instead I sat there consumed with dark thoughts, like the theatre director one day needing one of those electric stair chairs, and that the person in front of me wouldn't get an ice-cream in the interval... because I'd bought it all. Ha!

Ruffled, I tried to concentrate on the play, but it made no sense. Fifteen minutes later, I was none the wiser. I glanced at my parents who both had furrowed brows. Clearly they hadn't a clue either. I nudged Eleanor.

'What's going on?'

'What do you mean, what's going on?'

'Exactly that! What's going on? What the hell are the Three Bears doing in Fagin's School? And how does a bunch of pickpockets stack up with Christmas elves?'

'It's a spoof,' Eleanor whispered.

'It's rubbish,' I hissed.

'Shh,' said the person in front.

I narrowed my eyes and adopted a menacing tone. 'Ice-cream,' I hissed.

The person looked startled but left me alone.

The show went on. And on, and on. I closed my eyes and awoke half an hour later to the only bit of the show that was funny. The two main characters had got stuck in their flying harnesses and were spinning helplessly in the air while the Three Bears signalled frantically to somebody in the wings for assistance. Next year I won't be going. Sorry. Boo and hiss all you like but give me a decent British panto every time. Which reminds me.

Cinderella was very upset.

'The chemist has lost my photographs,' she wailed to her fairy godmother.

'Ah, there. Don't cry, Cinders,' said the fairy godmother, 'for some day your prints will come...'

What is insomnia?
The inability to sleep until it is time to get up...

Trying to get a good night's sleep is leaving me exhausted. Where am I going wrong? Well, I've only got to look a few inches to my right, and there lies the answer. Literally. Now please don't think that I'm about to write a *blue* chapter, because I'm not! Erotic writing is not my talent. Plus I'm the wrong side of fifty. Think slipper socks, PJ's and bobbly cardigans. The only time I get remotely hot and bothered is when I'm having a hot flush. But I'm getting ahead of myself here.

I've always found it hard to get to sleep at night. Ever since I was a little girl, I'd lie in bed at night hearing the sounds of the television as my parents watched *Van der Valk*, humming along to the opening bars of that catchy little tune as the credits later rolled. I'd often still be singing away to myself when my parents went to bed. I look back at school photographs in horror. I was the only kid in the school with bags under her eyes.

'Read a book before you turn out the light,' said a friend.

Yup. I do that. However, it's not easy concentrating on the plot when your husband is flat on his back, mouth hanging open and making the sound of a farrowing pig. This invariably leads to gentle prodding to get Mr V to turn on his side, thus bringing about a temporary halt to the snoring. However, when I do finally get to sleep, I'm invariably awoken at some point by the deafening noise my husband is once again making. Last time around, grumpy beyond belief, I gave him a hefty shove and shouted, 'For God's sake, man! You're driving me crazy!'

'The secret of a good night's rest,' said another well-meaning friend, 'is to get to sleep before your husband.

'Yes, but how? I'm not one of those people who crash out as soon as their head hits the pillow.'

'Have a mug of hot milk before bedtime. It releases dopamine and makes you sleepy.'

So I tried it. And it works! The first drawback is that a couple of hours later you will need to get up and empty your bladder. The second is, once back in bed, you'll lie there staring at the ceiling once again listening to your husband imitating that farrowing pig.

'Ear plugs,' said yet another friend.

No, because they're not comfortable.

'Listen to music.'

Er, no, music keeps me awake.

'Count sheep.'

Yes, been there and done that. I got bored after one thousand six hundred and twenty-four.

Even when I've had operations and been anaesthetised, I seem to take longer to knock out than the average person. I can still remember one blue-gowned chap sticking a needle in my hand and leaning over me.

'Count backwards from ten.'

So I did.

'Now what?' I asked.

I remember him looking faintly startled before I finally drifted off.

And why is it that when I *do* manage to sleep for a straight run of three hours without a hot flush... or having the duvet pulled off me... or receiving a prod in *my* back to stop *me* snoring (karma!)... then the pair of us are hauled out of sleep by the dog creeping in and gassing us out?

Actually the only guaranteed way to get a decent night's sleep is separate beds and preferably in separate bedrooms. Unfortunately, having now downsized house, there is no longer a spare room to escape to. Damn! Which reminds me.

A man went to the doctor complaining of insomnia. The doctor gave him a thorough examination. After finding absolutely nothing physically wrong with the man, the doctor said, 'Now listen to me. If you ever expect to cure your insomnia, you must stop taking your troubles to bed with you.'

'I know,' said the man, 'but that's simply not possible because my wife refuses to sleep alone...'

What sort of fish performs brain surgery?
A neurosturgeon...

This week has been hairy, and by that I don't mean there is a need to exfoliate (although a quick peek at the legs shows a wax is overdue). No, this week has been hairy for very different reasons.

Last Monday my son Robbie had brain surgery to "cure" the trigeminal neuralgia he's been suffering from for many months. To say he was nervous was an understatement. As his mother, it would be fair to say my own anxiety levels were on red alert.

We were up and out of the house at half past four in the morning, arriving at London's Wellington Hospital two hours later. A smiley-faced nurse checked my son in. The anaesthetist visited and discussed his part in the operation, and finally the surgeon popped in to reassure Robbie and explain what he was going to do.

'Are you sure you want to do this?' asked Mr Sabin. 'This is brain surgery, after all.'

Robbie has had almost a year of back-to-back attacks with pain that is reported to be worse than childbirth. He's been taking sixteen different medications in an attempt to gain some relief and, in the process, suffered horrible side effects. An allergic reaction to one drug put him in hospital overnight. An adverse effect to another saw him collapsing in the street with passers-by ignoring him because they assumed he was a drug addict. On another occasion, he experienced a reaction that rendered him 'drunk' just as he was crossing a busy road. When he turned to a stranger and asked in a slurring voice for assistance, he received a disgusted look and was left to stagger unaided to the other side. Was he sure about this operation? Definitely!

After listening to potential complications that included deafness, numbness, facial palsy and, at worse, death, he signed the consent form. My son might be a twenty-year-old but, understandably, he wanted his mum nearby, and I wanted to be there to support him.

The medical team then led us to the lift which

descended to the bowels of the hospital. When the doors opened, we stepped out and found ourselves in an artificially lit corridor. A powerful antiseptic smell instantly assaulted our nostrils. Doors led off to left and right, each being the entrance to an operating theatre.

'You're in Theatre 5,' said a nurse, leading us into the anaesthetic room (I was given permission to be with my son for this bit). Seconds later, we were joined by a man in scrubs.

'You'll soon be asleep,' he said cheerfully.

I stared at him. Who was this? He hadn't been one of the team who'd checked in with us earlier. Rob and I exchanged puzzled glances. At the same time, the anaesthetist leant close to the nurse and whispered in her ear. It was a very small room and he was so close I couldn't help but overhear.

'I don't recognise this young man. Where are his notes?'

'Oh my goodness, I'm so sorry,' said the nurse to Robbie, 'but you're in the wrong theatre!'

'Ha ha!' the anaesthetist laughed. 'Bit of a mix up, eh?'

Er, quite. Nothing like awakening in the recovery room to be told your trigeminal neuralgia hasn't been cured, but your heart transplant was a total success.

We joined in the laughter —in a shrill and slightly hysterical manner.

Moving into Theatre 6, our stomachs were churning like a washing machine on its final spin. Rob stretched out one arm and anxiously squeezed my fingers as the anaesthetist inserted a cannula into his vein. I averted my eyes and concentrated on not fainting. The smell of alcohol and general sterility mixed unhappily with worry about my boy. And suddenly my son was asleep and being trolleyed off through doors which swung back in my face. I promptly burst into tears.

Thankfully the operation was a total success. Thank heavens for the marvels of modern medicine and skilled surgeons. A couple of days later, other family members were allowed to visit.

'I packed something for my hospital stay,' Robbie

dimpled, 'and it is perfect for this moment.'

'Oh no,' his sister groaned. 'Please don't tell me it's *Monopoly*.'

Eleanor has never been keen on this classic property trading board game.

'Nope. This one is called *The London Board Game* and it's based on the tube system.'

As we'd just spent an hour battling our way around the underground, we really weren't that keen to play a board game based upon it! However, patients have perks and doing their bidding is one of them. So there we sat, throwing the dice, picking up our plastic train marker and moving it forward one, two, three stops before collecting a "Hazard Card" which then told us — much to Rob's glee — that we had to return to Liverpool Street which, naturally, due to engineering works was right on the other side of the board. It was all too near the mark for our taste. We were saved by a uniformed man coming into Rob's room bearing a tea tray. This he proceeded to set down... right on the board game, thus scattering counters and cards in all directions.

My son is now home and recuperating. All that remains is for us to enjoy Christmas. I know it will involve more board games! Which reminds me.

Parker Brothers have brought out a political version of Monopoly. Apparently all Members of Parliament get an instant "Get out of Jail" card...

For what we are about to receive, may the Lord make us truly grateful...
...apart from the sprouts!

Phew! The 25th of December has been and gone. I can now relax and reflect on the day of festivity without feeling flustered.

It was the first Christmas in our new home. My daughter was adamant everyone come to us.

'This house is a clean canvass,' Eleanor declared, 'and it needs to gather memories, so what better way to start than by having the entire family here for Christmas dinner?'

Amen to that. Except we'd downsized and I was a bit twitchy about how everybody would fit around the dining table.

'Why don't you come to me?' said my sister during a phone call. 'My dining table extends.'

'But Eleanor is insisting everybody comes here. It's important to her,' I hissed into the mouthpiece.

'I've lived in my house for eight years and nobody has ever come to me for Christmas Day,' said my sister, sounding peeved. 'Boxing Day, yes, but not Christmas Day. I think you should assert yourself as a parent and tell Eleanor she must do as she's told and everybody is going to Aunty Janice's.'

'Are you mad?' I said, gripping the handset. 'She's a *teenager*. You try going head to head with a sixteen-year-old.'

You see! Arguments already, and the big day hadn't even started.

'Oh, for heaven's sake,' Janice snapped. 'Okay, we'll come to you. What are you cooking?'

'What do you mean *what am I cooking?* Turkey, obviously.'

'Yes, yes, yes, what I meant is, from *where* are you buying the turkey?'

Ah! I suddenly realised where this conversation was going.

'Asda,' I mumbled.

'What? I can't hear you! Please don't tell me you're buying the bird from a supermarket. I really can't face sitting down to a flavourless piece of meat that's spent several days in a foil tray on a refrigerated shelf.'

'What's wrong with—?'

'*I'll* buy the turkey,' my sister interrupted. It's a shame she never had children. They'd have been incredibly obedient. Either that or seriously rebelled.

'There's a farm down the road which sells free range turkeys. All of them have been raised with love and slaughtered humanely. It will cost eighty-five quid, but will be worth every penny. Right, now that we've sorted that bit out, what about veg?'

'Well, I thought sprouts, carrots, roast potatoes and—'

'That's not what I meant, Debbie. Will your vegetables be organic?'

I gulped.

'I'll buy the vegetables locally,' I said, failing to mention they would be from the supermarket and covered in a residue of pesticides.

A sigh of annoyance whistled down the handset.

'*I'll* buy the veg,' said Janice. 'It will come from the farm shop. It's organic and absolutely beautiful.'

I resisted the urge to ask if the carrots and swede would be plucked from the soil with love and placed in paper rather than plastic bags.

'What size is your new oven?' asked Janice.

'Well, you know, it's just a regular sort of size.'

I wandered over to the oven and peered within its depths. We'd yet to bond.

'It's too small, isn't it?' my sister said knowingly. 'You see! If you'd asserted yourself to that daughter of yours and agreed to come to me for Christmas Day, it would be so much easier. My cooking range has three ovens and five gas rings.'

Three ovens? I had enough trouble dealing with one. My sister gave a heavy sigh.

'I'll cook the turkey here, then wrap it in foil and towels and bring it over in a big bag.'

'Okay,' I said.

'You do the roast potatoes and parsnips, and I'll bring the rest of the veg.'

'Okay,' I said again. That would be easy-peasy. *Aunt Bessie* did a cracking selection of pre-prepared potatoes and honey-smothered parsnips. Ooh, and Yorkshires too. Yum!

'And no *Aunt Bessie* stuff,' said Janice, cutting my thoughts. 'I don't eat factory prepared food, and neither should you.'

And so it was on Christmas Day that I found myself peeling a mountain of parsnips and potatoes, manhandling a vast vat of water for par-boiling, heating up oil in my immaculate oven and trying not to cry as it spat everywhere, then got incredibly red in the face as I alternated between steam from the hob and furnace-like blasts from the oven. On the worktop, in a slow cooker, was a *real* Christmas pudding. I couldn't help but weep at the hours and hours of cooking it required compared to a "luxury" jobbie from *Tesco* which needed only three minutes in the microwave.

When my sister arrived, she dragged into the hallway what can only be described as a body bag.

'The turkey is in here,' Janice nodded.

I shuddered and crossed myself, glad to be vegetarian. My brother-in-law followed Janice into the hallway.

'I was up at seven o'clock this morning,' he said, 'and outside in the garden with a torch picking herbs to stuff this with.'

More fool him.

Janice strode into the kitchen and I scuttled after her.

'The Christmas pudding is coming along just fine,' I gabbled, 'and the roast potatoes are perfect, as are the roast parsnips.'

'And the Yorkshires?'

'Sorry, I ran out of time.'

I rummaged in the freezer and, like a magician producing a rabbit from a hat, defiantly slapped down several packs of *Aunt Bessie's* finest battered puddings. My sister rolled her eyes.

'Right,' she said. 'Let's get this veg on.' She set down

plastic containers on the worktop. There were six different varieties of peeled vegetables. 'Where are your saucepans?'

'In the cupboard to your left.'

She bent down. 'There's only one saucepan in here.'

'Er, yes.'

'*One* saucepan?' said Janice incredulously.

'Well I didn't know you were going to bring so much veg!'

'How do you manage to cook anything, Debbie, with one saucepan? Thank goodness I bought my steamer along. Now, pay attention' — she waggled a finger at me — 'watch and learn.'

In no time at all a tottering pagoda of stainless steel was bubbling away on the hob. A delicious smell rose up into the air... apart from the sprouts which, it has to be said, smelt a bit farty.

But for all my sister's bossiness, she turned out a cracking Christmas dinner, and Eleanor had her wish that memories have now been made in our new house. Which reminds me.

Here is a tried-and-tested recipe on how to cook a turkey:

Step 1: Go buy a turkey

Step 2: Take a drink of whisky

Step 3: Put turkey in the oven

Step 4: Take another two drinks of whisky

Step 5: Set the degree at 375 ovens

Step 6: Take three more whiskys of drink

Step 7: Turn oven the on

Step 8: Take four whisks of drinky

Step 9: Turk the bastey

Step 10: Whisky another bottle of get

Step 11: Stick a turkey in the thermometer

Step 12: Glass yourself another pour of whisky

Step 13: Bake the whisky for four hours

Step 14: Take the oven out of the turkey

Step 15: Floor the turkey up off the pick

Step 16: Turk the carvey

Step 17: Get yourself another scottle of botch

228

Step 18: Tet the sable
Step 19: Pour yourself a glass of turkey
Step 20: Bless the saying, pass and eat out...

My New Year's Resolution is to get a personal trainer.
I shall insist that a bag of crisps is necessary for doing crunches...

It's 2014! The New Year is now well and truly underway. It would seem that many of us were pleased to say goodbye to 2013. Certainly, I was one of them! Let's keep our fingers and toes tightly crossed that 2014 will be kinder. New Year's Eve at *Casa Viggiano* was a quiet one.

My sister telephoned on New Year's Day.

'How was it for you?' Janice asked.

'Very quiet,' I said.

'Oh, you mean *boring*.'

'No, I mean quiet,' I said through slightly gritted teeth.

'You should have gone out, like us. We went to a black-tie event. A ball no less. It was wonderful. I've never had so much fun. It was brilliant dancing non-stop for three hours.'

Well obviously it would have been fun to go out. What woman doesn't want to put on a glam frock and rock like nobody is watching. Especially when I'm so good at the Birdie Dance. However, I was on taxi duties to my sixteen-year-old, and that rather put a lid on any party frivolity. I explained this to my sister.

'You should have told Eleanor, "Too bad, *I'm* going out, not you." If she'd thrown a wobbly, then so be it.'

My sister, never having had children of her own, certainly isn't au fait with the highs and lows of living with a teenager. If I'd told my darling girl what her aunt had just told me, it would *not* have been a fab start to the New Year. The last thing I wanted when Big Ben bonged the midnight hour was dealing with a massive teenage strop.

'So what did you do on your fabulous quiet night in?' asked Janice.

'I watched a funny film. That one with the bumbling detective, you know, *Clouseau*.'

'Peter Sellers?'

'No, Steve Martin.'

'I've seen it. God, it was dire.'

'I loved it,' I protested. 'You know me, I like a bit of silly humour.'

My sister snorted. 'I'll bet Mr V loved you for appropriating the television so he was unable to watch football.'

'He didn't mind at all,' I lied.

In fact, my husband had watched the film under duress. My sense of humour isn't his. He doesn't do slapstick. Or farce. Or... well... anything that isn't sport. I'd left him working his way through a few beers while I'd creased up at two grown men wearing pink outfits and blending in with curtains before launching into a routine as Beyoncé's backing dancers.

'Sounds riveting,' said my sister sarcastically. 'What did you do after that?'

'I took Eleanor and her boyfriend to their party, came home, went on Facebook, took my on-line Scrabble moves, chatted to people near and far, and then watched the fireworks. They were absolutely spectacular.'

'Wow, how exciting. Not. And what time did you go to bed?'

'Um, it was quite late. I think it was after two in the morning before I turned off the lights.'

'Really? Did you go somewhere after the fireworks then?'

'Yes, I went to pick Eleanor and her boyfriend up from their party.'

There was a stunned pause.

'So, let me get this straight. You went to bed really late but didn't actually *go* anywhere other than up and down a motorway?'

'Yes, but that's what parents do,' I said evenly, 'especially on occasions like New Year's Eve.'

'Thank heavens I never had children,' said my sister faintly.

Anyway, I've more than made up for any dancing deprivation since New Year's Eve. You see, the children gave me an iPod for Christmas. It's fabulous. I now dance all over the house — up the stairs as I dust, round the table as I set it for supper, over to the dishwasher, you get the picture. And when I can't dance — like when ironing for example — I sing instead. Which rather unnerves the family if they don't realise I'm plugged in.

'Can I have a lift?' asked my son. 'Mum? Did you hear me? Can you take me to Ebbsfleet Station? Mum? MUM!'

'I said I loved yooooo... *warble warble*... but I lied.'

'Does that mean you won't give me a lift?'

'What?'

'A lift?'

'What?'

'To Ebbsfleet?'

'What?'

Followed by two earpieces being wrenched from my lugs and my son repeating his request at "bellow" volume.

'I'm not deaf, you know!'

'And what is that terrible song you're singing?'

'It's by Michael Bolton. You're probably too young to know of him. He has lots of hair. And a fit body,' I added.

'Eww, that's not how I want to hear my mother talking. Are your hormones playing you up again?'

Which reminds me.

Many of us will have made a New Year's Resolution to get fitter. If, like me, you don't want to shock your middle-aged body, try the following:

Day 1
Beat around the bush
Jump to conclusions
Go over the edge

Day 2
Drag your heels
Push your luck
Put your foot in your mouth

Day 3
Make mountains out of molehills
Hit the nail on the head
Open a can of worms

Day 4
Jump on the latest bandwagon
Run around in circles
Lift a glass of your favourite tipple

Day 5
Start the ball rolling
Go to pieces
Blow your own trumpet

Day 6
Raise the roof
Skip the washing up
Add fuel to the fire

Day 7
Kneel in prayer
Raise hands in praise
Wade through newspaper to conclude
What an amazing workout!

**Have you heard the joke about the dirty car?
It's pure filth...**

Earlier this week I took my very grubby vehicle to the car wash. When I say "car wash" I don't mean the local garage that has a drive-in drive-out mechanical affair complete with whirling brushes. Oh no. I mean one of those car washes where six burly guys brandish pressure jets all at the same time. Have you noticed how these outfits have sprung up all over the country? Our local one isn't the most salubrious looking with its mismatched corrugated roof and rusting shelf units, and I'm a bit wary of "the boss". There's something unnerving about a man dressed in a balaclava with an accent like Vladimir Putin. It makes you jumpy.

Mr Grisly: *Meaty fist banging against driver's window.* 'Oi, lady.'

Me: *Feeling anxious.* 'Yes?'

Mr Grisly: *Sounding fierce.* 'Park car here.'

Me: *Apprehensive.* '*Right* here?'

Mr Grisly: *Stabs finger at me.* 'Face car other way.'

Me: *Dithering.* 'Why?

Mr Grisley: *Sneering.* 'You drive through wrong entrance. You all back to front.'

Me: *Uneasy at having to do a three-point turn in a narrow area.* 'Okay.'

Mr Grisly: *Irritated.* 'I no have all day.

Me: *Swiftly executes a thirty-eight point turn.*

Mr Grisly: *Summons gang... I mean "crew".*

Me: *Presses central locking button.*

Mr Grisley: *Bangs on sparkling window.* 'Gimme money.'

Me: *Hands over entire contents of purse which turns out to contain just two pennies because, unbeknownst to me, Eleanor "borrowed" my last tenner.*

Mr Grisley: *Sounding like General Grubozaboyschikov.* 'You come back.'

Me: *Gibbering wreck.* 'Yes, of course, I wouldn't dream of not paying because "Honesty" is my middle name and—'

Mr Grisley: *Violent arm gesture.* 'Move. Next customer, he waiting.'

Needless to say, because these pop-up places aren't exactly a soothing experience I don't frequent them very often. Nonetheless these chaps do give a mean car wash worthy of show room quality. And, boy, did my car need a good clean.

After weeks of endless rain, the roads have been awash with filthy water, grit and mud. The first clue that my car needed a good clean was because, after almost a month, it was no longer silver but matt brown. The second clue was more obvious. Some kind soul had licked their finger and written a message in the muck. It said *I wish my wife was this dirty.* Even worse, somebody else had licked their finger and added a postscript. *She is.*

I'm not the only one in the neighbourhood to be on the receiving end of this car graffiti 'wit'. Whilst passing a stationery lorry emptying a nearby school's septic tank, some wag had written on the lorry's rear *No stools left in this vehicle overnight.* And whilst stuck in the local rush hour, I was sitting behind a van on which somebody had put a signature. It said *R. Send.* Others, more predictably, had: *Clean me; Also available in white;* and *Driver lexdyslic.*

Despite the terrible weather, I suspect car washes all over the country have been doing a roaring business. Which reminds me.

A blonde heard that a new car wash was in her neighbourhood.

'How convenient,' she said to a friend, 'because I'll be able to walk to it...'

What kind of drama teachers do you find at the South Pole?
Cold ones...

Last September my daughter enrolled at our local college to study Performing Arts. Earlier this week she took part in her first show. It was an amazing play, very sensitive and full of emotion. The audience were in tears — as were many of the young actors and actresses. Nor were these tears fake. They sprung forth as a result of the lines they'd learnt touching their soul. Being in tears day in, day out, whilst rehearsing can't be very uplifting. So seeing the performance made us realise why Eleanor has been tricky to live with for the past month. Rewind to four weeks ago.

'Hi, darling,' I trilled, as Eleanor slumped into the front seat of the car. 'Good day at college?'

There was an unintelligible grunt while I did the mirror-signal-manoeuvre thing with the car and then edged out on to the main road. Eleanor gazed stonily out of the window. Eventually she spoke.

'I think I might have made a massive mistake opting to study Performing Arts.'

'Why?'

'It's not what I thought it would be. We did a workshop today. Everyone was given a soft piece of cloth. We were told to hold it and think of somebody very dear. We had to interact with the cloth. We hugged it. Laid it down on the floor. Went through a long visualisation exercise with our eyes tightly shut. It was all very beautiful and uplifting. But our director then tip-toed around each and every one of us, and she snatched the cloth away telling us that this wonderful connection had now been severed and we'd never, ever have it again. Everybody started crying. Even the lads.'

We rolled to a stop at some traffic lights, and I glanced at my daughter.

'Can I ask who you were thinking of when you were doing the attachment exercise with this piece of cloth?'

But I knew the answer before Eleanor spoke.

'My dad,' she whispered, as her eyes started to brim.

No wonder she felt so emotional. My daughter's father is deceased. Acting out losing him all over again in a 'learn how to cry' workshop must have been tough. The students were told to detach from the exercise and file it away in readiness for an acting experience which might one day require producing real tears on stage. They didn't have long to wait.

A week or two later, the students were told they would be doing their first ticketed performance. They were excited. What would it be? A comedy? A thriller? But it was neither of those things. Instead they would perform a drama based on true events which would include Hitler's era, concentration camps, and the death of millions of innocents.

The director was a formidable no-nonsense woman who stomped about in her Doc Martens, barking orders and berating the students. If she didn't get the desired results, her sentences would become littered with the F word.

'F*ck*ng call yourselves f*ck*ng actors? You're all a f*ck*ng load of f*ck*ng rubbish!'

Eleanor was shocked at the director's outburst and unimpressed that someone they were meant to respect wasn't just foulmouthed, but used swearing and criticism to supposedly get the best out of her students, whereas in fact it had the opposite effect and demoralised them. After all, if you continually tell someone they are 'rubbish', might not they eventually believe that?

My initial reaction was to ring up the college and complain bitterly about this member of staff. However, I didn't. This wasn't school.

The traffic lights flipped to green and we set off again. Picking my words carefully, I cleared my throat.

'I'm sorry you're having to rehearse such a heavy subject in such a negative atmosphere' — I reached across the handbrake and patted Eleanor's knee — 'but I have a feeling this is a learning curve. It might well be that this is how a lot of directors speak and therefore serve as a lesson. Do you think you can toughen up and grow an extra layer of skin?'

A lone tear rolled down Eleanor's cheek, and then plopped on to one leg.

'I'll try,' she said.

That evening I rang my mother to let off some steam about the whole thing.

'Oh dear,' said Mum, 'I'm so sorry to hear that Eleanor isn't currently enjoying the acting. Who is the woman that's making all the students so miserable?'

'The director,' I sighed.

'Can't you have a word with her?'

'Hell, no!' I clutched the phone in horror. 'She's really scary. She might gore me with her spiky hair or stamp on my feet with her Doc Martens. The only time she takes them off is when she goes to her kick-boxing class.'

'Kick boxing?' said mum in confusion. 'Is Eleanor studying kick boxing?'

'No, Mum. I was talking about the director.'

My mother is eighty-one. Sometimes her concentration wanders.

The director continued to terrorise her students, eventually telling them their acting was so f*cking dire there would only be the one performance. And so, tickets bought, I sat with my family in the audience as the spotlight hit the stage and the drama began.

I was stunned. Gobsmacked at the brilliance of these young people. Astonished at their ability to literally morph into the characters they were playing. And they all carried a piece of cloth that represented something very meaningful to them —a dog... cat... mother... father... sister... a baby. And when the cloth was snatched away to be brutally executed, every single one of those students cried. As did the audience. As the play finished, the audience erupted with tumultuous applause.

Needless to say, it wasn't a one-off performance and the show is still running as I write this.

'I have to take my hat off to your director,' I said to Eleanor, as she came out from backstage to greet us all. 'She might be a cow, but she did a brilliant job with you all.'

My mother toddled over on her walking stick.

'Well done, dear,' she said, kissing her granddaughter on the cheek, 'but I'm a little confused. I thought you were playing the part of a spiky-haired woman who likes wearing big boots?'

As I said, my mother is eighty-one and her concentration wanders.

Meanwhile, Eleanor has decided she hasn't made a mistake choosing to study Performing Arts. I reckon she's just grown her first extra layer of skin. She's now looking forward to embracing the next performance with a new director. Let's hope the language will be a little sweeter. Which reminds me.

Did you hear about the director who said, 'Sticks and stones will break my bones, but words will never harm me.' She was proved wrong when an irate parent hit her over the head with a dictionary...

What do cars do at a disco?
Brake dance...

It's been a very sociable week. Hurrah! A meal out at a favourite restaurant, followed by an outing to *The National Television Awards*, another restaurant, then a club and, later this evening, yet another restaurant. Wow! I'm still reeling in astonishment because, until very recently, my social life was comparable to a drought.

In the run up to Christmas I was convinced a party or two might be on the cards. Having moved to a new house a few months ago, there was an anticipation of housewarming get-togethers or a New Year's knees-up. But it turned out our neighbours were either very young with little kids and wanted peace and quiet, or very old, and ditto.

'How I wish,' I said to my husband, 'that we were still young enough to go to a club. I'd give anything to have a good dance.'

'I'm done with dancing,' said Mr V.

He's been saying that for the last decade. A few years ago, I managed to bully him into taking up *Ceroc* as an evening class. We did this for several months until Mr V confessed he wasn't enjoying it. So we switched to salsa. Who can resist such sexy music or watching pin-thin women blend their bodies with snake-hipped guys? It's not called "dirty dancing" for nothing! So, can we salsa? Of course not. Mr V kept reverting to Eighties' disco moves, and I didn't progress beyond the forward and back steps. And that, I thought, was that. Until last night.

Wham! Suddenly we were in a club. The location was Leeds, so a long way from home. It was a leaving 'do' for some of Mr V's colleagues at head office.

'Can you salsa?' asked a female colleague of my husband.

'Can I salsa?' Mr V repeated in an *of-course-I-can-salsa-any-idiot-can-salsa* voice. He then swiftly declined the offer of a salsa dance with his colleague on the grounds of having just bought a drink. 'Debbie will salsa with you instead.'

The female in question was quite happy to dance with another woman.

'You'll have to lead,' I said, 'as I can only go backwards and forwards.'

And we were off. Forwards, backwards, strut, strut, a messy twirl, forward, backwards, hip swing, strut, strut, oops wrong direction, forwards, backwards, a bounce off each other's tummies, swing, swing, fling arms up and, oops, punch somebody walking past, and forwards, backwards, feet protesting, strut, strut, ouch, going to have to stop, feet are really not liking this...

So I resorted to wiggling. For the uninformed, this is my own version of dancing but standing on the spot. The feet do not move and therefore do not protest. Two hours later I was all wiggled out. There's only so long you can stand there impersonating a tree in a gale force wind.

By this point many of the gathering were the worse for wear.

'We've had enough of the music in this club,' said one merrymaker. 'We're going to another where the music is a mixture of' — she frowned and did an expansive gesture — 'just *everything*.' Fabulous. Except my feet were having none of it. I was also stone cold sober thanks to consuming gallons of water. An earlier attempt to enjoy a rum and coke — which, for health reasons, I haven't touched since last summer — resulted in a head rush after three sips. It was only half past one in the morning but suddenly we both felt hideously tired.

'We'll say goodnight,' said Mr V.

Saying goodnight took a while. In England you hear talk of the North/South divide. This relates to several things, from the scenery and house prices, to politics and employment. I would like to add something else to the North/South divide list. *Friendliness*. I should have been born a Northerner. They are so much friendlier than Southerners. How many times have I been friendly to a fellow Southerner and had it misconstrued for either being a bit eccentric, totally bonkers or even flirting? Numerous times. But in the North? Saying good-bye is something else. You hug. You fully embrace. You wrap arms around each other. You ruffle hair. You promise everyone — even if you don't really know them — that you will see them again. And if you really feel so inclined, I suspect you could even get away with a lip lock!

Once back at the hotel, I pulled off my stilettos and limped across the carpet. My feet felt like they were on back to front. So for now we are all danced out, but if anybody out there is having a party, we're still up for it! Which reminds me.

What kind of dance do mothers do best?

The Mum-bo...

When are your eyes no longer eyes?
When a cold wind makes them water...

Weekends are precious. After working hard from Monday through to Friday and often being short on sleep, we welcome the arrival of Saturday and Sunday with open arms. Oh, the bliss of a lie in! Unfortunately, more often than not, the longed for lie in doesn't always happen because our brains are still in weekday wake-up mode. Either that or Trudy Beagle and HRH Dolly have barged into the bedroom respectively demanding breakfast at an unearthly hour. But the *idea* of a lie in is wonderful. And of course we live in hope that *this* weekend might be the one where a lie in proves successful.

I personally love the weekend because it means dawdling over breakfast, having time for that second cup of tea, catching up with my online Scrabble moves, chatting on social media, and generally wasting quite a bit of the day. My husband, thrilled to bits knowing his wife is occupied elsewhere, usually jumps on the sofa, grabs the remote control and then assumes a horizontal position. In recent months this has become a pattern and, without either of us realising it, a precious Saturday has been frittered away. Three weeks ago, I decided to tackle the issue.

'We should be enjoying our weekends,' I said, waggling a finger at Mr V, 'and *doing* something.'

'I *am* doing something,' he replied. 'I'm watching football. And rugby. And racing. And golf.'

'I'm talking doing something *together*. Other couples go jogging or have a day out visiting places of interest.'

My husband looked alarmed. 'Why?'

'Because that's what other couples *do*!'

Mr V heaved himself off the sofa.

'Okay, okay,' he said, putting his hands up in surrender. 'I can take a hint. You want me to go to the supermarket with you. Not a problem.'

'No, not the supermarket. I'm talking about getting *out*. Having *fun*.'

The pursuit of fun is what took us two-hundred and

fifty miles north to Leeds last weekend to say goodbye to a colleague and enjoy a curry and club. However, this weekend's first choice of entertainment didn't come off. We were meant to visit Knole Park in nearby Sevenoaks. I've never been there, and yet it's a place virtually on our doorstep. The idea of a winter's walk and feeding the deer appealed immensely. However, the relentless rain and flooding of the last few weeks literally reduced this whim to a wash-out. Mr V looked secretly relieved.

'Not a problem,' I said. 'Let's go in the opposite direction and instead stroll around Greenwich Park.'

'As long as we're back in time to watch the Six Nations and Man U who are play—'

'Yes, yes, yes' — I flapped a hand dismissively — 'come on, let's go.'

'Are we taking Trudy Beagle?'

'Yes, I think her legs are up for it if we just stroll.'

I reached into the cupboard under the stairs for our pooch's doggy coat.

'She won't need that. It's eight degrees.'

'Yes, eight degrees. Not eighty degrees. The sun might be shining but there's a nippy breeze blowing. Greenwich Park is very open so take into consideration the wind chill factor.'

'Well I'm not wrapping up,' said Mr V, slipping a summer jacket over his t-shirt, 'because I don't think it's remotely chilly.'

'It is.'

'It isn't.'

'Is.'

'Isn't. And anyway, I'd rather look cool than resemble a human marshmallow,' he said, nodding at my own jacket, a billowing quilted affair which I'd bought for a tenner in a ski shop sale but never worn for fear it might inflate like a parachute when skiing down a steep run.

'You'll regret it.'

'No I won't.'

Underneath the jacket I was wearing fleece-lined joggers and a cosy sweatshirt. Winding a soft fluffy scarf around my neck, I then donned a matching bobble hat and pair of gloves. Mr V took one look at my attire and rolled his eyes, before strolling out the front door in his thin jeans and even thinner jacket. Fashion was all.

Greenwich Park was busy, and the car park was stuffed with vehicles. Spotting the last available space ahead, I ground the gears of my car into reverse and did some very messy parallel parking. Ten minutes later, the car was shoehorned into its space.

Locking up, Trudy Beagle and I snuggled into our coats and the three of us set off. Within seconds Mr V had pulled up his collar and stuffed his hands into pockets.

'Warm enough?' I asked cheerfully.

'Yes,' he said through gritted teeth.

'Well at least you look good. Very *cool*,' I quipped.

Two hours later my husband wasn't so much cool as totally frozen.

'I'm cold,' he bleated.

'Well you should have listened to me and wrapped up warmly.'

Sometimes I feel like my husband's mother instead of a wife, and I could have sworn even Trudy Beagle rolled her eyes. Which reminds me.

What's the difference between a new husband and a new dog?

After a year, the dog is still excited to see you…

What does an eighty-year-old mother do if her children are still at home?
Watch them for signs of improvement...

Next Tuesday my son will celebrate his twenty-first birthday. However, because he will be at university, we chose to celebrate the event three days earlier, on Saturday night.

It was a noisy family party entailing a visit to our favourite Italian restaurant, several bottles of wine, lots of good food, a birthday cake and a compulsory rendition of "Happy Birthday" sang at top volume. My daughter took lots of pictures, and precious moments were turned into picture memories to be enjoyed and mulled over again at some point in the future.

Twenty-one is a blissful age. You are truly an adult. People take you more seriously. You have your looks, youth and a bit of wisdom in your back pocket. There is a feeling that the world is literally your oyster and you can carve out any future you desire.

Well, that's how it seems to me when I look back with rose-tinted specs on being twenty-one. The actual reality is that you're usually broke! My son is a dental student. Robbie lives on a tight budget in digs with other students, and budgets his social life via "Wowcher" deals. Unlike my son, I didn't go to university. I was working, but still broke. This is because I'd bought my first home – a one bedroomed apartment. A huge portion of my salary went on paying the mortgage and putting petrol in an ancient Morris Minor. Back then any social life revolved around a neighbour throwing an *Avon* party and wondering if enough money could be scraped together to order a nice shiny nail polish. It's only now, so many years later, that I look back and realise those were happy, carefree days. I'm sure Robbie will one day look back on his student days in the same way.

'Believe you me, Mum, I won't,' he declared. 'I can't wait to be able to afford to live in a place without mice under the bed, damp on the walls, and an idiot of a plonker in the flat below playing his base at three in the morning.'

My son and his flat mates have been knackered thanks to Mr Plonker's last musical session not finishing until six in the morning. As Robbie and his pals wearily filed past the downstairs apartment, one of the students paused.

'Hang on a minute, there's something we should do.'

With a great deal of whispers, giggles and snorts, revenge took place by taking it in turns to lean on Mr Plonker's doorbell. There then followed a mad scramble out the main door before they were caught.

And THAT is the very sort of my memory my son will one day hazily recall with great fondness and say, "Do you remember when...?" Which reminds me.

There was a Scottish student, Donald McDonald, who went to study at an English university. He lived in the halls of residence with the other students. After a month, his mother came to visit.

'How are you finding the other students, Donald?' she asked.

'Mother,' he replied, 'they are such terrible, noisy people. The one on that side' — he pointed — 'keeps banging his head on the wall and won't stop. The one on this side' — he pointed again 'screams all night.'

'You poor thing! How do you manage to put up with it?'

'I just ignore them and stay here quietly, playing my bagpipes...'

What did the boy bird ask the girl bird on Valentine's Day?
Will you be my Tweet-heart...?

On the eve of Valentine's Day, my husband came home from work with a freshly licked down scarlet envelope and half a dozen red roses in cellophane.

'I have to be up early tomorrow morning,' he said, 'so have these now.'

'Wow, thanks!' I said, taking the roses and waiting for the accompanying three important words.

'Nice, eh?'

Only two words.

'Yes.'

'Red roses.'

Still only two words.

'Yes, I can see that.

'*Luxury* red roses.'

Okay, that was three words, but not the three words I was hoping for.'

I headed off to the kitchen in search of a vase.

'So why are they luxury roses?' I asked, running scissors along the cellophane.

'Because it says so here' — my husband pointed to a sticky label and read aloud — '*Luxury* red roses.'

I lifted the blooms out and instantly a flurry of petals and leaves fell at my feet.

'These roses are almost dead,' I said.

'Oh. Never mind. Anyway' — he sidled towards the lounge — 'I'll just pop the telly on. It's *Soprano* night.'

Viva la romance!

Meanwhile my daughter and her friends had a special visitor to their college on Valentine's Day — a National Health Service van and two hospital staff were offering free chlamydia tests. How romantic. Not. As a "thank you" to every female agreeing to be tested, there was the offer of a free pair of Valentine boxer shorts smothered in hearts. The girls dithered. Did they want to do the test? No. Did they want the free gift to give their boyfriends? Yes! So they all trooped into the examination room, took

the long-stemmed cotton tip, went behind the curtain —
and ran the cotton tip around their mouths. They then
accepted the boxer shorts and skipped off. I'm not quite
sure what results the NHS will get, but you must admire
the girls' strategic thinking. No doubt, all over Dartford,
puzzled lads are comparing Valentine gifts and
wondering if their girlfriends went on an en-masse
shopping spree.

My son's partner, however, knew how to celebrate in
style.

'I'm taking you to the most romantic restaurant in
London. But I'm not telling you the name. It's a surprise.'

I instantly hit the internet and Googled *most romantic
restaurant in London.* Up came the answer. I nearly fell
off my typing chair. Now *that* was indeed a romantic
restaurant. I shall keep the number and drop lots of hints
to Mr V for next Valentine's Day! Which reminds me.

Why did the banana go out with the prune?

Because it couldn't get a date...

What is a television?
A weapon of mass distraction...

I'm not really a watcher of television. During the day I'm working, then late into the night I write, and somewhere in between I look after my family and run the home. Sometimes I 'tune in' to what's on when cooking in our open-plan kitchen-lounge and Mr V is watching his beloved football. I can tell you the cast of Manchester United, but not of Coronation Street. On occasion, when I venture into my daughter's bedroom to pick up mountains of clothes or clean, I will catch snippets of programmes about fat people who want to be thinner, and thin people who want to be fatter; or people who have inked almost every part of their skin and are now begging for laser removal. But my relationship with the television is a very fragmented one, which is probably why I love going to the movies.

When Saturday night rolls around and it's time to relax, there's nothing better than visiting the local cinema, popcorn in hand whilst watching the latest heartthrob chasing baddies, or someone like Jennifer Aniston in a funny "chick flick". We don't watch too many of Jen's films as Mr V prefers Cameron Diaz. Our taste in films is not usually one that is mutual. Generally my husband prefers films like *Saw.* And *Saw 2*, and *Saw 3*, and *Saw 4...* you get the picture (no pun intended). I watched the first *Saw* film years ago and was so disturbed that, the moment we were home, I searched the inside of every wardrobe and under all the beds looking for hidden lunatics.

Nor am I a great fan of alien moves, unless you count *ET*. Mr V persuaded me to watch *The Fourth Kind* at the cinema. I'm not joking when I say that wretched film wrecked my sleep for weeks on end. Come bedtime, I was a nervous wreck, convinced that an alien would creep into the house the moment we succumbed to sleep.

Give me something silly and farcical to watch and I'm in my element. Which is why I was surprised when Mr V said he liked *Laurel and Hardy*. How had we been married to each other for all these years and only just found this out? So we settled down together and watched *Pardon Me*. What a pleasure it was. Neither of them resorted to one single swear word in order to raise a laugh, and absolutely no political correctness nonsense either. When the lads escaped from prison and hid with the cotton pickers and blacked themselves up to blend in, it was done innocently and was incredibly funny, whereas I'm not sure you could get away with that today without someone claiming it to be offensive. Which is just plain stupid. I certainly wasn't offended watching the film *White Chicks* where two black cops not only 'go white' but also 'go female' in order to solve a crime. If something is innocent and funny, what is there to be offended about? But back to Laurel and Hardy.

Desk Sergeant: What's your name?
Stanley: Stanley Laurel.
Desk Sergeant: Say "Sir" when you're addressing me. Now what's your name?
Stanley: Sir Stanley Laurel.

And from another film:
Ollie: What did she say?
Stan: She said we can't go out tonight, that we have to go right home.
Ollie: Why?
Stan: Because she's got a surprise for you.
Ollie: What else did she say?
Stan: She told me not to tell you she had a surprise.
Ollie: Well don't tell me.
Stan: I won't, I can keep a secret.

Which is more than I can. Which reminds me.
Did you hear about the butter's secret?
No, no, I mustn't tell you, in case it spreads...

What do you call a month's worth of rain? England...

The sun is shining and the daffodils are out. It is officially spring, hurrah! After one of the wettest winters in two-hundred and fifty years, it is almost a novelty to look at the sky and see a golden circle languishing alongside some truculent looking clouds.

The weather has been all over the place. It seems as though the 'four seasons' have been more akin to 'no rhyme or reason'. After a mad time of storms, endless rain, terrible flooding, and even freaky sink holes, the United Kingdom experienced an amazing aurora borealis. Usually this remarkable light show is seen in the polar regions, but this week everyone gasped as a rare and spectacular display was sighted from Scotland to as far south as Jersey. And did anybody else see the image of a face on top of a spectacular 'garment' of lime-green and strawberry-pink light? The newspapers were full of the story about this sighting.

If you are given to fancy (and I most certainly am!), you might ask what on earth is going on? Whizz back in time a few thousand years and we all would have muttered that God was angry in his heaven. The light show and 'face' would have either sent our ancestors running for cover or falling to the ground in worship. There are many legends from North America and Scandinavia about how dangerous it can be to not show respect for the northern lights. They are even mentioned in the bible's Old Testament, in the book of Ezekiel. Two thousand six hundred years ago, the description says, 'I looked, and I saw a windstorm coming out of the north — an immense cloud with flashing lightning and surrounded by brilliant light.'

Facebook abounded with jokey 'prophecy' cartoons, and I laughed along with others at the drawing of a wooden ark captioned *Also available as a flatpack from Ikea*. However, given that the Thames Barrier closed for a record twenty occasions last month, it did also uneasily seem that such 'prophecy' cartoons weren't such an amusing matter. Certainly, the many people who had to evacuate their homes did not laugh. There was nothing funny having all their belongings ruined due to roads turning into rivers which flooded so many houses. Their misery must have been as deep as the water whooshing through their local high streets.

But for now the rain has stopped, the light show is over, and God is happy in his heaven. I'm going to take advantage of the sunny spell and wash my car. At least the Government can't impose a hosepipe ban for now. Which reminds me.

What did one raindrop say to the other?

Two's company, three's a cloud...

How do you know you're getting old?
When it takes twice as long to look half as good...

My birthday is looming... and I'd completely forgotten about it. After all, surely it's only five minutes ago we celebrated Christmas?

This time of year always sees family celebrations within weeks of each other. The Christmas tree had barely been put back in its box when my mother celebrated turning eighty-one, and shortly after that was my son's twenty-first. The days are zooming by. If I were a cosmic policeman I'd flag down 2014 and say, 'Hey, do you know what speed you're travelling at? A hefty fine for you, and three points on your calendar!'

'Mum, can we celebrate your birthday at our favourite restaurant?' asked my daughter.

I did a rough head count of who would attend including those who are very good at ordering extra bottles of champagne without offering to pay for it. Too expensive.

'I think a birthday buffet at home will be much nicer,' I said.

'Oh, how disappointing' — Eleanor's teenage moodiness instantly let itself be felt — 'not to mention boring.'

But the truth of the matter is money doesn't grow on trees. There is always someone who takes advantage and "misconstrues" their invite as permission to bring along the entirety of their extended family. My credit card has only just recovered from forking out for Robbie's twenty-first. It wouldn't be so bad if some of the guests were a little more thoughtful, but one relative turned up and didn't even have the generosity to give Rob a birthday card. Rude!

'What would you like for your birthday?' said Robbie, during a late night telephone call.

'Your company,' I replied.

'Okay, I'll pop down for the weekend.'

'Fantastic!'

'Can we celebrate your birthday at our favourite

restaurant?'

Oh no. Immediate déjà vu.

'I need to watch my pennies at the moment, so there will be a birthday buffet at home instead.'

'Oh, how disappointing.'

More déjà vu.

'I know!' said Rob. 'What about we go out somewhere cheap?'

'Like where?'

'What about going to the local and having pub grub?'

'Yes, pub grub would be fine if W didn't drink like a fish, and X didn't order the most expensive thing on the menu twice over because of his huge appetite, and Y didn't want half a dozen shorts — and I don't mean trousers that end at the knee — not forgetting Z who is so miserly he even likes to have a laugh at my expense.'

Sigh. Perhaps I should just bash the credit card and be done with it. Which reminds me.

Living on Earth might be expensive, but it does involve a free annual trip around the sun....

What do you do when you see a spaceman? Park in it, dammit!

I had to take my daughter to hospital yesterday. Eleanor had a very early appointment and fortunately the traffic was so good we arrived with time on our side.

'There's a lovely little café around the corner,' I said. 'Let's grab a quick cappuccino.'

'And a nice fat slice of cake?'

'That sounds good. Let's get the car parked, and then we'll make our way to the café.'

Which was easier said than done for the only *cake* we ended up having was the bun fight in the hospital's car park. As I crawled through its narrow entrance, it was immediately apparent that the car park was full. I scanned the choc-a-bloc parking bays and offered up a few silent prayers. Yes! There, right in front of me, a woman was reversing her vehicle and getting ready to leave. However, she had a very tiny car whereas mine is designed to take the entire family, a heap of bikes and still fit in the dog. I squared my shoulders. Somehow I *would* make my car fit into that space. It just required some careful manoeuvring.

'I don't think you're going to get into it, Mum.'

'Nonsense. If I squeeze the car into this alleyway to my left, I can then reverse back and... oh!'

Someone had taken advantage of my sideways manoeuvre and zoomed into my space. Annoyed, I buzzed the window down.

'Excuse me' — I called politely — 'but that was *my* space. I was just preparing to reverse into it.'

My words were met with a glare.

'And now it's my space.'

Well there was no arguing with that, was there! I gave the person one of my own special 'looks' whilst sitting on my twitching hands lest they do the sort of hand signals that aren't part of the Highway Code.

'What a flaming cheek,' said Eleanor.

'Never mind,' I sighed. 'I've spotted another space.'

'Where?'

'Over there. Somebody else is leaving.'

'Quick.'

'On it.'

I rammed the car into gear and shot forward. YESSSSSS! A stream of cars were now coming into the car park, bunging up the aisles, causing chaos, with drivers' heads rotating three-hundred and sixty degrees in an effort to seek out that elusive empty parking bay —but I had *mine* covered. Any moment now and that space would be ready for me to zoom into. Except... what was that driver over there doing? A swish BMW had stopped and was signalling, letting me know he was after *my* space. More buzzing down of windows took place.

'Excuse me?' I smiled pleasantly.

The man blanked me.

'He's going to nick your parking space, Mum.'

'Oh no he's not.'

'He is.'

He was.

I jumped out of my car and marched over to the BMW.

'Hi.' My next attempt at a polite smile probably looked more like how the Joker greets Batman. 'This space that you're waiting for... well I saw it first... so it's mine.'

'But I'm closest to it.'

'I don't care. I was here before you and good manners dictate you acknowledge that and let me park my car here.'

'You ain't parking your car here, lady.'

'Oh yes I am. Watch me.'

'It will be my pleasure.'

'Good. Have fun watching.'

'Are you a magician or something?'

'What sort of daft question is that?'

'Because while you've been telling me that you're parking in this space, the original car has left and a Mini has parked there instead. So are you going to somehow magically park your car on top of that Mini?'

'Wha—?'

'Hurry up, lady. I'm waiting to be entertained.'

Muttering oaths under my breath, I returned to my

car.

'Mum, forget the coffee and cake because, at this rate, we're going to miss our appointment.'

'The next space is ours,' I snarled. 'And if anybody tries to stop me, I'll—'

'Look! He's leaving!'

'Who?'

'Him!'

'Where?'

'There!'

'Oh dear God and Mother Mary and anybody else up there listening, just get me into that parking space!'

A van was moving out of a sideways bay. This meant having to do what nearly every woman dreads. Parallel parking. I zipped over, put my hazards on, slammed the car into reverse, lined up my passenger door with a parked car's rear side door, swung the steering wheel hard left ninety degrees, and prayed very hard that my car would go in first time and... yes... yes... it was happening... absolutely fantastic... what a *sensational* bit of parallel parking... someone should film this and use it to demonstrate to all learner drivers exactly how to parallel park because this was beyond brilliant... except... what the hell was that?

Behind me a horn had sounded long, loud, and protesting. I craned my neck to see a little old lady in a Micra beeping me... and she was halfway into *my* parking space.

'I don't sodding believe this!' I fumed. 'Well two can play that game.'

I leant on my horn too. For a while, we duetted. After thirty seconds, lots of other horns joined in the racket because the stand-off over this parking space was causing major havoc with the other circling predators. And then the little old lady began edging forwards. Good heavens! She was calling my bluff and going for it! Ten out of ten to her for sheer bloody-minded courage. I instantly wimped out and drove forward again.

'What a nerve!' Eleanor said. 'And she's got to be at least eighty. You'd have thought the older generation had manners.'

'Unfortunately there are some members of the older generation who think that just because they are Golden Oldies, they have the right to be rude. Look at Victor Meldrew.'

'Who?'

'Ah, never mind.'

And then a miracle occurred. A man knocked on my window.

'Do you want my parking space, love, only I saw what happened there and I'm just about to go. And the wife is with me, so she'll make sure nobody barges in.'

You see! There is a God!

'Oh thank you, thank you, thank you,' I burbled to the nice man... and God... and Mother Mary... and all the parking angels in Heaven.

And so it came to pass that the sun shone, birds tweeted, flowers bloomed and I parked my car with no mishaps, while a huge thunderbolt burst out from nowhere and turned the little old lady's Micra to marshmallow. Okay, that last bit didn't happen, but I can't deny that the thought didn't enter my head. Which reminds me.

A group of pensioners were discussing their medical problems at the Day Centre's coffee morning.

'Do you realise,' said one, 'that my arm is so weak I can hardly hold this coffee cup?'

'Yes, I know,' replied the second, 'and my cataracts are so bad I can't see to *pour* the coffee.'

'I can't turn my head,' said the third, 'because of the arthritis in my neck.'

'My blood pressure pills make me dizzy,' lamented the fourth, 'but I guess that's the price we pay for getting old.'

'Well, it's not all bad,' piped up the first, 'we should be thankful that we can all still drive...'

How do bakers trade recipes?
On a knead-to-know basis...

In an eternal quest to be fitter and slimmer, yesterday I suggested another visit to Greenwich Park.

'We could do some exercise together,' I said to my husband hopefully.

'I'm not running,' said Mr V. 'I've only just got over my bad back.'

'Okay, that's fine' — I shrugged — 'I'll do on-the-spot jogging and keep pace with your walking stride.'

'Won't that be boring for you?'

'Not at all. I'll mix it up with little spurts of jogging ahead, and then back again.'

'Okay. Shall we take a picnic?'

'Good idea. After all, right now the weather is perfect.'

So we set off, picnic packed, and immediately it poured with rain.

'Fine picnic this is going to be,' growled Mr V, as the car's windscreen wipers swished backwards and forwards.

Fortunately, by the time we arrived at Greenwich Park, the sun was back in a pretty pale blue sky.

'I'm starving,' said Mr V.

'Me too.'

We wandered into the 'Flower Garden'. We've visited Greenwich Park many times but never set foot in this beautiful area. This is because, years ago, our children were riding the obligatory bicycles on stabilisers or, later, hurtling along on scooters or, later still, we had Trudy Beagle barking hysterically in our wake and dogs are not allowed in the Flower Garden. So today, without children or our ancient beagle present, we opened the wooden gate bearing the sign:

No dogs, no radios, no bicycles, no scooters, no wheelies, no heelies... no anything in fact other than yourself and peacefulness. Oh, and your picnic.

Clutching our tuna baguettes, we stepped inside this fragrant wonderland.

'Ooh, isn't this lovely!' I said, peering around and

admiring the manicured parkland and taking mental notes. Would a circle of hyacinth bulbs interspersed with nodding daffodils work in our postage stamp of a garden?

'Look' — my husband pointed to a bench — 'let's sit over there and eat our picnic.'

So we sat. Unwrapping the foil from my baguette, I gazed at an impressive pine to our left.

'How majestic is that tree,' I said. 'Look at those huge branches and the way they almost bow to the ground as if in worship. Oh, and see there! A dear little squirrel… and he seems so tame. Look how close he is to us.'

'Mmm,' said Mr V, mouth full of tuna and bread.

'In fact, I can't believe how daring he is. How charming and endearing. And—'

I broke off. Because, actually, this charming and endearing squirrel was starting to look like he was on a mission. I rather suspected that, if he'd been human, right now he'd be rolling up his shirt sleeves. Never had I seen a squirrel look so intent as he scampered purposefully over, eyes fixed firmly on my lunch. I clasped my baguette to my bosom.

'Evacuate,' I squeaked.

'What?' said Mr V looking puzzled.

'Evacuate the Flower Garden.'

'No, that song was called *Evacuate the Dance Floor*.'

I stood up. 'Forthwith.'

'Forthwith? Sit down you daft mare.'

By this point the squirrel had a 'hand' on one of my hiking boots and was all set to do his squiggly walk up my leg. I hastily pulled off a bit of baguette and lobbed it. Exhaling with relief, I watched as the squirrel shot off after the bread, looking for all the world like a dog running after a ball.

'You shouldn't have done that,' Mr V mumbled, shaking his head.

'Why ever not?'

I didn't have long to find out. Another squirrel had appeared, and he was bringing reinforcements. A pigeon landed at my feet.

'Coo, coo,' said the pigeon.

You didn't need to speak pigeon to understand what it was saying. "Hand over the food, dude."

'Now look what you've done,' Mr V complained.

Five more pigeons fluttered around my feet. It's astonishing how much racket half a dozen birds can make. And then, like something out of a Hitchcock movie, the air was filled with birds all hovering above my baguette.

'I'm out of here,' I said, jumping to my feet.

The pigeons and squirrels weren't interested in my husband or his baguette. Their focus was solely on me and my lunch. I took off at a sprint with a stream of pigeons and squirrels dashing after me. In that moment I can honestly say I now know how Snow White felt when she made friends with all the woodland animals who followed her everywhere. Perhaps I should have turned around and sung to them? Which reminds me.

Why does Snow White always treat each of the seven dwarfs equally?

Because she's the fairest of them all...

What do dour skiers who dislike children, cats and dogs use for birth control?
Their personalities...

This time last week I was with my daughter skiing in France. Like any longed-for trip, it came and went too quickly.

Upon arriving at the hotel, Eleanor and I grabbed our skis and wasted no time in getting on to the slopes. We were tired from a very early start, but reckoned we could squeeze in a couple of hours before heading back to our village for après-ski drinkies.

'Where do we go from here?' asked Eleanor, as we paused on a mountain to get our bearings.

'Les Menuires,' I replied.

'There are no signposts with that name.'

'Yes there are. Look' — I gestured with a ski pole — 'right there.'

'That says "Lez Manure".'

'Well that's where we want to be.'

I gazed around cluelessly. We'd wanted to ski to Meribel, but had somehow ended up in Courchevel. That's the great thing about skiing — there is a huge area to explore, but getting lost is quite easy because one mountain looks very much like another. Thankfully, we did find our way back before the chair lift staff clocked off.

Our trip had started with high anticipation. I'd deliberately booked a chalet after having rose-tinted visions of sitting around a scrubbed pine table making friends with like-minded people who were happy to buddy up on the slopes and generally share a giggle. The reality is always different.

We'd left home for Gatwick Airport at four in the morning There was a moment of angst on the plane when I realised I'd forgotten to put on my in-flight socks. Okay, they were actually surgical stockings, swiped after a spell in hospital last year, and I was being a cheapskate recycling them.

'Oh no' — I wailed to Eleanor as the plane rumbled down the runway — 'I'm not wearing my in-flight socks.'

'Does it matter?'

'I don't know. Possibly. My legs were always swelling up last year and flying aggravated it.' Memories of nearly being denied a flight home from Crete had my stomach knotting with tension.

'That was when you had leukaemia, but now you're in remission.'

'I'd be happier if I had them on.'

'Where are they?'

'In my handbag under the front seat.'

'Then get them out and put them on' — Eleanor rolled her eyes — 'but hurry up.'

However, donning long surgical stockings whilst wearing jeans and sitting in an economy seat of an aircraft isn't easy. Not unless you are six inches wide and more bendy than a gymnast. Which I'm not. There then followed a lot of ankle grappling and muttered oaths as I creaked my feet up to my nose, wrestled with the surgical stockings and elbowed the woman to my left more times than was polite. By the time the wretched things were on, I was wet through.

'Done,' I muttered to Eleanor.

'Pull the legs of your jeans down, Mum!'

'Ah, yes.' I leant forward and tugged at the denim. Regrettably the surgical stockings rolled down with them.

'Now what's the matter?'

'They've fallen down.'

'They can't have fallen down. They're skintight!'

'They got caught up with the denim' — I hauled one leg on to Eleanor's lap — 'look.'

My daughter lifted the hem of my jeans and regarded a neatly rolled surgical stocking.

'You'll have to leave them like that.'

'I can't,' I gasped. 'They're miles too tight like this. They might cut off my circulation or something.'

'Then take them off' — said Eleanor looking exasperated — 'and put your socks back on.'

'Good idea.'

There then followed more huffing and puffing as I pulled the wretched things off, much to the irritation of the woman sitting next to me.

'*Now* what's wrong?' asked Eleanor.

'I can't find my socks.'

'Well they can't be far away because you haven't gone anywhere!'

Cue more contortion as I went into the brace position and peered under our row of seats. Two familiar stripy socks were under my neighbour's chair and *j-u-s-t* out of reach.

I came up for air, hit my forehead on the seat in front, and was nearly knocked out by a dinner tray unfolding on my head.

'Terribly sorry' — I said to the tutting woman next to me — 'but you appear to have my socks.'

She gave me the sort of look reserved for the mentally unhinged before reaching down and gingerly picking up my socks. She dangled them between thumb and forefinger before depositing them in my lap.

'God, Mum, you are so embarrassing.'

'I know. It's embarrassing to be so embarrassing. I think I ought to disown myself.'

'Can you now just sit still? Please?'

So I sat still. For about thirty seconds.

'For goodness sake, what's the matter now?'

'I want to read my Kindle.'

'Then read your Kindle.'

'It's in the overhead locker, which means I'll have to ask the woman sitting next to me to move.'

'You really know how to annoy people, don't you?'

So after more faff with the woman next door shuffling in and out of her seat, then a rucksack falling on her head — yes, mine — retrieving the Kindle and shoving the rucksack back, but then stripping off my jacket because all this Zumba on an aircraft had once again left me dreadfully hot and bothered, the woman next to me sank back into her seat to enjoy the rest of the flight. By that point, of course, it was all over and we were being told to get ready for landing. I never did get to read my Kindle.

At the chalet Eleanor and I oohed and aahed with happiness.

'Look' — I said, pointing to the scrubbed pine dinner table in the lounge — 'it's just as I thought it would be. I can't wait to make friends with the others.'

Unfortunately, the scrubbed pine dinner table was the only thing in my rose-tinted vision that actually came true. That evening, most of the people who joined us weren't very friendly. In fact, their manner was as chilly as the air outside.

'Hello' — I said, smiling at two of the women — 'I'm Debbie.'

One gave me a tight smile. The other said nothing and stared. Seemingly they didn't pal up with women like me. They also gave the cold shoulder to a single mum and her two young boys sitting at the far end of the table. The women scuttled over to their husbands and clung possessively to their men's arms. Clearly they suspected the single mum and I were man-eaters, possibly with a penchant for ravishing the opposite sex on scrubbed pine tables, scattering crockery in all directions. A heavy silence prevailed.

Awkward or what?

Eventually our chalet maid arrived and set steaming bowls before us.

'Ooh, yummy' — I said to nobody in particular — 'homemade vegetable soup.'

Whereupon the two married women suddenly decided I was a friend after all. They confided they couldn't abide vegetables and were more than happy for me to eat their soup. So I did. The next course was salmon with masses of broccoli. Suddenly my plate was full of greenery. However, giving me their veg was as far as their friendship extended. They made it plain to both me and the single mum that they couldn't abide children or pets. The single lady and I immediately chummed up, whipped out our mobiles and shared two thousand pictures of our respective children and pets. Revenge is sweet. Which is more than I can say about those women.

On the last day, one of the men helped me wrestle two

vast suitcases down the chalet's wooden staircase. Judging by his wife's expression, she wasn't happy he was helping out another woman. Her mouth took on the sort of shape that resembled Trudy Beagle's bottom. I gave her a neutral smile and wished her a pleasant trip home.

It is the Law of Sod that when you want to get away from someone, life has a joke and makes sure you are thrown together. Of all the people taking that packed flight home, who was sitting next to me?

'Oh no,' — I whispered to Eleanor — 'I've forgotten to put on my surgical stockings.'

'I'm having a déjà vu moment,' she sighed. Which reminds me.

What do you call a second moment of déjà vu? Déjà two.

What do you call being on the same plane as before? Déjà flew.

What do you call a woman who doesn't like you? Déjà moo.

What do you call elbowing the woman next to you? Déjà ooh.

What do you call lost socks under an airplane seat? Déjà poo.

What do you call a menopausal hot-flushing passenger? Déjà phew.

What do you call an exasperated daughter? Déjà disowning-yooo...

Why did the boy cut the joke book in half?
His mum said to cut the comedy...

According to Wikipedia, Mother's Day is, "A celebration honouring mothers and motherhood, maternal bonds, and the influence of mothers in society".

The reality is that there are many women out there who might not have physically given birth to a child, but they are still in a mothering role. For example, the childless woman who, in later life finds herself in a role reversal situation nurturing the frail old lady who once nurtured her. There are also childless women who foster kids, and some adopt. One of the most famous mothers of all was a convent school headmistress. She experienced a "call within a call" to leave the convent and help the poor whilst living amongst them. Somewhere in that moment, Sister Teresa became *Mother* Teresa. And there are other women still whose pet becomes their baby. I know numerous women who are "Mum" to budgies, rabbits, guinea pigs, cats, dogs, hamsters and horses. The bottom line is... mothering is about loving and nurturing. I am blessed with a son, a daughter, a step-daughter, a dog and a cat and mother them all.

On days like today I love looking back at the time I became a mother... that particular point where your own personal world was upended on its axis. Being a mother has many joyful moments. Equally, tearful moments. And let us not forget all those tear-your-hair-out moments. But, essentially, we love to love — no matter what.

Earlier this week I had to catch a train to London. A harassed mother puffed her way on to the train. A little boy was on her hip. She plonked him down opposite me and then slumped, exhausted, on the seat next to him. The little boy gazed at me enquiringly and asked a question. As it has been a great many years since I was fluent in baby babble, I hadn't a clue what the little chap asked, so was unable to answer. Instead I smiled. Instantly bored, the tot stood up on the seat and looked out of the window.

'Duck,' he said.

My eyes swivelled sideways searching for a duck. However, at this point we'd gone into a tunnel. Ah! Not "duck", but *dark*. I closed my eyes and relaxed against the seat, listening to the little boy's babble and trying to work out what he was saying, with the occasional helpful prompt from his weary mother.

The years peeled away and suddenly I could understand him. "Dwink" was *drink*, "twee" was *tree*, "seep" was *sheep*, and so on. Finally he said the magic word that every mummy understands and really doesn't want to hear on a packed train to London.

'Poo.'

Well we won't go into what happened next, but let's just say that every parent has been there, done it and, as they say, bought the t-shirt. And no I won't tell you about the time my young daughter uttered the same magic word just as the aircraft we were on charged down a runway and flung itself into the sky.

So whatever you are doing today, whether it is blowing a kiss to the heavens for a beloved mother no longer with you, or letting your children kiss you, or your precious pet slobber all over you, make sure you have a Happy Mother's Day — and that your other half spoils you too. Which reminds me.

Fred was thirty-two years old but still single. One day a friend asked, 'Why aren't you married? Can't you find a woman who will be a good wife?'

'Actually,' said Fred, 'I've found many women I've wanted to marry, but whenever I've taken them home to meet my parents, my mother always announced that she didn't like them.'

His friend thought for a moment before saying, 'I have a perfect solution. Find a girl who is just like your mother.'

A few months later they met again, and Fred's friend said, 'Did you find the perfect girl and, if so, did your mother like her?'

Fred frowned and answered, 'Yes, I found the perfect girl. She was just like my mother. And you were right, Mum loved her. But I didn't marry her.'

'So what's the problem now?' asked the friend.
'Because,' Fred explained, 'my father didn't like her...'

What is marriage?
Marriage is the only war where one sleeps with the enemy...

Three days ago, on the third of April, my parents celebrated sixty years of wedded bliss. Okay, let me rephrase that. They celebrated sixty years of marriage. I don't think any marriage — let alone one that has lasted six decades — has been all bliss. Indeed, as my mother recently quipped, 'I don't know how we made it to sixty years because I always meant to leave him.'

Marriage is a juggling act at the best of times. You must work at keeping someone happy. They, in turn, must work at keeping *you* happy. Then just when you think you are both happy, children come along and shift the balance and you have to re-think the whole *keeping each other happy* thing all over again.

My parents had a nine year wait before I came along and they were indeed happily married. At that point my father was in the Merchant Navy. He spent months at a time at sea — which is probably another reason for their happiness... they rarely saw each other! There would be long intervals between them being reunited.

When my mother gave birth to me, my father was on leave until I was nine weeks old. The next time he saw me, I was nine *months* old. What a change! And after that, the next time he saw me I was eighteen months — and would have nothing to do with him! He was devastated. Apparently I would scream if my father hugged my mother, and I'd scream again if he tried to cuddle me. This was stressful for both parents.

Eventually my father made the monumental decision to leave the Merchant Navy and find alternative work. However, there wasn't any local work. So, there was another period of stress as unemployment was experienced before making one more colossal decision — selling up and moving close to London where my father found work behind a desk.

Marital harmony was restored. The family settled into their new abode, in a new area, and my father adapted to

271

his new career. And, in time, I became accustomed to this man-person who was apparently my father. The marriage ticked along nicely... until my sister arrived.

The effect of a new baby on an older child is colossal. One moment the child's life is akin to a smooth pond, the next a pebble has plopped into it causing major ripples. Once again, my parents' marriage became a little stretched.

But eventually all these ripples subside, and once again there is a period of calm... until the oldest child becomes a teen. And all hell breaks loose. This is where a marriage is sorely tested as a manipulative teenager constantly tests the boundaries. These boundaries usually involve playing one parent off against the other, and I'm ashamed to say I was no different to your average scheming teen. One memory that sticks in my mind (and makes me cringe with guilt all these years later!):

Me: Can I go to a party on Saturday night?

Mum: Ask your father.

Me: Can I go to a party on Saturday night?

Dad: Ask your mother.

Me: I did. She said it was fine, but only if you give me a lift home afterwards.

Dad: Okay. I'll pick you up at eight o'clock.

Me: The party *starts* at eight.

Dad: In that case ask your mother to collect you.

Me: Dad says I can go but he's tired so you must collect me at midnight.

Mum: Flaming cheek — I'm tired too! Where is he?

Me: Watching telly.

Mum: *Bustling into lounge* Tony! YOU collect Debbie at midnight, do you hear?

Dad: Yes, dear.

Wasn't I horrible! And just when I'd stomped off into the big wide world at eighteen, my parents had about six months of peace before my sister turned into a walking hormonal gland and once again put my parents through their paces.

This pattern repeats when grandchildren come along. But we won't go there. Least said and all that and, anyway, the grandchildren are now young adults.

'You can finally enjoy your marriage,' I recently said to my mother.

'I'm now too knackered to enjoy anything,' she retorted.

Well, she is eighty-one.

However, knackered or not, you absolutely have to celebrate such a lengthy marriage. Even the Queen sent an anniversary card to my parents congratulating them and urging them to party. So they did.

Last night my parents took to the dance floor as their youngest daughter serenaded them. It was unbelievably touching to watch the silver-haired gentleman holding the tiny lady with a stoop. Love conquers all. As well as endurance! Which reminds me.

'Some people' — said an elderly gentleman — 'ask the secret of a long marriage. The secret is this. We take time to go to a restaurant twice a week. A little candlelight. Good food. Soft music, and even dancing. She goes Tuesdays, and I go Fridays...'

How does a teapot address its lover?
Oh, Darjeeling...

Earlier this year, my son gave me a birthday present never experienced before. Tea for two at a posh hotel in London. Tea is possibly my favourite drink. Recently, when out with family, a cousin asked if I wanted tea or coffee.

'I'm always up for some teabagging,' I said happily.

This produced some sniggers until another cousin quietly brought me up to date with some changes to the English language. Apparently my teabagging reference means something very different to being a tea addict. So, as my son and I emerged from Marble Arch tube station into spring's bright sunshine, I reminded myself that at no point should I tell hotel's tearoom staff that I was up for a spot of teabagging.

Robbie and I had a short walk to the venue which was down a little side road off Oxford Street. Ahead was a boutique hotel snuggled against wrought iron railings lavishly decorated with frothing flowerboxes. We went up some stone steps and stepped into a hallway where we were greeted and directed into a tea room straight out of a bygone era.

'This is nice,' said Robbie.

'Indeed,' I agreed.

As we sat down, I was captivated by the wall opposite me. It was smothered in framed portraits, prints, paintings and something that particularly caught my eye — an intricate tapestry. Now anybody who can painstakingly produce the tiniest of cross-stitches into a work of art needs, in my opinion, a massive gold medal. The only time I ever attempted embroidery was when pregnant with my daughter. I had purchased a personalised tapestry kit of a rocking horse complete with two cute teddy bears cuddling each other in the saddle. This, you understand, was a gift for my unborn child to one day exclaim over and say, 'Good heavens, Mum, you did this amazing bit of needlework for me? It's incredible!'

In fact, it's incredible I finished the wretched thing. I spent the next nine months going cross-eyed as I counted tiny holes for different coloured threads, muttering oaths when I realised the saddle was four squares out and the stirrup didn't quite line up. By that point I'd decided cross-stitch was thus named because it made you very cross.

Years later, instead of exclaiming in amazement over my sewing, Eleanor still doesn't quite believe I spent all those months stitching. Indeed, her last comment about it was, "Come clean, Mum. Your sewing just about covers putting a button on a shirt, so who *really* did this tapestry?" Which is why, when I looked at this particular wall-hanging, it was all the more amazing because it was signed and dated — in cross-stitch —1806 by a little girl aged ten. *Ten*! It was so beautiful and so incredibly complex, conjuring up a long-ago moment in time where little girls sat quietly and used their fingers to intricately sew rather than stab the screen of an iPhone.

But I digress. Our afternoon tea was delightful. For two hours Rob and I ate tiny crustless sandwiches and teeny cakes set upon fancy china whilst sipping a perfect brew from wafer-thin porcelain cups, all the while putting the world to rights. Which reminds me.

Make tea, not war.

~ Monty Python…

Do not touch my iPad. It's not an *us*Pad, a *we*Pad, or an *our*Pad.
It's an *i*Pad...

'I've done it!' I cried, coming in through the front door.

'Done what?' asked my daughter.

'Bought a mini iPad.'

'You mean an iPad mini,' Eleanor corrected.

'That's what I said' —I reverently set my purchase down on the kitchen table — 'and *this* time, it's mine.'

'Let me see?'

'No,' I said, snatching up the little white box with its bitten apple logo.

You see, this isn't the first time I've bought an iPad. My initial attempt at acquainting myself with the gadget was a couple of years ago. Except my daughter suggested we "share" it. And then, of course, the purchase just happened to coincide with her fast approaching birthday, so it ended up being her birthday present with me supposedly having a go on it every once in a blue moon. Except, as you know, the moon never really goes blue so I never got to use the iPad.

The second time I bought an iPad was last year. My son took one look and said, 'You know how you always insist that you treat me and Eleanor the same?'

'Er... yes,' I said, looking at Robbie warily.

'Well, that's not strictly true.'

'What do you mean?'

'I mean that my sister has an iPad, but I don't.'

'It was her birthday present.'

Rob grinned broadly.

'So I thought I'd remind you that I have a birthday looming.'

I sighed, and wrapped up the latest iPad in gift paper. After all, what did I want with such a gadget? I couldn't even send an email via my Smartphone, let alone talk to *Siri*.

However, I revised this drop-out attitude after my parents' recent sixtieth wedding anniversary party. On that night, I'd been very cross with myself for failing to charge my digital camera's battery in order to take pics at the celebration. Now it doesn't seem *that* long ago this camera was hailed as "the bee's knees". After all, it had come in a box with a vast sticker screaming *FIVE MEGAPIXELS!* I realised how lacking it now was when someone mentioned that Nokia's new *Lumia* phone has an inbuilt forty-one megapixel camera. And, as I'd glanced around at the many guests taking pictures of my parents as they'd cut their diamond anniversary cake, half of those guests hadn't been snapping away with a five megapixel digital camera. They'd been using iPads. When I'd spotted my uncle strolling past clutching such a gadget, it was the last straw. My uncle is nearly eighty. If an *eighty*-year-old can keep up with technology, then surely to goodness so should I —especially when I'm off to Canada later this year to visit precious family and friends. I want to capture the memories!

So yesterday, for the third time, I bought an iPad. This smaller version is much more suitable for slipping into my handbag.

'Ooh, isn't it a lovely size,' said Eleanor, after grappling the box from my grasp. 'It's perfect for slipping into my handbag.'

Was this kid a mind reader?

'Indeed. Except it's going in *my* handbag.'

'Wow, sixteen gigabytes,' said Eleanor, ignoring me. 'Mine is only eight.'

I kept my silence and waited. I wasn't the only one who could mind read, and knew what was coming next.

'You know, Mum, you'd be much better off having my old iPad to mess about on, and give this new one to me.'

'You don't say!' I said, making wide eyes at my daughter. 'Tell you what... I'll share it with you. But only when the moon turns blue.'

'Eh?'

I left my daughter to think about my comment. Which reminds me.

If Apple made a car, would it have windows...?

Roses are red, violets are blue, garbage gets dumped...
...just like you!

My son, having been unceremoniously dumped by his latest, has been home for the last couple of weekends looking for a shoulder to cry on. Well, *cry* isn't strictly true. But you know what I mean. He's looking for comfort. Distraction. So, last Friday, Robbie and I went out for a pizza. Having some mother-and-son time isn't something I'm often honoured with. My kids still regard me as "a very embarrassing parent" and not really someone to be seen publicly hanging around with.

'I do hope' — said Robbie as we sat down at a table in the pizza parlour — 'that you won't be embarrassing when we go to Canada and meet our relations.'

'What do you mean?' I said, a teeny bit hurt.

'Well, you know, Mum, you have a habit of just coming out with things.'

'Like what?'

'Like... "Oh please excuse me everyone, I'm having a hot flush" and then you start dramatically fanning yourself with whatever you can get your hands on.'

'Honestly, what do you take me for?' I said, picking up the menu and flapping it about.

'Look! You're doing it now!' my son hissed. 'It's so embarrassing.'

'Don't be ridiculous,' I snapped. 'Look around this restaurant. Every woman my age is fanning herself with the menu.'

'But not setting fire to it,' said Rob, snatching the menu from me. He bashed it against the table. 'You constantly set fire to menus.'

'It's not my fault the menus are tall, made of paper and that there's always a candle burning in the centre of the table.

'I just wish you were, you know, a bit more composed.'

'You mean *seen but not heard*.'

'No, I mean composed.'

'I am who I am and can't pretend to be something I'm

not.'

'Why not?' said Rob with a sigh.

'Because I tried doing that a long time ago and it's impossible to keep up.'

I was instantly transported back to my late thirties, when I started dating again.

'Never tell a man that you are a rubbish cook,' advised a friend.

So there I was ordering take-outs from restaurants, sneakily transferring the food to my saucepans and pretending to be the next Nigella.

'Good heavens,' said the nice man I was so desperate to impress, 'you make a mean curry. It tastes just like the one from my local.'

That's because it was.

And when I produced an Italian three course meal right down to "homemade" tiramisu, my date thought he'd died and gone to heaven. At last, a woman who cooked like his mama! It was *un miracolo*.

'Tell me, you don't happen to play golf, do you?'

'Do I play golf?' I repeated, rolling my eyes. 'That's like asking me whether I can cook!'

'I knew it!' said my date, sighing happily. 'I'll book us a round.'

'Lovely,' I said, privately thinking it would be anything but. 'Excuse me for two ticks. Just need to freshen up.'

Cue belting into the bathroom, locking the door and then whispering down the phone to the local golf club.

'Hi, I need to book some golf lessons.'

'Sure. We can have you achieving a decent handicap in six months.'

'Make it six days' — I hissed — 'because it's an emergency.'

Seven days later, my date took me to the local club where, thank God, there was a friendly nine-hole option. Having made out I'd not played for years and was very rusty, my date was happy to leave the far more challenging eighteen-hole course for another day.

The fact that I teed off and promptly did a freak hole-in-one had my date in raptures. At the second tee I wasn't so lucky and ended up in a bunker. However, the gods were looking down on me favourably and, miraculously, I chipped the ball out of the bunker, onto the green and watched it rattle straight into the hole.

'One under par! Is there no end to your talent?'

I think it was at that point I collapsed on the green in a gibbering heap and said something like, 'Yes, I'm also brilliant at pretending to be something I'm not.'

Needless to say my fluky good luck then abandoned me and I annihilated not just my game but also the golf course. Sand and divots everywhere. Fortunately, my date saw the funny side and went on to marry me. But it taught me a valuable lesson.

I looked across the table at my son.

'Trying to be something you're not is exhausting,' I advised. 'Honesty really is the best policy.'

Well, most of the time anyway. Which reminds me.

A wife looked in the mirror and didn't like what she saw.

'I'm old, wrinkled, grey, and fat,' she said to her husband. 'Give me a compliment to make me feel better.'

'Well,' he said cautiously, 'there's nothing wrong with your eyesight...'

Did you hear about the guy who lost the whole of his left side?
He's all right now...

This time last week my eighty-one-year-old mother was rushed to hospital by ambulance. She required urgent surgery and was warned of the risks and potential complications. However, if she hadn't had the operation she would have died, so she signed the consent form and we all kept our fingers tightly crossed that she would come through.

Thankfully Mother Bryant survived the op. Physically she is on the road to recovery. Mentally it's a different story. Anaesthetic and morphine have blurred the lines between reality and dreams. Apparently this is very common in geriatrics. It is called "postoperative delirium" and it's making Mother Bryant very paranoid.

'Shh' — said Mum as I greeted her — 'the nurses don't like me. In fact, they don't like any of us. They know absolutely *everything* about all of us. There must be a hidden microphone somewhere. I don't want them listening to me telling you this. Come closer.' She beckoned me towards her, and I leant in. 'They're all in cahoots with each other and as for you'— she jabbed a finger at my chest 'they think you're a trouble-maker.'

'Right,' I said, worried about my mother's ramblings and mentally offering up a prayer for swift recovery.

'Do you know,' she hissed, 'at night there is bedlam in this ward. The nurses do *terrible* things.' My mother leant back, tapping the side of her nose. 'You ask Iris. She'll tell you.'

'Iris?'

My mother jerked her head.

'In the next bed. She knows what's been going on. She and I talk, you know.'

I looked at the little old lady one bed along. She was staring vacantly at the ceiling, mouth hanging open, and looked beyond having any sort of conversation.

The thing is, I've been listening to this nonsensical chatter throughout the entirety of the week. Some of the

281

things Mother Bryant has come out with would have been quite funny if we weren't so concerned. To say she is muddled is an understatement. It is also quite astonishing how the *energy* of somebody's confusion can rub off. Let me give you an example.

On Thursday I went to the hospital with my father and sister. By the time visiting came to an end, Mother Bryant had given all three of us monumental headaches.

'I don't know about you, girls,' said Father Bryant as we stood in the hospital corridor, 'but I need a cup of coffee and some paracetamol. Fancy joining me?'

'Yes,' Janice and I chorused.

We made our way to the hospital's on-site Costa and joined the queue. When our turn came, the young lady behind the counter asked us what we would like.

Dad: I'll have a black coffee.

Me: Tea, please.

Sis: Hot chocolate for me.

Me: Ooh, that sounds nice. Cancel the tea. I'll have hot chocolate too.

Dad: Something milky sounds appealing. Change mine to a latte, please.'

Sis: Can I have soya rather than milk?

Me: Yes, make mine with soya too, please.

Costa Lady: So that's two hot chocolates and a latte, all to be made with soya?

Dad: Milk.

Costa Lady: Sorry, two hot chocolates and a latte, all to be made with milk.

Sis: No, two with soya.

Dad: I'll have milk, please.

Costa Lady: So that's two hot chocolates with soya and you, sir, are now having hot milk?

Dad: No, coffee.

Costa Lady: Americano?

Dad: No, I'm English.

Sis: She means filter coffee, Dad.

Dad: Oh, I see. Actually, I think I'd rather have a latte.

Costa Lady: (*confused*) So that's one latte with soya

and two hot chocolates with milk?

Me: No. One latte with milk, two hot chocolates with soya.

Costa Lady: Got it! What size?

Dad: I'll have a medium.

Sis: I'll have a small.

Me: Medium, please.

Sis: Actually, stuff the diet. I'll have a medium too.

Me: Oh, that's a point. I'm meant to be weight watching. Make mine a small.

Dad: How big is a medium?

Costa Lady: (*waggling paper cup*) This big.

Dad: In that case I'll have a small.

Costa Lady: To have here or take away?

Me/Sis/Dad: (*all at same time*) Here/take away/um-?

Costa Lady: (*looking frazzled*) Go to the till and pay, please.

Lady on till: I've no idea what you want or what you're going to get, so have it on us!

Dad: That's awfully generous of you. Are you sure?

Sis: Have we muddled you?

Lady on till: I think we're all confused. Let's see what the boy on "drinks" produces.

We turned to see a young lad setting down the tray. It contained one vast hot chocolate in a soup bowl, one tiny hot chocolate in a glass, and one medium latte in a paper cup. All made with soya. But we didn't care. We just wanted something to wash down our paracetamol. The Costa lady looked wistfully at our painkillers.

'Would you like one?' I asked.

It's probably the closest I've ever come to drug dealing. Which reminds me.

Did you hear about the duck with a drug problem?

He was a quack-head...

I now pronounce you dumped and single.
You may kiss my...

Following the recent hospital havoc with my mother's delirium, disruption has since descended upon my private life too. Things have been.... testing.

Mr V attempted making the peace by presenting me with a dozen red roses. The cat shredded them on my behalf. And on top of that, my daughter's two-year romance with her school sweetheart came to a very abrupt big fat full stop.

'I can't understand it,' Eleanor wailed.

Unfortunately I could.

'You don't think' — I suggested cautiously — 'it could be something to do with you being a bit, um, bossy?'

'*Bossy*?' My daughter's head rotated one-hundred and eighty degrees. 'Are you saying it's all my fault?'

'Okay, forget I said that.'

'No, I won't,' Eleanor hissed. 'That's an awful thing to suggest — and from my own mother! I thought you'd at least be on my side.'

'I'm not on anyone's side, and nor am I taking sides. I'm merely pointing out that you should speak to others in the same way as you'd like them to speak to you.'

'I SPEAK TO EVERYBODY EXTREMELY NICELY!'

'I rest my case.'

'I've had enough of this conversation' — Eleanor snapped, ready to flounce off to her room — 'and roll on Saturday. Newly single, I shall go to a party with my college friends. Ha!'

Saturday arrived, and with it my son. Robbie wanted company following his own recent relationship going down the plug hole.

'I still don't know where I went wrong,' he said mournfully.

As my children are two peas in a pod when it comes to temperament, I had an inkling of what had gone wrong, even if Robbie hadn't.

'Could it have ended because you're, well, just a tad, you know, a teeny weeny bit—'

'Spit it out!'

'Ok. Bossy.'

There, I'd said it.

'Bossy? *Bossy*?' Rob's eyes widened incredulously. 'How can you suggest such a thing?' This was followed by a bossy rant about me not being supportive enough.

On Sunday morning there was a shift in the household's mood. Rob was nursing a stonking hangover, and Eleanor was tearful and subdued. The three of us sat around the kitchen table having breakfast together. Actually, let me rephrase that. Eleanor was nursing a mug of tea after declaring she was too upset to eat anything, while I tucked into a mound of toast, and Robbie told me off for crunching too loudly.

I looked at my daughter's unhappy face. 'Didn't you enjoy your party last night?'

'Oh, yes, I actually had a lovely time. It was good fun.'

'So why the long face?'

'Because we all played *Spin the Bottle* and I had to kiss H.'

'I see,' I said, not seeing at all. 'So what's the problem?'

'Because now I feel so guilty!'

'Why? It was only a game you were all playing.'

'I know! But I've been going out with M and never kissed anyone else before!'

'But you're no longer going out with M.'

'Yeah, but you don't understand. It seems wrong, even though it was just a stupid game and meant nothing.'

'Oh my God,' said Rob, interrupting. 'My fingers have gone numb.'

'I just can't stop feeling guilty about that kiss.'

'Well you must.'

'My fingers are tingling like crazy.'

'So what shall I do about this guilt feeling?'

'Ignore it.'

'It's spreading to my hands.'

'Do you think I should tell M?'

'Why? It wouldn't change anything.'

'And now my hands have gone numb.'

'Maybe if I tell him, the guilt will go away.'

285

'Don't be silly. After all, you're now a free agent.'

'It's spreading up my arms. Help! Help me!'

'I feel so miserable.'

'Time is a great healer.'

'I've just Googled this and I think I'm dying.'

'So what do you think I should do?'

'Stop fretting. I tell you, there is nothing to feel guilty about.'

'Call the emergency doctor!'

'Do you think M and I will ever get back together?'

'I don't know, but right now you both need time apart.'

'Call an ambulance!'

'I feel like I can't cope with anything right now.'

'I've felt like that for ages.'

'I NEED MY HANDS FOR MY PROFESSION!'

'I feel funny.'

'I've felt funny for weeks.'

'THIS ISN'T FUNNY.'

It was with a sense of relief that I greeted Monday. Which reminds me.

If you ever think everything seems to be going well, then you have obviously overlooked something...

Stress is when you wake up screaming
— and realise you haven't fallen asleep yet...

Somebody once said, "Stress doesn't kill. What *does* kill, is the way stress is handled."

Currently I'm not sure whether my stress levels are being handled brilliantly or whether, due to irregular and almost painful heart palpitations, my plan to live to one hundred might end in the next one hundred seconds.

We all suffer stress, many of us on a daily basis. We deal with work, kids, spouse, home and chores on automatic pilot. However, if you add too many extras into that juggling act, there is a danger of everything tipping over.

When my mother was rushed into hospital a few weeks ago (where she remains), everything I'd been juggling started to wobble. In order to find considerable time to visit her every day and see to her personal needs, something had to give. The ironing was the first to go. Like a rolling snowball, it quickly gathered momentum. Within days a huge pile of crumpled clothes had accumulated.

'I've nearly run out of shirts,' said Mr V whilst lying on the sofa in front of the television.

'How shocking!'

He glanced up, uncertain whether I was being flippant or serious, but opted for the latter.

'I know. My wardrobe is nearly empty.'

The shopping was the next thing to slide.

'What's for tea?' asked my daughter. 'I'm starving.'

I peered inside the freezer.

'Brussel sprouts, peas and roast potatoes.'

Eleanor looked confused.

'Isn't there something to go with that?'

I looked inside the freezer again.

'Yes. Ice-cream.'

The next thing to lapse was housework.

'Mum, there's cat hair everywhere,' said Robbie, when he visited last weekend. 'You haven't vacuumed, and you know how allergic I am to Dolly's hair.'

The washing was the next thing to be abandoned.

'I'm out of socks,' Mr V complained.

'I'm out of pants,' said Eleanor.

'I'm out of allergy tablets,' said Robbie.

'And I'm OUT OF PATIENCE,' I yelled.

It was at that point everybody ran for cover. Like a dropped bottle of fizz, stress bubbled up, whooshed to the surface and exploded out of me.

Suddenly my son was vacuuming as if his life depended upon it, my husband was whizzing an iron backwards and forwards over the mountain of crumpled clothes, my daughter tidied her room and walked Trudy Beagle, and then everybody shot off to the supermarket to do a mammoth shop. I left them all to it and rushed off to the hospital to speak to doctors about unchanged dressings, potential cellulitis, an absence of bed bathing, drug changes, care assistance and ongoing post-operative delirium — only to have my confused and angry mother berate me for "interfering".

'Thanks for nothing,' she ranted, 'because now my life won't be worth living. They taunt me, you know.'

'Who taunts you?'

'Everybody. And one of the nurses here is absolute *poison*. And she hates your guts. She's reported you to all the national newspapers. Do you realise everyone is reading about you? Your name is mud.'

'Yes, Mum,' I said. 'I do believe you told me all this yesterday.'

And the day before. And the day before that. And the day before that one too.

'You've got to stop causing me trouble.'

I knelt before my mother and cupped her face in my hands.

'Listen to me, Mum. Try and hang on to what I'm saying. I care about you. I love you. I'm "interfering" — as you call it — because I love and care.'

She gazed back at me with vacant blue eyes. The lights were on, but nobody was home.

The time I gave in to tears was upon mislaying my mobile. It's silly how something so trivial can open the flood gates but, for me, losing the phone was the breaking point. I needed that phone! I couldn't function without it. Where the flipping flaming hell *was* the wretched thing? Too bad, I'd have to go without it. Visiting time had already started. So I dashed off to hospital, alternatively crunching the gears of my car and trumpeting into a packet of tissues, but minus the phone. In the hospital's foyer, I met my father.

'I've mislaid my mobile, Dad. Can I borrow yours? I need to text Eleanor to say I will be late picking her up from college.'

'Of course,' said my father. 'You can use my new mobile.'

'What happened to the old one?'

It wasn't that long ago my father upgraded to a Smart phone.

'I couldn't get on with it.'

'Really? Oh, that's a shame. Well, never mind, let me borrow your *new* new mobile.'

And with that my father placed a tiny clam in the palm of my hand. It was, possibly, the very first mobile ever invented. Wait, the first mobile had been the size of a brick. Okay, perhaps this was the second mobile ever invented.

'How much did you pay for this?'

'Oh, it was a bargain,' he assured.

I bit my tongue and silently cursed the salesman who had fleeced my father. Now wasn't the time to fight another battle. I opened the clam and tried to remember how to use such a phone. Good heavens. Where was the internet? It didn't even have a camera!

'Okay. I need to text. Do you know how to message on this thing?'

'I'm still finding my way around it,' said my father vaguely.

'Right. Not to worry. Ah. Found it.'

I began to tap out a message to my daughter.

'Blast. How do you backspace?'

'I don't know.'

'Damn. All the words are joining up. Any idea which

289

key might be the space bar?'

'I don't know.'

'Doesn't matter' — I assured, whilst inwardly screaming — 'I think Eleanor will understand the gist of my message.'

I pressed the send button.

Later that day Eleanor found my "lost" mobile. It was where I'd left it, on my desk, next to a brochure about a nursing home for my mother. Back home again, I picked up my mobile and stared at its screen. There were thirteen missed calls, one voicemail and a text. Twelve of the missed calls were from my mother. So was the voicemail. I pressed the button and listened to her quavering voice.

'Please tell me. Please, please, please.'

I shook my head. *Tell you what, Mum?*

As if on cue, she continued. 'Tell me whether your private life is in all the newspapers and if your name is mud.'

I gave a weary sigh and deleted the message.

The other missed call was from Eleanor, followed by a text. It read:

Grandad sent me a weird message. Please can you translate:

Ellie

I

have

lostomyomobileowillobeooutsideoyourocollegeoaro undofiveoxxx

Well it made perfect sense to me. Which reminds me.

Did you hear about the two mobile phones that got married?

The wedding was terrible, but the reception was terrific...

We had a new postman, but he quit.
He looked at his first letter to deliver and thought, "This isn't for me…"

There is a man in my life who sees me in ways that only a husband should — and a husband of longstanding at that. What a shameful thing to confess. Every morning, not long after Mr V has left for work, I greet this other man with dishevelled hair, a naked face, and dressed in the seductive attire of pyjama bottoms with a mis-matched top. Our relationship is now in its eighth month. Sometimes he leaves me little notes too. *There's a parcel behind your wheelie bin.* Yes, I'm talking about my postman.

Earlier this week, I greeted my postie possibly looking like his worst nightmare. No doubt postmen all over the country see many ladies looking — let's not mince words —*rough*. I know for a fact this is true because I recently bumped into my postie at the supermarket, said hello, and he didn't know who I was.

'It's me,' I said, beaming away. 'You don't recognise me with my clothes on!'

It was only then that I registered the flabbergasted woman standing next to him.

'He's my postman!' I explained.

'He's my husband,' she snapped.

'Well, yes, of course, and rest assured I have my own husband,' I gabbled.

'Excellent, although I'm sure you wouldn't want me greeting *him* in my birthday suit every morning, eh?'

'Oh, no, I mean yes, but I haven't. I mean didn't. I wear pyjamas you see. And a mis-matched top. Well, apart from the time your husband got me out of the shower. On that occasion I was wearing a towel.'

Mrs Postie looked outraged.

'Lovely to meet you,' I trilled. 'I'm just off to dig a hole for myself in the tinned soup aisle.'

Ok, I didn't really say that last bit although, at the time, I'd fervently wished it had been possible to do such a thing. Why is it that the most innocent things can become a minefield?

In my old house, the hallway was large enough to open the front door without being seen, poke your head around it — like a lollipop on a stick — and take the proffered parcel. Unfortunately, in our current house, the hallway is the width of the front door and there is no hope of opening it without first revealing yourself.

The dustmen haven't escaped my early morning dishevelment either. There has been many an early Friday morning where it's dawned on me that neither of us have put the bins out the night before. Last week was no exception.

'Damn, the dustmen are here,' I said to Mr V. 'Quick, go and put the bins out.'

'But I'm not dressed. You put the bins out.'

'I'm not dressed either. I'm wearing my pyjama bottoms and mis-matched top.'

'And I'm in my underpants.'

'I don't care. You're the man of the house. You do it.'

'You're always telling me that you run this house, so *you* do it.'

'Oh for—'

Followed by a crazed blonde catapulting out of the house and legging it after the dustcart with wheelie bins bouncing along in her wake.

In the early days of my mother's marriage, there was yet another man who used to regularly see ladies in a state of undress. The milkman. These days everybody buys their milk in cartons at the supermarket but, when I was a child, the sound of the electric milk float was commonplace. My mother would greet the milkman every morning, a vision in bathrobe and hair curlers. Sometimes, if it was the weekend and she was hoping for a lie-in, she'd leave a note folded into one of the empty glass bottles.

Dear Milkman. Please leave an extra pint today.

On one occasion, her note was misunderstood.

Dear Milkman. I missed you yesterday. Do you have any strawberry yoghurts?

His reply:

Strawberry yoghurts behind the planter. And I missed you too.

Our milkman had a sense of humour.

One evening, my mother put out the empties and scribbled another of her hasty notes. Never great at spelling, she didn't realise she'd asked him to leave an extra pint of "paralysed" milk. Which reminds me.

Here are some genuine notes that have been left in milk bottles for milkmen:

I've just had a baby. Please leave another one.

Cancel one pint after the day after today.

Please close the gate behind you as the birds keep pecking the tops off the milk.

Do not leave milk at Number 14 because he is dead until further notice.

My child wants a milkshake. Do you deliver? Or do I shake the bottle?

Please leave details about cheap milk as I'm stagnant...

How do monsters like their eggs?
Terri-fried...

Earlier this week, my daughter and I — due to an uncharacteristically early start to the day — popped in on my parent and ended up having breakfast with them.

My mother, unused to being awake at "the crack of dawn" (it was nine in the morning) was still floating about in her nightie. She is now fully recovered from her emergency surgery and, thankfully, about seventy per cent better regarding the postoperative delirium.

'Put the kettle on, Debs, and help yourself to food,' said Mother Bryant. 'I'll just pop upstairs and get dressed. You know where everything is.'

'Sure,' I said. 'What do you want to eat, Ellie?'

'What is there?' asked Eleanor.

My mother immediately did a U-turn and shuffled back into the kitchen.

'I have ten different varieties of cereal, or there's muffins, or bread for toasting — you can choose from brown, white, oatmeal or gluten-free — there's also croissants... plain or almond, or there's scones with currants or cherries, or you can have teacakes, or fresh fruit... bananas, blueberries and strawberries.'

Only my mother can offer such a choice.

Eleanor considered. 'Is there anything else?'

Only my daughter can remain indecisive.

'Boiled eggs and soldiers?'

Eleanor's face lit up. 'Yes please!'

'I'll let your mother take care of it for you. I *must* go and get dressed.'

Father Bryant came into the kitchen.

'Are you giving Ellie some breakfast?' he asked.

'Yes. She's having boiled eggs. Would you like a couple?'

'No, thanks. I fancy toast.'

My mother once again did a U-turn and shuffled back into the kitchen.

'Oh no you're not, Tony. You're going to finish off the yoghurt. It's two days out of date and needs eating up.'

'Right, dear.'

'Do you think it's wise to eat dairy that's out of date?' I asked.

'Certainly,' said Mother Bryant. 'When you've been through a war, you'll eat anything.'

'Do you want to share some yoghurt?' Father Bryant asked Eleanor.

'She's not having yoghurt!' cried Mother Bryant. 'I'm not risking my granddaughter getting listeria.'

'Oh, but it's okay for me to get listeria?' asked Father Bryant.

My mother thought about this for a moment.

'Yes,' she said. 'Now you really must all excuse me because I *must* get dressed.'

There then followed a couple of minutes where I side-stepped my father to reach the hob, and Eleanor danced around her grandfather to fill the kettle, and my father jiggled around the pair of us to open the fridge, and then my mother shuffled back in again, *still* in her nightie.

'Dear Heart,' said my father (you can tell he's irritated when he refers to Mum as *Dear Heart*), 'there isn't enough room in this part of the kitchen for all of us. What are you doing?'

'I want to warm the bowl for Eleanor's eggs.'

'Surely the eggs will go into eggcups?' said Father Bryant.

'No, Ellie likes them turned out. Now get out of my way, please. I want to warm the bowl.'

'You don't need to warm the bowl, Grandma,' said Eleanor.

'I'm warming the bowl!' said Mother Bryant, her tone defying any argument.

There then followed sixty seconds of us all holding our breath while Mother Bryant, daring us to interfere, picked up the boiling kettle and, with a violently shaking hand, slopped scalding water into a china bowl.

'There!' she said triumphantly, banging the kettle back down on the worktop. We all exhaled with relief. 'Now excuse me, because I *must* get dressed.'

I then waited for the water to boil in the egg saucepan,

set the timer, and eventually turned the eggs out into the warmed bowl.

'Oh dear.'

'What is it?' asked Father Bryant.

'The eggs aren't cooked enough. They're all watery.'

'Oh nooo, Mum' — Eleanor peered over my shoulder — 'they look revolting.'

'Not to worry,' said Father Bryant. 'I shall put them in the microwave.'

'How does it work?' I asked, peering at the old-fashioned oven.

'Everybody out of my way,' said Mother Bryant, lurching back into the kitchen and grabbing hold of door handles and backs of chairs for balance. She was still in her nightie. 'I'll sort out the microwave. Do you think ten seconds will do it?'

'I'm not sure,' said Eleanor.

'We'll try it,' said Father Bryant, pressing the start button.

'Stop! STOP!' shrieked Mother Bryant. 'The timer says nine minutes fifteen seconds.'

'No, it doesn't, Dear Heart.' (Uh-oh. Another "Dear Heart". See above.)

'Yes it *does*,' said Mother Bryant, pointing one knobbly finger at the microwave's digital display. 'See? Or are you blind?'

'That's the clock, Dear Heart' (said in an ominously growly voice).

'It isn't.'

'It is.'

'It isn't.'

'It is.'

'It isn't.'

'It *is*.'

'Grandma' — interrupted Eleanor— 'I don't think it can be the timer because nine minutes and fifteen seconds in a microwave would cause the eggs to explode.'

My mother thought about this.

'Don't you want the eggs well cooked?'

'I think thirty seconds will suffice. Let me do it while

296

you get dressed.'

'Yes, good idea. I keep meaning to get out of this nightie, but everybody keeps interrupting me.'

My mother then shuffled over to the kitchen table before pulling out a chair and sitting down. 'Actually, I'm too exhausted to get dressed right now. I'll do it in a little while.'

The eggs came out of the microwave looking extremely unappetising.

'Are they okay?' said Father Bryant, showing a grey, congealed mess to his granddaughter.

'Um, they look a bit dodgy, but it will do.'

'What about some marmalade?' asked Mother Bryant, hauling herself upright and shuffling across to the larder.

'Not on eggs, Grandma.'

'No? Well what about something else? I've got Nutella, Marmite, strawberry jam, or peanut butter.'

'I think I'd just like butter, Grandma.'

'Okay. I've got Lurpak, Olivio or Flora.'

My daughter took the Lurpak, dolloped it over the grey mess, and we all finally sat down to eat.

'How is your breakfast?' Father Bryant asked Eleanor.

'If I don't look at it, then it's passable.'

I put down my piece of toast and glanced around the table.

'I've just remembered the dream I had last night.'

'Oh? Did it feature microwaved eggs?' Father Bryant asked with a guffaw.

'No, it had angels in it.'

Dad and Eleanor exchanged a look. One that clearly said *she's away with the fairies again*.

'*I'm* listening to you, dear,' said Mother Bryant indulgently, 'even if these two aren't.'

'I went for an amazing journey around the globe with these two massive angels. It was a really uplifting dream. And as we flew through the air, they kept chanting over and over three words.'

'Which were?' Mother Bryant prompted.

'Love, mercy and forgiveness.'

'Probably in relation to your egg cooking skills,'

muttered Eleanor.

Which reminds me.

What day do eggs hate the most?

Fry-day...

What is the best way to diet?
To eat on the run...

Yesterday my daughter offered me three pairs of her old shorts. When I say *old*, I don't mean *ancient*. I use the word more in the context of 'no longer required'. After an intense year of pole fitness and physical theatre, Eleanor's weight has dropped to eight stone seven pounds. She has an enviable pencil-slim body.

'Try these on,' she said, pulling the unwanted garments from her wardrobe.

'Don't be daft,' I said. 'They won't fit me.'

'Yes, they will. They're *huge*.'

They are not huge. The label says "Size Small". They are only huge to Eleanor because she is wearing clothes with labels that sport the letters "XXS".

'Here,' she said, 'these were my favourite.'

'I'm not sure.'

'Why?'

'I don't think they'll look right on me.'

'Ok.'

Somehow I couldn't see myself in sawn-off leopard print unless I wanted to look like a fifty-two-year old hooker.

'What about these? They cost a lot of money.'

She proffered some black hot pants smothered in silver spikes and tiny metal skulls. They harked back to her 'emo' phase. I arched an eyebrow by way of response.

'Ok,' she said, discarding them. 'I'm absolutely certain you'll love this last pair.' She passed me some blue denim. 'They're boring as anything. Just like y— I mean, they'll totally suit you.'

I peered at the label. Levi Strauss! And look at the lovely soft frayed hemline. This was more like it!

I stuck one foot through the leg hole, then the other, and pulled them up. There was a pause as the denim hit my thighs. A bit of a tug. You can suck in your stomach but unfortunately not your thighs. A firm yank, and they shot upwards nearly garrotting my private parts.

'Very nice,' said Eleanor with approval.

'Yes, but unfortunately they're way too tight. Let me get them off.'

My son chose that moment to wander into his sister's bedroom, a vague expression upon his face.

'I'm revising, but stuck.'

'I think these shorts are stuck.'

'I've gone blank on the definition of *volatile*.'

'It means tense or uncomfortable. A bit like shorts on me.'

'I'm talking about the word in *chemistry* terms.'

'Don't take them off, Mum,' said Eleanor. 'I'm sure they fit you.'

'They don't. Look.' I lifted up my t-shirt hem and revealed a gap between the stud button and buttonhole. 'I can't do them up.'

'Oh, I remember now,' said Robbie, as he hastened back to his revision. 'It means a liquid that easily evaporates at room temperature.'

'I wish my waist would evaporate at room temperature.'

'Oh, shame,' said Eleanor, trying not to look appalled at my waist impersonating a particularly porky sausage in the grip of a very tight bandage. 'Ok, take them off. They can all go to the charity shop.'

Removing the shorts was not an experience I ever wish to repeat. As I went to pull them down, they jammed over my hips. How on earth had I ever got into them?

'Help,' I wailed.

'Keep still, I'll tug with you,' said Eleanor.

So we tugged. Nothing happened. Visions of reaching for the kitchen scissors and cutting them off danced through my mind.

'One more try,' said Eleanor.

Thankfully the next attempt had the shorts coming down. Along with my pants.

'Do not ask me,' I gasped, trying to protect my modesty, 'to ever attempt getting into your clothes again.'

'Well, you could always go on a diet,' Eleanor sniffed.

Which reminds me.

I'm going to try that new pasta diet. The Italians have

been using it for centuries. You walka pasta da bakery.
You walka pasta da sweet shop. And you walka pasta da
ice-cream van...

What do you call an irresponsible dog owner?
Too many choice names to mention here...

I wanted to end our chick-chat with something cheerful but life is full of bumps and, accordingly, so is this final chapter.

At the time of originally writing this, our darling Trudy Beagle was ancient, arthritic, and recovering from being attacked by two other dogs whilst out walking. The whole incident left me seething with anger and a need to let rip!

If you are thinking about getting a dog, or have recently acquired a dog, please take on board that it is your responsibility — no, DUTY — to teach your dog basic obedience, manners and respect.

Over the years I've owned many dogs and, with the exception of one, they were all rescue dogs. I had no idea of their background or why they were no longer wanted. It is a tough decision taking on a rescue dog when the animal is an *unknown quantity.* Has the animal been badly treated? Could it, as a result, bite? If you have children, is the dog going to be good with them? If you have a cat, will the dog be tolerant? There are several questions you need to ask yourself and these are just a few. Ironically, the only dog I ever had a problem with was one I welcomed as a puppy.

Several decades ago, our family dog — an old mongrel by the name of Bobby — fathered a litter of twelve puppies. He was immensely proud of himself, but the effort might have taken it out of him because, not long afterwards, he keeled over. The owner of the bitch that Old Bob had wooed was, understandably, aghast at having so many pups on her hands, but blamed herself for not getting around to having her girl spayed.

'Can you help me out here?' she asked. 'I'd be very grateful if you could give one of these puppies a home.'

So we chose a pup, telling ourselves it would be like having a little bit of Old Bob always with us. We named our bundle of cuteness "Max". He was adorable and so sweet-natured — until a friend's child tripped over and fell on him. From that moment, Max couldn't abide kids.

And when I say *couldn't abide*, I actually mean *detest*.

When my baby son came along, I dithered about whether to rehome Max and tormented myself in the process, telling myself I'd failed as a dog owner. And, anyway, what if the rehoming centre failed to pass on vital information about Max's loathing of children? What if Max's new owner let him off the lead at a local park and he frightened a child? Perhaps I should even consider putting him to sleep? But no, no, no, that idea instantly had me in tears. This was a young, fit dog with years ahead of him. And — argued my conscience — despite him loathing children, he'd never actually bitten one, had he?

So Max stayed with us, and I made sure he not once had an opportunity to be alone with my baby son. Robbie grew up alongside Max and, in truth, Max never gave Rob a second glance, although he remained a nightmare regarding other people's children.

There was one heart-stopping moment when an unsolicited visitor — a woman with a toddler in a buggy no less —ventured through our garden gate when Max was out, despite a huge sign screaming PRIVATE PROPERTY, NO UNSOLICITED VISITORS and BEWARE OF THE DOG.

Horrified, I shot out the front door just in time to witness Max whooshing towards the trespasser at a speed that rivalled a racing greyhound after the lure. He skidded to a halt in front of the buggy, gave one deep baritone bark at the tot, then zoomed back to me. I was expecting hysterics from the mother and, shaken, thought, "This is *it*. The mother is going to report me to the police, and I'll be forced to put Max to sleep."

Fortunately, the mother acknowledged she had stupidly entered private property with visible warning signs, and I silently thanked God that her child was unharmed. But it was a horrendous moment.

The whole situation about Max and his abhorrence of children was unexpectedly resolved when he began limping. Shockingly, he was diagnosed with bone cancer and this time there was no choice about saying goodbye.

Despite the tears, I would be a liar not to admit there was also an element of relief.

If you know your dog is unpredictable and can't stand the postman, the dustmen, bike riders, or has serious issues with other dogs, cats, or children, then it is up to you to take every possible step to ensure your dog doesn't cause an accident or bring harm to others. Letting your dog off the lead and "hoping for the best" just isn't on. Which is what a young man did while I was walking Trudy Beagle.

This man was allowing his dogs to romp off-lead in a children's play area — which was prohibited to the likes of him anyway. As a nod to this, he'd left the playground gate open. Upon seeing Trudy Beagle, the two dogs shot out the play area and hurtled over, all the while barking and snarling. It was obvious they meant business. The man saw what was happening, but deliberately looked away, as if pretending not to notice.

The ensuing noise was awful. The first dog set about attacking Trudy Beagle's ears, muzzle and shoulders, and the second clamped its huge teeth around the base of her tail. Her screams, as those two dogs attempted to pull her apart, were beyond upsetting — and *still* that man ignored what was going on.

I was left with no choice but to risk being bitten myself and began lashing out at the dogs with my feet, attempting to kick them off. I hasten to add that I didn't hurt them enough to injure them. There were no broken ribs. It was only when I dared to retaliate, that the man ran over. I was then subjected to a swearing rant because, would you believe, he insisted his dogs had only been "playing".

Fortunately, the vet who later stitched up Trudy Beagle didn't agree her wounds had been sustained from "playing", nor did the police. Yes, I reported the incident. I only saw the man and his dogs one more time after that, and both were muzzled and on a lead. Good! Which reminds me.

Mrs Brown was standing in the queue at her Post Office when a neighbour came in.

'Hello, Mrs Brown. How's your dog? I saw it yesterday chasing an old man on a bicycle.'

'That wasn't my dog,' said Mrs Brown indignantly.

'Are you sure?' asked the neighbour.

'Most definitely,' said Mrs Brown. 'My dog can't ride a bicycle...'

A Letter from Debbie Viggiano

I want to say a huge thank you for reading *Cappuccino and Chick-Chat* which I really hope you enjoyed. If you did, it would be great if you could write a review. I'd be thrilled to hear what you think, and it makes such a difference helping new readers discover one of my books for the first time.

I always love hearing from my readers, so do look me up on Facebook, Twitter, Goodreads or my website.

With love,

Debbie

Acknowledgements

I am deeply grateful to the amazing Rebecca Emin of Gingersnap Books for working her magic and turning this manuscript into a proper book.

Likewise, I would like to thank the fabulous Cathy Helms of Avalon Graphics for producing a wonderful cover.

Finally, I want to thank *you*, my reader. Without you, there is no book.

Debbie xx

Also by Debbie Viggiano

Lucy's Last Straw
The Man You Meet in Heaven
What Holly's Husband Did
Stockings and Cellulite
Lipstick and Lies
Flings and Arrows
The Perfect Marriage
Secrets
The Corner Shop of Whispers
The Woman Who Knew Everything
Mixed Emotions ~ short stories
The Ex Factor (family drama)
Lily's Pink Cloud ~ a child's fairytale
100 ~ the Author's experience of Chronic Myeloid Leukaemia